Jewish Wayfarers in Modern China

Jewish Wayfarers in Modern China

Tragedy and Splendor

Matthias Messmer

LEXINGTON BOOKS
Lanham·Boulder·New York·Toronto·Plymouth, UK

Published by Lexington Books
A wholly owned subsidiary of The Rowman & Littlefield Publishing Group, Inc.
4501 Forbes Boulevard, Suite 200, Lanham, Maryland 20706
www.lexingtonbooks.com

Estover Road, Plymouth PL6 7PY, United Kingdom

British Library Cataloguing in Publication Information Available

Library of Congress Cataloging-in-Publication Data

Messmer, Matthias, 1967-
Jewish wayfarers in modern China : tragedy and splendor / Matthias Messmer.
p. cm.
Includes bibliographical references and index.
ISBN 978-0-7391-6938-4 (cloth : alk. paper) — ISBN 978-0-7391-6939-1 (ebook)
1. China—Description and travel. 2. Jewish travelers—China. I. Title.
DS712M47 2012
305.892'4051—dc23 2011032547

∞™ The paper used in this publication meets the minimum requirements of American National Standard for Information Sciences—Permanence of Paper for Printed Library Materials, ANSI/NISO Z39.48-1992.

Printed in the United States of America

Contents

Illustration Credits

Figures 1.2, 1.3, 2.4, 2.9, 4.1	From the author's collection
Figure 1.1	Courtesy of the collection of Peter Hibbard, Shanghai
Figure 2.1	George Sokolsky Papers, 1916–1962, Box 392, Envelope A, Hoover Institution Archives, Stanford University, Palo Alto, CA
Figures 2.2, 2.3	Courtesy of the collection of Peter Rand, Belmont, MA
Figure 2.5	Courtesy of Marta Balinska and Institut Pasteur, Paris
Figure 2.6	Courtesy of Dr Yee Wah Foo (Fu Bingchang Collection, Bristol University), Bristol
Figure 2.7	Courtesy of Carol Lew Simons, Southold, NY
Figure 2.8	Courtesy of US National Archives, College Park, MD
Figures 2.10–2.13, 3.8	Courtesy of the collection of Prof. Gerd Kaminski, Vienna
Figures 3.1–3.4	Courtesy of Lydia Abel, Nuremberg

Figures 3.5–3.7	Courtesy of the collection of Paul Rosdy, Vienna
Figure 4.2	Courtesy of Martina Fluck, Heide (photography by Jürgen Hoffmann)
Cover	Courtesy of Chiang Yeng-Fong, Shanghai ("A Healthy Beauty," Da Hwa Offset Press, 1930s) and Hoover Institution Archives, Stanford University ("If China Goes")

Names and Orthography

The problems of spelling Chinese names and words in the Roman alphabet are almost insurmountable. In this text, I use the modern *pinyin* spellings (e.g., Chongqing rather than Chungking) wherever possible. (*Pinyin* is the most commonly used Romanization system for standard Mandarin Chinese.) However, I deviate from this rule with the original titles of books and in contemporary quotes (e.g., Rayna Prohme's description of "Canton," a city we today call Guangzhou). In cases that would still be unclear to the reader, I have added the name or word in *pinyin* in parentheses. I also use some standard spellings of Chinese names that came into use in Western literature many years or even decades before the *pinyin* system was introduced (Chiang Kai-shek, or Sun Yat-sen and not Jiang Jieshi or Sun Yixian). I use this principle as well with geographical names (e.g., Yangtze, not Chang Jiang).

Preface and Acknowledgments

It all began ten years ago when I became interested in images, particularly in the ones Westerners have formed of the Chinese and their country. *Jewish Wayfarers in Modern China—Tragedy and Splendor* grew out of my research on the history and traces of the Jewish presence in China in the last century and the images that Jewish visitors formed of China and the Chinese.[1]

I dedicate this book to those Westerners who with their individual experiences in the Middle Kingdom can give readers the unique possibility to relive a special aspect of twentieth-century history and thereby savor not only the better known, but also the more exotic fruits of these Westerners' encounters with China and its people. All the personalities presented here were of Jewish origin and through their life and work in some way made a more or less important contribution in China; or thanks to their stay in the Far East, they brought the Western public closer to the Middle Kingdom and thereby contributed to demystifying China and the Chinese.[2]

Even if it is an unusual approach, my concentration on persons of Jewish origin has much to recommend it: First, this group offers an unsurpassed variety of national, cultural, and ideological backgrounds and worldviews, which makes it possible to create an exceptionally diverse panoramic mosaic of respective encounters with China and its society. Second, in a large number of cases, the "double exile function" plays a significant role. As outsiders in China, these individuals saw, from the perspective of their own exile, a country in upheaval and in search of the "right" relationship with the West. Third, some of the persons described here were especially qualified to think in universalistic terms, which gave them an immeasurable advantage in coping with the interplay of various cultures and societies.

Many readers of this book already know that thousands of Jews survived the Holocaust because they found refuge in China. Some readers may be surprised to discover, however, that in the twentieth century, many other Western Jews visited or resided in China for a variety of different reasons. This book offers a panoramic view of these different persons and their connections with China by means of a collection of short biographies situated in the context of Chinese and Western history. Among the men and women included are those who came as children with their families, diplomats sent by their governments, scholars, poets, artists, photographers, writers, composers, journalists, anthropologists, linguists, entrepreneurs, adventurers, revolutionaries, doctors, nurses, health professionals, Zionists, Marxists, devout believers, and international social activists. Some had a personal interest in China, others were altruists or desired to change the world, others worked in the interest of Jews living abroad, and still others simply wanted new experiences or sought to understand their world better. In many cases, the reasons changed in the course of their stay.

I could only reconstruct many of the biographies presented in this book with the greatest effort, and then only thanks to additional, sometimes fragmentary information provided by other researchers and colleagues. Biographical statistics alone cannot capture some of these intercultural life stories. As hard as I have tried, I still do not know many important and interesting aspects of these life stories. The turmoil and disruption of the twentieth century were determining factors in the lives of many of these Western visitors, and yet in most cases their stay in China was a central life experience. In studying them, it was not my aim to expose weaknesses or political mistakes so that a know-it-all contemporary reader could look back in smug disapproval, but rather solely to accurately portray the respective individual's relationship with China.

Similar to Chinese cuisine, the reader of this book can savor a wide range of different flavors and impressions, for instance, as evoked by the impostor Trebitsch Lincoln, the insightful and sensitive scholar Willy Tonn, or Julius Tandler, the type of person whom today we would call a human-rights activist. As the reader will quickly begin to realize, a great number of persons of Jewish ancestry played important roles in enabling us in the West to understand Chinese "sights and sounds." By contributing in diverse ways to Chinese life or by helping or befriending Chinese officials and opinion makers, they mediated between China and the West. This book consists of four parts: In the first part, I present biographies of Jewish "Old China Hands." The second part deals with travelers who went to China voluntarily and stayed for some time. The third part presents persons who literally felt that China had saved their lives: persons fleeing from Nazi terror in Europe. The fourth part, finally, focuses on the so-called "foreign experts": those persons who decided to stay in China even after the Communists took power.

Travel to and within China was considerably harder to organize in the past than today, when every businessperson and almost all tourists can arrive and depart by airplane. The advantage of the past was that the Western visitor sometimes approached the Middle Kingdom more cautiously and accordingly could become aware of the others' perspectives. In the twentieth century, the paths of many persons led to the Middle Kingdom, and it is likewise one of my concerns that persons who at the time undertook the adventure of going to China would find their deserved place in this book. I have chosen to reconstruct their biographies as a contribution to keeping alive memories of persons who during their lifetime received little or no recognition.

This extensive study was only possible due to a wealth of documents and works by scholars and "ordinary people" from all over the world. Without the aid and support of dozens of friends, colleagues, and other good souls from almost every continent, today's reader would not have available this book, with its many descriptions of diverse Jewish visitors to twentieth-century China. Retrospectively, it is almost impossible to determine who led me via whom to which persons and how the intertwined paths of "discovery" of China travelers progressed. What I can definitely say is that neither computers nor other technical aids are sufficient to trace the life or even survival situation of a Samuel Sokobin in Manchuria or the adventures of a Harold Isaacs on the Yangtze River.

I cannot here acknowledge everyone who contributed to this work as a "helper." Nevertheless, I would like to name a few persons and express my sincere gratitude to them. These include, first of all, Rabbi Marvin Tokayer (Great Neck, New York), who encouraged me to carry out this project and supported me in every possible regard; Professor Tom Grunfeld (New York), who accompanied me and my research for the last ten years; the translator, James Stuart Brice (St. Paul), who did his work quickly and yet very thoroughly; the editor, Justin Race from Lexington Books, who from the beginning thought this project "offbeat but most worthwhile"; and naturally my partner Hsin-mei Chuang, who has patiently stood by me at all times, with deeds and advice.

NOTES

1. This research culminated in my book *China—Schauplätze west-östlicher Begegnungen* (published by Böhlau, Vienna 2007). The reader of that book will find many details on the historical and societal settings of these East-West encounters, as well as more biographies of Jewish wayfarers in Modern China and their images of the Middle Kingdom.

2. The concept of "Jewish origin" is defined as "according to the Jewish tradition," that is, a person is regarded as a Jew if his or her mother is Jewish, or if he or she has converted to the Jewish religion in accordance with the formally prescribed Jewish rites. Many of the persons presented in the second part of the book would perhaps not (or no longer) identify themselves as Jewish, would deny their religious roots, or would even claim to be nonbelievers.

Introduction

Individuals, Biographies, and *Lebenswelten*

For centuries, China has aroused the outside world's interest and curiosity, and especially that of a broad and diverse range of visitors. Travel reports from China have been reaching the West ever since Marco Polo's thirteenth-century journey to the court of Kublai Khan, the Mongol ruler of China. For centuries after that, missionaries and the diplomatic representatives of Western powers shaped the image of China in the West. The philosophers guild, including names such as Voltaire, Montesquieu, Hegel, Herder, and Marx, who never set foot on Chinese soil, also participated in the discourse on China, its people, customs, laws, and philosophy. Particularly with the spread of the *Chinoiserie* cult in nineteenth-century Europe, many poets and writers (such as Mark Twain, Pierre Loti, Paul Claudel, or Karl May) likewise joined the ranks of those who chose China for study or respectively fictional representation. Finally, Western advisors in the most diverse services and positions in China imparted their personal impressions of a country where they were active for various periods.

Twentieth-century Western perceptions of China differed from those of previous centuries, because, due to the Boxer Rebellion and its subsequent suppression by the Baguo Lianjun, the allied troops of the intervening eight powers, for the first time a widespread awareness of China arose even among ordinary people. In Germany, Kaiser Wilhelm II encouraged a negative image of China in the famous-notorious "Hun Speech" that he gave in Bremerhaven on July 27, 1900, to troops en route to fight the Boxers. To the German Chancellor's dismay, the Kaiser exhorted his soldiers to avenge without mercy the death in Peking of German envoy von Ketteler, so that no Chinese would ever again dare to harm a German or even to look askance at one. At about the same time, China was increasingly drawing the attention of the English and French, so that in the years before the First World War, people speculated out loud about the rise of the yellow race(s): In 1905, Japan became the first Asian nation to defeat a European nation (Czarist Russia). Fear of an anticipated loss of territories acquired in the Far East also spread in Western capitals like Paris and London.

During the Great War, large numbers of Europeans had their first frequent and personal encounters with the Chinese, as thousands of workers, mostly from China's North, labored in Allied industries, particularly in munitions production. At this time, the speculation also became very widespread in the West that the Chinese were profiting from the narcotics trade with Europe. Furthermore, the thought of Chinese men having sexual relations with white women scandalized conservative Western circles. Various reactions to these East-West encounters found expression in literature: *The Yellow Danger* (M. P. Shiel, originally Matthew Phipps Shiell, 1898), *Limehouse Nights* (Thomas Burke, 1917), *The Tomb of Ts'in* (Edgar Wallace, 1916), or the legendary *The Insidious Dr. Fu-Manchu* (Sax Rohmer, the pseudonym of Arthur Sarsfield Ward, 1913). In these and other tales, Chinese villains, seducers, or conspirators dominated the action, and they not infrequently forged their base, deceitful plans in opium dens and other morally reprehensible establishments. Even in America, which unlike the European countries did not have a reputation in China of being a colonial power, anti-Chinese images enjoyed a heyday in public opinion. The threat that allegedly emanated from the yellow race mutated there into fear of an invasion of coolies, the labor forces from China who worked for near starvation wages. At least in the United States, the figure of the would-be world conqueror Dr. Fu Manchu had a positive counterweight in Charlie Chan, a perceptive, good-natured detective who in dozens of popular films represented a different, more "appealing" image of the Chinese.

The collapse of the Qing Dynasty, the founding of the Republic, the Versailles Peace Treaty, and, linked with them the rise of Chinese nationalism, increased the interest of broader circles in the West for events in distant China. The "yellow-peril" literature subsided a bit in the 1920s and 1930s, as more sophisticated authors took up the then "in" topic: In several popular novels, including the widely read *The Good Earth*, Pearl Buck, who was herself born in China, described in great detail and with a sense of timelessness a range of Chinese characters, from poor peasants to wealthy landowners. In his novel *La condition humaine,* André Malraux condemned the heinous policies of the West and the betrayal of the Revolution. Paul Claudel's friend Victor Segalen, an art historian, archaeologist, physician, and author, created with his semi-autobiographical novel *René Leys* a picture of fading grandeur and decadence in the days of the declining Imperial dynasty.[1]

In the nineteenth century, missionaries (James Legge, W. A. P. Martin, Karl Gützlaff and others) and diplomats (Sir Thomas Wade, Lord Elgin, Rutherford Alcock and Anson Burlingame) contributed to the development of Western interest in China. In the twentieth century, by contrast, not only the actors, but also the forms of East-West encounter changed in many ways: Missionaries no longer enjoyed the positive reputations of their Jesuit predecessors at the courts of the last Ming and first Qing emperors. To the contrary, most Chinese now viewed them primarily as hindrances to their own national emancipation. This again also influenced perceptions of them in a country that had grown tired of foreign missionaries. In the nineteenth century, diplomats had had a relatively free hand in structuring the extraterritorial areas: From the Qing they took whatever seemed particularly right and cheap to build up a Western treaty port culture. The strengthening of the Chinese central power and respectively the increasing politicization of Chinese society strongly limited the natural scope for action of many diplomats in the first third of the twentieth century. It was not rare for them to become prisoners within the Peking embassy quarters, which became miniature Western enclaves. Only a few inquisitive persons were willing and able to break out of this freely chosen isolation and encounter the foreign China (as for example the American envoy Paul Reinsch or his Italian diplomatic colleague Daniele Varè).

In the twentieth century, not only the way of looking at China in the West, but also the range of observers changed. Given the Western sense of superiority to the Chinese, steadily increasing efforts were made to share with them Western knowledge and achievements in the technical and theoretical domains. While Jesuit missionaries had already made their debut as advisors four centuries earlier, it was not until the nineteenth century that Western countries or institutions sent higher numbers of advisors to China. Most of the Western "helpers"—trained professionals as well as charlatans—remained anonymous. Among the best known were Sir Robert Hart, Inspector General of the Chinese customs system; Charles Gordon (also known as Chinese Gordon), commander in the war against the Taiping; and Gustav Detring, who served Li Hongzhang, one of the most competent officials and diplomats in all of China.

The integration of China into the international rail network with the Chinese Eastern Railway, the increase in shipping routes from West to East, as well as finally the commencement of regular air traffic between Europe and China furthered the wanderlust and travel possibilities of curious Westerners, who thought and reacted differently than earlier travelers. Missionaries and diplomats, who had held a monopoly on China reportage into the twentieth century, seemed only to a limited degree capable of conveying "objective" images of the Middle Kingdom. Other advisors replaced them (such as, for example, the political scientist Frank J. Goodnow, a constitutional law advisor, and "General" Homer Lea, one of Sun Yat-sen's many military advisors); they streamed into China in droves, and not just on their own initiative. Along with them came Western scholars, explorers, students, adventurers, writers, and finally refugees. In contrast to the missionaries or diplomats, who had come with a clear pre-given assignment from a government or religious denomination, they usually had the advantage of being more independent and accordingly freer to perceive China and its world in many different ways. Common to, for example, a Sir Harold Acton or a Sir Osbert Sitwell, was, first of all, that they came to China in order to understand, not to change anything. They did not have the sense of superiority that seduced so many Westerners to, consciously or unconsciously, act like members of a master race in dealings with the Chinese. Contact with the Chinese was not foreign to them; their aim was not distance, but rather closeness.

In this book, the biographies of persons who participated in this unique meeting of East and West in the twentieth century are set against the background of the special Chinese context that shaped the spirit of the age. They all possessed, besides the fact that they were of Jewish origin, an individual relationship to China that enabled them to gain valuable experience in the Middle Kingdom. The reader will find among them persons of every national, societal, and professional origin. Biographies not only capture the reader's interest in great themes, they also help to explain the subject's times, even his entire age. In the following, the attempt is made to represent these often disjointed life courses, which often crisscross several continents, from the viewpoint of their relationship to China, and where the persons encounter Eastern *Lebenswelten*, to pause for a moment to capture what it was that informed their impressions and images of the Middle Kingdom. I did not choose the subjects of this study arbitrarily. I followed a principle that historian Dan Diner states at the beginning of his universal historical interpretation of the twentieth century: "What . . . is held to be essential is left to the judgmental power of the historians. . . . [It is a matter] of meaningfully reducing the complexity and variety of historical realities."[2]

NOTES

1. Buck, *Good Earth* (1931); Malraux, *La condition humaine* (1933); Segalen, *René Leys* (1971).
2. Diner, *Jahrhundert* (1999), p. 9.

Chapter 1

The Long Established: Jewish Old China Hands

I. DESCENDANTS: JEWS WITH SEPHARDIC ROOTS

The oldest Jewish community residing in Shanghai consisted of Sephardi Jews (they called themselves Baghdadi Jews) who, chiefly for economic reasons, between 1820 and the start of the First World War reached India and traveled on to the Far East from Baghdad, which was then under Ottoman rule. The majority of the Abrahams, Kadoories, Ezras, Solomons, and Sassoons belonged to the professional category of businessmen who had become wealthy by trading in opium, tea, silk, and real estate. Not all, however, disposed of such fantastic sums that permitted them to call street blocks, banks, and even electrical works their own. The majority of the Sephardi Jews—their number in Shanghai probably never exceeded eight hundred—belonged, relative to the other foreigners residing there, to the lower middle class. They earned their living as blue- and white-collar workers, chiefly employed by the companies of their rich fellow Jews.

The Sephardi Jews in Shanghai were in many ways outsiders among outsiders. They belonged to one of the numerous minorities in the Shanghai of those years, and if individual representatives had not been literally conspicuous in the architectural streetscape of Shanghai through their enormous financial strength, they would have had the status of an insignificant marginal group.[1] The partly voluntary, partly obligatory search for their own identity and the meditation on their roots made the Sephardic community a markedly coherent construction. Many maintained their religious customs and practices: They went to the synagogue, lived according to the Jewish holiday calendar, observed the dietary rules, and tried to put into practice the biblical wisdom of their ancestors. Marriages between Sephardim who considered themselves Orthodox and members of the Ashkenazi community were rare; still rarer were marriages between Sephardim and non-Jews.

Sir Victor Sassoon

Sir Victor Sassoon was not a man to choose his words diplomatically, especially not when speaking of "his" China: "Sir Victor Sassoon's talk is giving us endless worry."[2] This expression of concern by a representative of a Shanghai aid committee was a response to anti-Japanese comments made by Sassoon during his February 1940 visit to America.[3] If today it is the pronouncements of a George Soros that throw the financial world into a state of turmoil, at the time it was not only the financial markets in Shanghai, but also his fellow Jews in China who responded to his comments with some consternation. Given the superior strength of the Japanese, the Jews viewed their—in any case precarious—situation as further endangered. "It is with reverence and gratitude to the Nipponese Empire that Far Eastern Jewry once again reiterates its unshaken belief and also its readiness to co-operate and assist in establishing the peace for East Asia towards which the great Nipponese nation is leading us."[4] In contrast, Sir Victor, who was born in Naples, educated in England, and served in the British Army during the First World War, was extremely unsuited for such bowing and scraping.

Equipped already in his young years with an extraordinarily astute feeling for economic relationships, Sir Victor took over the business empire of E. D. Sassoon & Company in the Far East, with bases in Bombay, Hong Kong, and Shanghai. Sir Victor had the reputation of a pioneer in sponsoring social assistance for his employees and their health benefits, for which purpose he initiated various aid programs. After transferring his headquarters to Shanghai in the early 1930s, Sir Victor immediately became entangled in the political constellation of that literally explosive atmosphere. When the Japanese occupied Zhabei, the Chinese part of Shanghai in 1932, there were shoot-outs. One occurred near the Cathay Hotel, the "Sassoon House," precisely when Sir Victor was enjoying his midday meal. In the following years, Sir Victor often found himself confronted with events that reinforced his fear of a Japanese occupation of the city.

Sir Victor was not a practicing Jew, although he did not deny his roots. Up until his mother's death, he refrained from using his Saturdays to pursue his interests in business and horseracing, the pastime he loved above all else. Many also thought that he should have insisted on having a traditional Jewish funeral service.[5] While Zionist ideas for solving the "Jewish Problem" seemed to have been foreign to him, he worked especially hard to aid the Jews escaping to Shanghai from Nazi Germany. The luxurious parties organized by Sassoon in the Cathay Hotel had a legendary reputation, whereby Sir Victor especially liked the company of attractive women—the decked out wives of diplomats, as well as Eurasian beauties. Yet Victor Sassoon also got along well with the Chinese: H. H. Kung, who was educated at Yale, Chiang Kai-shek's brother-in-law and for a time the Finance Minister, was his friend and patron and insisted on personally awarding Sha Sun (Sassoon's name in Chinese) a gold medal for his generous support of the Chinese Red Cross Hospital.

Surprisingly, there are no studies of two financial enterprises' involvement in Chinese domestic politics: D. Sassoon Sons and Co., and E. D. Sassoon and Company. It is certain that after their founding both enterprises worked closely with Chinese *maibans*, the compradors (natives who acted as agents for Western companies), as well as granting generous loans to various Chinese governments from the late nineteenth century until Chiang Kai-shek's Kuomintang government. It is likewise no secret that, at least until the time of the "warlords," these two financial empires also traded in opium and thereby accumulated immense fortunes. The firm of E. D. Sassoon, very probably *the* trigger of the 1920s Shanghai real estate boom, urged the Bank of England to rescue China from collapse in the mid-1930s economic crisis.[6] Not only representatives of D. Sassoon Sons and Co., but also of E. D. Sassoon served as members of the supervisory board of the banking empire of the Hong Kong and Shanghai Banking Corporation, the former without interruption from 1864 to 1956.[7] They thereby enjoyed, until war broke out in the Pacific, an excellent rapport with the innermost Chinese economic and governmental circles.

After the Sino-Japanese War began in 1937, Sir Victor held lavish parties in the Cathay Hotel to create a mood of sympathy for the Chinese cause. He was convinced even then of Chiang Kai-shek's future victory over the Japanese and prophesied that the Japanese army would eventually bleed itself white in China. Nevertheless, Sir Victor finally yielded to Japanese threats and intimidation attempts and left his beloved city on the Huangpu River, which had made him the "J. P. Morgan of the Orient," just in time before Pearl Harbor. Back at the starting point of his economic expansion in Bombay, he mourned for China or respectively for those of his assets that were falling into hostile hands there.

Sir Victor was of course glad when Japan capitulated, but he was quite aware that "his" China was forever lost: Extraterritoriality had been abolished, the railroad system was devastated, gasoline was very scarce, the black market was in full swing, and inflation was already beginning. To be sure, the Japanese had in the meantime vacated the Cathay Hotel, but now General Wedemeyer, General Stilwell's successor, occupied Sir Victor's Suite on the top story of the Sassoon House. The open outbreak of the Civil

Figure 1.1
"I gave India up, and China has given me up" is supposed to have been Sir Victor Sassoon's comment on the end of his East-West career. His financial enterprises first and foremost in Shanghai were closely linked with Chinese domestic politics.

Figure 1.2
The Cathay, also called the Sassoon House, was completed in 1929. It was then the most luxurious hotel in Shanghai.

War and the increasingly precarious situation in Shanghai were further reasons for the once richest man in China to take leave of the Middle Kingdom. With the entry of the communists into Shanghai, the activities of E. D. Sassoon & Co. came permanently to an end, and not without the usual intimidation and extortion on the side of the new masters of China. "I gave India up, and China has given me up," is supposed to have been Sir Victor's comment on the end of his East-West career.

Sir Elly Kadoorie

Overall, the Kadoories deserve the highest honors for their philanthropic work to aid the Baghdadi Jews who were at one time resident in China. Like the Sassoons, Abrahams, Gubbays, or Sophers, the Kadoories originally also came to China from Baghdad. Sir Elly Kadoorie (1867–1944) began his career with E. D. Sassoon and Co. in Hong Kong, which he soon represented in the treaty harbors of Shanghai, Tianjin, and Ningbo. Even at that time the family undertook, beyond their widely ramified interests and relationships, charitable activities in Hong Kong, Mesopotamia, and India, and later also in Shanghai and Canton (Guangzhou). What was different about the Kadoorie family's approach was that they chiefly benefited the natives—above all the education of children and youth—to which some of their co-religionists reacted with a certain disappointment. Thus, for example, Elly's brother, Sir Ellis Kadoorie, had already built six schools for the Chinese in the early days of the Republic, but not even one for Jews.[8] By sponsoring free education for the less prosperous, the Kadoorie family offered Chinese pupils a good alternative to the Christian mission schools.

Perhaps Sir Elly Kadoorie did not love the limelight quite as much as Sir Victor, but he also had a fondness for ostentatious architecture, at least when it was a matter of his own residence. In Shanghai, where Sir Elly settled in the closing years of the Great War, this was the Marble Hall on the Great Western Road (today Yan'an Xi Lu). The white classical show palace boasted a ballroom that, if desired, could be lit up by thousands of differently colored incandescent bulbs. Here Sir Elly entertained his guests—for example, the Indian Nobel Prize winner Rabindranath Tagore, who visited the Huangpu metropolis in the 1920s and proclaimed his interest in Zionist ideas.[9] Sir Elly became the President of the Shanghai Zionist Association starting in 1915, but he alienated himself from this movement as a consequence of a dispute over the construction of a "garden city" that he proposed for what was then Palestine. In Sir Elly's Marble Hall, the lord of the manor also signed checks to aid the Chinese civilian population, so distressed after the Japanese attacks.

In contrast to Sir Victor, Sir Elly and his family do not succeed in leaving the Far East in time before the outbreak of the war in the Pacific. While Sir Elly dies in Stanley Camp, the Hong Kong internment camp for citizens of the Allied countries, his son Lord Lawrence Kadoorie—"a true Hong Kong native"—survives the hardships of Japanese internment and indeed, after 1943, in the Zhabei Camp in Shanghai and later under house arrest in his own Marble Hall. After the war, Lord Lawrence Kadoorie does not wait—like Sir Victor—for the arrival of the communists, but instead immediately moves to Hong Kong, where he contributes to the flourishing of China Light and Power, Hong Kong's largest electric utility company, which his father had founded. "My chief asset was my father's good name," affirms Lord Kadoorie on many occasions.[10] Unlike many of his co-religionists who left China's harbors at the latest toward the end of the Civil War, Kadoorie is convinced that when the time comes he can find a *modus vivendi* with the communists.

The "Asian Rockefeller," as Lord Lawrence Kadoorie is called in his lifetime, understands China like no one else. He, who has enjoyed no great formal higher education, disposes of rich experience in dealing with the Middle Kingdom. He has great confidence in the Chinese, and he is aware that most Westerners had made mistakes at the time when Shanghai was being lost: "Western investors . . . should not behave as if they owned Hong Kong. It was that kind of attitude in Shanghai that brought down the Bamboo Curtain."[11]

Lord Kadoorie correctly points out that during his lifetime, Chinese leaders had primarily oriented themselves to practical considerations. Consequently, he does not share the doom and gloom pessimism of many businesspeople, according to which Hong Kong would lose its economic position after its return to China in 1997. "Here in Hong Kong, we continue to build on a foundation of uncertainty, but I remain convinced that this city has an important part to play in the contacts between East and West and that in this changing world we may look forward to the future with optimism."[12]

Lord Lawrence was proud of his Jewish roots, which at the start of the 1970s cost him his seat on the board of directors of the Hongkong and Shanghai Banking Corporation.[13] In conversations, he characterizes himself as a reform Jew. For years, Lord Lawrence, "almost one of us" as an Englishman once said, presided as the president of the Hong Kong Jewish community.[14] He served as chairman of China Light & Power, which provided the entire electricity supply of the former Crown Colony, as well as being the majority stockholder of a wide range of Hong Kong's trademarks (for example, the Peak Tram on Victoria Peak, the Star Ferry between Hong Kong and Kowloon and the prestigious Peninsula Hotel). He thereby found himself again in the position of his father, who with his fortune—"Money has not been my master"—had sponsored large philanthropic projects. One of the doubtlessly greatest contributions of Lord Lawrence and his brother Horace was the 1951 founding of the Kadoorie Agricultural Aid Association.[15] This fund enabled millions of refugees, following the defeat of Chiang Kai-shek in the Civil War, to cultivate the steep, fissured hillsides of the New Territories, the border area of Hong Kong with the People's Republic of China (PRC), as well as to engage in poultry and hog breeding. Thirty-five years later, Kadoorie's China Light & Power signed a contract with the government in Peking for the construction of a nuclear reactor near Hong Kong. By this time, the government had long since transformed Sir Elly's Marble Hall in Shanghai into a Children's Palace for gifted children.

Silas Aaron Hardoon

The list of Sephardic tycoons in twentieth-century Shanghai would have an inexcusable gap if no mention were made of Silas Aaron Hardoon. However, only in his geographic and religious origins does his biography resemble the life stories of a Sir Victor Sassoon or a Sir Elly Kadoorie. The personal fates and individual encounters with China were too different for significant parallels to be obvious, and yet his reputation for philanthropic work competed with those of the two other Sephardic greats of Shanghai: "Mr. HARDOON . . . has received several decorations from the Chinese Government for his philanthropic work in China. He is advisor to the Tuchun [dujun, i.e., military governor) of Kiangsu, to the government of Anwei and others. He is probably the best and most widely known foreigner in China amongst the Chinese."[16]

Hardoon possessed certain remarkable characteristics that distinguished him from other Old China Hands, Jews and non-Jews alike. "Mr. Hardoon was loved and hated, cursed and praised, but few people knew him well. Few understood his many eccentricities. Mr. Hardoon was a symbol of the white man's position in the Far East. . . . He was a blend of all faiths and hopes, a talented man who lived his life in an exotic setting as he thought best."[17] This eccentricity included, for example, that twelve years after he reached Shanghai from Baghdad via Bombay in 1886, he married a Eurasian, Luo Jialing (Liza Roos), which given the treaty port mentality of the time was quite surprising and rare.[18] She, the illegitimate daughter of a Chinese woman and a French police official, was to introduce the former employee of E. D. Sassoon & Co. and later manager of the Hardoon Real Estate Company to a world of foreign customs and practices, Chinese moral conceptions, and the Buddhist faith of her ancestors.

Completely captivated by the Chinese spiritual and intellectual world, the unconventional couple resided in a house set in the midst of a traditional Chinese landscape, the Aili Yuan ("ai" for love, "li" for beauty and "yuan" for garden), also called Hatong Huayuan (Hardoon Garden). The garden was the brainchild of Huang Zongyang, a Buddhist monk who until 1914 or 1915 was also Hardoon's most influential advisor for all "Chinese matters."[19] In accord with the classical rules of geomancy ("fengshui"), numerous pavilions, pagodas, ponds, artificial hills, cliffs and grottoes, a Buddhist temple, a small theater, and even a stone ship fit harmoniously into the garden landscape, which was located in the western part of the International Settlement on the Bubbling Well Road (now Nanjing Xi Lu). One might say that in this way Hardoon's aesthetic sensitivity—similar to his matrimonial choice—strongly contrasted with the tastes of the rest of the Anglicized group of Sephardic big names. Whereas it was usual for Western businesspeople to create an oasis of European culture in the treaty port of Shanghai and to distance themselves as much as possible from the Chinese population, Hardoon attempted to assimilate himself into the Chinese world across an entire range of ideas and activities.

Figure 1.3
"Silas Aaron Hardoon was loved and hated, cursed and praised, but few people knew him well." The Baghdad-born Hardoon was regarded as a person with a preference for the eccentric, someone to whom the so fitting expression "going native" applied completely.

To be sure, similar to Lord Kadoorie, Hardoon did not enjoy a high level of formal education, and like the members of the Sassoon Dynasty, he scaled the ladder of financial power chiefly through the opium trade. Still, already at the time of the proclamation of the Republic, this eccentric among the Sephardic tycoons had a comprehensive political and cultural grasp of Chinese circumstances. From 1911 on, many considered the Aili Garden as not only a place of refuge for the defeated mandarins of the Qing Dynasty, but also for revolutionaries of the first hour.[20]

In the years between 1916 and 1925, dismissed military potentates are included among Hardoon's various guests, with whom he, to some extent, engaged in patronage-like relationships. Overall, in the years 1920–1925, he placed bets on various different wild cards, just to be certain of being on the winning side after a war. After the successful end of the Northern Expedition (a military campaign led by the Kuomintang from 1926 to 1928 to unify China) under Chiang Kai-shek, it became increasingly difficult for the Sephardic entrepreneur to gain advantages from his network of connections. Because of his long years of supporting prominent military leaders, for example General Sun Chuanfang, Hardoon became a prisoner of his own "policy," to be sure not directly harassed by Nanking (or Nanjing, the capital of the Republic of China), but also no longer courted.

No less spectacular is the guest list of people gifted in the arts at Hardoon's house. By means of broadly positioned patronage and generous sponsorship, Hardoon personified the typical Chinese role of a merchant and philanthropist: Under the influence of his wife and a new advisor for "Chinese affairs," he tried, particularly between 1915 and 1922, to expand the Aili Garden into a center for traditional Confucian studies. Because his efforts to revive the values and moral conceptions of the classics, especially of Confucius, were in conflict with the then prevalent spirit of the times, his ideas and actions appear even more eccentric. Around the turn of the century, Hardoon and Luo Jialing had even supported the foundation of one of the then most modern educational institutions for girls and women. However, after Hardoon's advisor, Huang Zongyang, had to leave the country briefly because of his progressive ideas, the remarkable couple began to concentrate on supporting Buddhist projects.[21]

To visitors in those days, the Aili Garden may have seemed like an anachronistic survival of the nineteenth century in the great pulsing metropolis. An almost surrealistic atmosphere prevailed in this "forbidden city" within modern Shanghai, in comparison to the events happening outside this little world. However, the walls of Hardoon's property were not entirely impenetrable. A few of the students there caught the spirit of the May Fourth Movement, the cultural, political, and anti-imperialist movement that grew out of student demonstrations in Beijing on May 4, 1919, and so at the beginning of the 1920s there were likewise demonstrations and accusations against the school direction in the Aili Garden. It was chiefly a protest against the poor quality of the meals, linked to the question of the logic of the strict rules of the almost cloister-like school routine.[22]

Therefore, many Chinese regarded Hardoon's Aili Garden as a refuge for the preservation of their rich cultural heritage. The scion of Sephardi Jews and former watchman in the service of D. Sassoon & Co. had—by trading in opium, acquiring real estate, and above all through an exotic marriage with an Eurasian woman—succeeded in becoming one of the few foreigners who actually gained admission to the Chinese business and social world, generally inaccessible to Westerners. As a successful entrepreneur, the "richest man east of Suez" assumed the role of a valued, albeit rather taciturn patron of the arts. If necessary, he enhanced his performances with a deliberate sartorial tactic: At public events in his Aili Garden, he preferred to appear in the garb of an educated Confucian scholar or a Qing official (he chose such attire because Chinese philosophy assigned the merchant the lowest rank within the social classes). Even in his office on Nanking Road, he reportedly wore a long, if necessary thickly quilted, Chinese gown (*pao*). Among the foreigners, Hardoon, who actually held British citizenship, was regarded as rather odd, a person with a preference for the eccentric, someone to whom the so fitting expression "going native" applied completely.

Although Hardoon did not speak Mandarin—perhaps he spoke the Shanghai dialect—he assimilated himself to Chinese thinking and Chinese modes of behavior. It was important for him to enhance his status with the Chinese by assuming the appropriate demeanor and practicing the right symbolic rituals. Even former employees of the Peking Imperial Palace, among them not a few eunuchs, belonged to the personnel of Hardoon's Shanghai residence.[23] Politicians, soldiers and literati from the Middle Kingdom—they all flattered him, the benefactor and patron who offered them in the Aili Garden a world in miniature format that elsewhere was doomed to decline. The lord of the manor lived and thought in a border region that enabled him, at least as seen from outside, to assume a place in the Chinese *Lebenswelt*. Perhaps self-interest did not lead him to adopt his behavior. Rather he may have wanted to overcome the barriers between East and West and to himself experience the cosmopolitanism of the Huangpu metropolis—the dream of an idealist.

Hardoon, like Sir Victor, permitted posterity to learn nothing about his personal encounters with China. Today's contemporary can merely read *about* him, nothing *by* him. Hardoon apparently did not want, and could not bear, to leave behind written testimony about his experiences in China. In the Shanghai Jewish community he did not have the best reputation, above all because after his death in 1931 it was found that he had not left any of his fortune to the Jewish community, for which many could not forgive him.

> He lived to a good old age, leaving behind him mammon Korah! Lavish sums were spent to build this mausoleum, a monument to the man who hoarded a vast wealth, leaving not a penny for charity, Jewish or otherwise. . . . Many have forgotten the late Mr. Hardoon already, there being no footprints of history left by him on the pages of time. The late Mr. Hardoon was ruined by success![24]

Even his funeral, on June 19, 1931, outraged some in the Jewish community. Although Hardoon was buried with Jewish rites, Buddhist monks took part in the funeral services, and still worse things were yet to come for orthodox Jewish souls: A month later the monks held their own "observance" with the participation of Taoist priests, who performed rituals to enable the soul of the deceased to waft away on the breeze.

Hardoon was the only foreigner who served on both the Shanghai Municipal Council (SMC) and the French Conseil Municipal, the two (foreign) official bodies governing the International Settlement and the Concession Française. That a Shanghai street was named for him (today Tongren Lu) gave him in retrospect a lasting monument, not only among his co-religionists by birth, but also among the Chinese he so admired.

Probably no other foreigner was able to leave behind him more traces than Hardoon. Already during his lifetime, and above all after his death and up until today the figure of Hardoon was and is regarded as not only a philanthropist and patron of the arts, but also—in a consciously negative, because politically opportune stereotypification—an adventurer (*maoxian-jia*), exploiter (*boxuezhe*) or even "bloodsucker" among the Chinese (*xixue-gui*).[25] We can best regard Hardoon's endeavors to establish his Aili Garden as a traditional center for the preservation of the Chinese cultural heritage as the striving of a Westerner to attain a highly esteemed status among his Chinese friends and partners.

N. E. B. Ezra

Nissim Elias Benjamin Ezra, for short N. E. B. Ezra, was the editor of *Israel's Messenger*. Founded in 1904, this newspaper for the Sephardi Jews was his baby, in which he regularly published contributions to the West-East dialogue. In an editorial under the title "Buddha, the Light of Asia," for example, Ezra, who was born in Lahore (now Pakistan), expounds the universal validity of ethical laws.[26] While he finds few friendly words for the West ("the West where the engines of destruction are ready to inflict harm and injury"), he extols the East as a refuge of humanity ("East is yeast to humanity"). In view of the inhumane regimes in Germany and Moscow, the time was right to decide for the fundamental tenets of faith inherent in all religions—"either God or ba'al!" Ezra, not entirely free of controversy in the Shanghai Sephardic community, pleads for the advent of a new Buddha who, like Moses and the prophets, Confucius and the Zoroastrians, or Jesus and Mohammed, would pour out the sacred spirit on humanity, threatened by tyranny.

In his editorials, N. E. B. Ezra often recalls the special task and pride of the Jews in helping to modernize China. "It may be said without exaggeration that Jewish enterprises, Jewish skill and Jewish brain had contributed immeasurably in developing the latent resources of the country and stimulating trade, industry and commerce."[27] Ezra thought of Confucius as like Buddha, the savior of the Chinese nation who would lead the country out of its difficulties and move the world as a whole: "Guided by the spirit of her great Sage, the difficulties ahead will be avoided and subdued. Confucius pleaded for justice and righteousness; he made morality and good government synonymous. If the country is willing to follow him and adopt his teachings then China will be able to 'move the world' in the real sense of the word."[28]

If in view of the Japanese threat, Ezra's ideas may have seemed all too idealistic for Eastern and Western ears at that time, and if they were definitely classed as blasphemous during the first forty years after the founding of the PRC, they would probably meet with agreement among contemporary "modern neo-Confucians." Since the late 1980s, the Chinese Communist Party has attempted to portray Confucianism as the quintessence of Chinese culture.

II. RUSSIAN JEWS ORIGINATING FROM THE CZARIST EMPIRE

The group of Russian Jews who reached Shanghai in various sequential and local stages was clearly numerically larger than their Sephardic co-religionists (before the outbreak of the Second World War about 4000 Russian Jews lived in the coastal city). The settlement of Russian Jews ran parallel to the cycles of political and social developments of the Czarist Empire. In times of oppression, revolution, war, and economic need, all not atypical phenomena, not only in old Russia, but also in the young Soviet Union, the distant, and for Russian standards unlimited, freedoms of China attracted people with a less favorable lot. Traders, grocers, members of the Czarist army (after the 1905 Russo-Japanese War), political exiles, and persecuted persons (especially after anti-Semitic pogroms and anti-Jewish campaigns between 1905 and 1917), artists and adventurers were among those who sought their fortune in the "Wild East."

The social composition of the Russian Jews entailed that they were not exactly received with open arms by their Sephardic co-religionists. Among the many upright emigrants there were some dubious figures, for whom the "swamp" of lawlessness in Shanghai was ideal for their not always reputable business activities: Trade in narcotics and weapons, human trafficking, blackmail and extortion, or the operation of disreputable bars. Beyond this, the Shanghai Municipal Police (SMP) seemed to be of the view since the beginning of the 1920s that among the Bolshevist agitators working in Shanghai there were also many Russians of Jewish origins.

The majority of the Russian Jews were for various reasons not especially religious, which did not exactly simplify the relationships with the old-established Sephardi Jews, who were often skeptical of the newcomers. The Russian Jews had the one advantage in contrast to their rich Sephardic brothers that after the outbreak of the Pacific War they were not classified as citizens of the enemy states, and thereby were not interned, but rather could move about the city and pursue their business relatively freely.

Rena Krasno

Strangers Always is the title of the autobiographical story of Rena Krasno, a Russian-Jewish woman born in 1923 in Shanghai.[29] The author, who later lived in the United States until her death in 2009, thereby implies that the majority of the Russian Jews in China generally had less contact with the Chinese than their Sephardic co-religionists. Overall, they did not establish close economic relationships to China like the famous tycoons; nor did any of them seem to have a particularly marked journalistic curiosity that would have gone beyond the treatment of internal Jewish topics.[30] Although no one discussed God in Rena Krasno's home (her father was David B. Rabinovich, editor of the Russian newspaper *Nascha Shisn / Our Life*), the family identified passionately with the Jewish people. Rena Krasno's report of her story and her experiences in Shanghai, based on neatly arranged, detailed diary entries, offers contemporary readers a vivid excerpt of a life in the Huangpu metropolis.

Yet the eyes and ears of the stateless Russian woman are hardly committed to following the Chinese world of Shanghai. For her, Chinese people are merely insignificant extras, so to speak "the huge, massive, subdued background."[31] Her interest, sometimes also curiosity or even respect, centers much more on the Westerners in Shanghai: Kadoorie, Sassoon, Hardoon, and other Shanghai "celebrities." A different sort of Russian Jewess, *Anna Ginsbourg* (Frenkel), described by Krasno as a young woman full of vitality and enthusiasm, did not belong to the group of these human "emblems" of Shanghai. She represented an exception in the Russian-Jewish community, because she had sought and found a closer relationship to her Chinese environment.

Anna Ginsbourg

Born in 1911 in Samara, Anna Alexandrovna Ginsbourg lives initially in Harbin in Northeastern China, where she attends the law school of the Oriental University and graduates as an attorney in the same year as Hitler comes to power. In Shanghai, according to a report of the Shanghai Municipal Police, the Soviet citizen tries to work as an independent legal advisor, while her father serves as a judge on the highest court of the province.[32]

In 1935 Anna Ginsbourg becomes the secretary of the International League for Cultural Cooperation, located in Shanghai. This association sets as its aim, besides better understanding between China and the West, the "revitalization of the Chinese nation by means of elements from modern Western civilization."[33] The members include, in addition to Chinese academics, a range of Westerners with an interest in China, such as the American journalist Wilbur Burton, the Austrian refugee and dentist Herbert Wunsch, or the Russian architect Emmanuel Gran. In 1937, Anna Ginsbourg receives an invitation from the University of Suzhou to give lectures on law. We do not know whether she accepts. In any case, in those years she frequently publishes articles on legal topics in *The China Weekly Review*.

"Law is Life" is the title of an article that the then 26-year-old Anna Ginsbourg writes as a plea for the recognition of law as a "comprehensive life science."[34] In another contribution, written with no less commitment, Anna Ginsbourg draws attention to the debate, which is today once again current and topical, about the definition of universal justice. "Justice is universal, but its application differs depending on the general conception of every individual nation."[35] She was already convinced that China, if it wanted to become a member of the world community, would have to adopt Western legal conceptions. However, she was sufficiently familiar with Chinese culture and history to recognize that China itself possesses a long legal history with great continuity that would make it possible for both conceptions to coexist. Thereby she approaches the view of Joseph Needham, who thought that, "Europeans should cease to think that they have nothing to learn from the legal systems of Asia."[36]

After WWII she moved to Australia and was particularly interested in the fate of her persecuted co-religionists stranded in Shanghai. Even during the Japanese occupation, she edited a small booklet by Julius Rudolph, *Shanghai—City of Refuge*, for which she also wrote the foreword.[37] An interview with Trebitsch-Lincoln (discussed below), shortly before his death, is still regarded as a unique and simultaneously quaint document of this incident.[38]

Judith Hasser

A no less dynamic personality was *Judith Hasser*, a member of the Zionist Beitar youth movement. Her family moved to China even before the October Revolution of 1917. Through trade with Russia, the stateless Hassers acquire so much wealth that they are able to purchase the building that once housed the Austrian consulate in Shanghai, with no less than 23 rooms and 10 servants. In her sweet and light, somewhat novelistic autobiography, *Shanghai Lost, Jerusalem Regained,* Hasser, who was born in 1927, contrasts Western luxury and quantity with the Chinese *quality* of human relations: "The less fortunate Chinese, who had to pack several families into very cramped space, developed a communal life and got along. . . . They cooked their meals together and seemed most congenial. All this was in marked contrast to the tense and unhappy home atmosphere I endured."[39]

Judith Hasser, who after the war built up a branch of the Jewish underground movement Irgun Zvai Leumi in Shanghai, certainly took more interest in Jewish affairs than in her immediate Chinese surroundings. She spent a few of her summer vacations in Qingdao, which China's last Emperor, Pu Yi, also occasionally visited. In her direct manner, tackling things unconventionally and circumventing overly strict protocols, she often met Chinese businesspeople and politicians, hoping to gain their support for Zionist positions—as in the time after the 1917 Balfour Declaration became public.[40] In 1948 Hasser left Shanghai for Israel, with no premonition that the Middle Kingdom would so soon be communist ruled.[41]

Georges Spunt

"J'ai plus de souvenirs que si j'avais mille ans" (I have more memories than if I were a thousand years old) is the epigraph from Charles Baudelaire in a book entitled *A Place in Time*. To Westerners who lived for many years in China during the first part of the twentieth century this would seem no exaggeration, certainly not for the author of this work, Georges Spunt, a connoisseur of life, born in Shanghai in 1923. His thoughts are an expression of an eccentric spirit that with a child's eyes, on the one side, and the mind of an adult, on the other, tries to gain a feeling for and understanding of his unfamiliar surroundings. In his autobiographical writings, he packs his impressions into a minimal space not unlike the Babylonian language confusion of Russian, Italian, French, Yiddish, and (pidgin-) English spoken in the Spunt family home in Shanghai.

His mother's family came to China from Berdichev, a city in Northern Ukraine, and Odessa via Egypt, where she was educated in a Catholic convent. Her first contact with the apparent opposition between East and West occurred in the harbor of Shanghai, where she saw colorful junks with eyes painted on the bows sailing past British gunboats.[42] Initially the relatives of Georges' mother, like most Russian Jews at the start of their Shanghai odyssey, live in the Hongkou district (northern part of Shanghai). After the grandmother finds a suitable husband for her daughter (Maximilian Spunt, an Austrian with a French passport), they move to the French Concession. Maximilian Spunt is the owner of the Laou Kung Mao Mills, a cotton mill, and often travels throughout the interior of China, while Georges and his two brothers are entrusted to the care of Chinese servants and other members of the family. They observe Jewish commandments only to a limited degree: "What a family—only in birth and in death are you Jews," an aunt is supposed to have declared at Georges Spunt's circumcision.[43]

Already at a tender age Georges begins to listen to the political discussions of his father with various illustrious personalities of Shanghai society. He thereby learns that there are nationalists, communists, and people from the North ("Northerners"), but they are, however, all Chinese and hate the white man.[44] To be sure, Maximilian Spunt is an exception among the Old China Hands: He knows the value of honor and saving face and accordingly cultivates his Chinese friends—and he understands the Chinese rage against foreigners. Of course, Georges Spunt hears, during debates at home on concessions, revolutions and civil war, of Chiang Kai-shek, Du Yuesheng, the notorious gangster, and other foreign sounding names; but these recede into the background behind the more familiar names like Elman and Moiseevich, Dickens, Hardy, and Defoe. There is scarcely any visible evidence in the Spunt household that they are in China. Georges' mother continues to enjoy convivial gatherings, at which one could chat about the latest Parisian fashion over a glass of Moët et Chandon champagne (after Maximilian's death this was replaced by Asti Spumante sparkling wine, because Georges' mother had an Italian lover) and a little Beluga caviar. Certainly, Georges and his two brothers also learn a few scraps of Chinese and sometimes even of Shanghaihua, the local dialect, but do not retain much more than the expression "nahkuning" (the native designation for a foreigner).

A Place in Time also means for Georges Spunt a confrontation with just those anti-Chinese taunts or even diatribes that his father had rejected during his lifetime. In the Cercle Sportif Français (a French social club on Rue Cardinal Mercier in Shanghai which was only accessible to Chinese with special authorization), he hears others express contempt for his Chinese friend Didi: They talked of "littee Chinee," who is "velly, velly yellow" or of "chink members" who have no business in foreign clubs.[45] During the following row and the usual defensive Chinese outbursts like "Foreign pigs!" or "Parasitic turtles!" Georges does not hold back from energetically supporting his Chinese friend. A few months later, after the outbreak of the Sino-Japanese War, the idealistic Georges Spunt must come down to earth, however. Didi tells him, the Westerner who was born and grew up there, that in the future Shanghai would be for him merely a sentimental memory. He was doubtlessly right: "Writing this makes me long for those days of youth and I'm saddened by the thought that the Chinese seem determined to make a modern city out of what was truly a unique one."[46] Perhaps precisely in order to preserve something lasting for posterity from the Chinese tradition, decades after his departure from China, Georges Spunt publishes a successful book on Chinese cuisine.[47]

Aaron Avshalomov

"He must not eat . . . any dish that lacks its proper seasoning," Confucius is supposed to have once admonished.[48] This applies *mutatis mutandis* as well to the musical sounds with which Aaron Avshalomov (Avshalomoff) occupied himself during his stay in China and afterward. Born in 1895 in Russian Nikolayevsk-on-Amur (a town near the Pacific Ocean on the Amur River in Siberia), already as a small child Avshalomov encountered Chinese culture. As a prosperous fishery owner, his father, the son of a mountain Jew from Derbent in Dagestan (now part of the Russian Federation located in the Northern Caucasus), disposed of the financial means and the confidence to entrust little Aaron to the care of a Chinese "factotum" from Shandong Province. Dung Fa, the name of the Chinese man, was a living remnant of the time when the area was still Chinese, before the Czar acquired it from the Emperor in the mid-nineteenth century. Dung Fa loves to entertain little Aaron with the most varied gestures and performances. For example, he dresses up as a warrior of the Han period, with a false beard and flourishing a sword, and he knows how to play a drum, sound a gong, and sing Chinese opera arias. One day when the Chinese man is away on business for Aaron's father, a Japanese nursemaid substitutes for him. She consoles the Jewish lad with melancholy tones from ancient Japan. Already then fantastic worlds open up for Aaron that are alien to the majority of the Old China Hands.

Aaron's next assignment is to study Hebrew at the local synagogue, where he imagines he hears the singing of Dung Fa when the rabbi recites the Bible. In view of the impending Russo-Japanese War, Aaron's father decides as a precaution to evacuate the family to the interior of Russia, specifically to Kazan on the Volga (capital city of Tatarstan), where Aaron attends his first opera performance (Tchaikovsky's "The Queen of Spades") and his first symphony concert (Schubert's "Unfinished"). Then they travel, by way of European detours, from Karlsbad (Karlovy Vary in the Czech Republic) to Khabarovsk (a Siberian administrative city near the northeast Chinese border), where Aaron reads biographies of Beethoven and other composers. Although his father presses him to study medicine in Switzerland, Aaron prefers music to the healing arts. Just before the First World War, his father calls him back to the Far East and immediately sends him—to avoid his being drafted into the Czarist army—to China. First, he goes to Harbin and then to Tianjin, where by playing the violin in a musical ensemble at the Victoria Hotel, he saves the necessary funds to finance a ship crossing to San Francisco.

Shortly after the Russian October Revolution, Aaron, in the meantime married to Esther Magidson, sets foot on Chinese soil for the second time. In the cities of Tsingtao (Qingdao) and Tientsin (Tianjin) he wants to at last systematically study Chinese music, but must, however, first concentrate on earning his daily bread: in a slaughterhouse, as a cattle dealer, and as a member of the British Tientsin Volunteer Corps. Like many other visitors to China before and after him, in 1921 Avshalomov is finally drawn to Peking, where he finds a place to live on legendary Morrison Street—today Wangfujing Dajie. Here he works, among other things, as a book dealer for the well-known French journalist Henri Vetch, who published, for example, the classic *In Search of Old Peking* (1935) with Arlington and Lewisohn. In Peking, Avshalomov realizes his long cherished dream of writing a Chinese opera: He completes it in 1925, with the title *Kuan Yin* (Guanyin, a Buddhist deity of mercy), and it is first performed in the ballroom of the Grand Hôtel de Pékin. The composer himself casts the roles in the Russian exile community in Harbin. In 1926, the arrival of Zhang Zuolin's troops in Peking briefly interrupts Avshalomov's creative work in China, which forces him to return to the United States for a short time.[49]

In the New World, the Russian Jewish artist attempts to make the fruits of his creative musical work appealing to the public. As a pioneer of East-West symbiosis in the domain of music, he is several years ahead of his time. To be sure, he still cannot count on the great enthusiasm of a later globalized society and above all not on its extravagant patronage of exotically inspired, multiculturally tinged foreign musical harmonies. On the other hand, however, he makes a few contacts in the Jewish community of Portland, Oregon, that will aid him later in the course of his career in China. Avshalomov probably privately senses that what he is and can become are inseparable from his being physically present in the Middle Kingdom:

> I have had no noted teachers, and inasmuch as my whole output is Chinese in character and represents an attempt at the fusion of Chinese thematic and rhythmic elements with the Western media, I had to teach myself through trial and error the hows and whys of the specific musical task. For it was not of the variety inspired by a trip around the world, but came as a circumstance of my environment, in which I found the dialect of Chinese music to be the most natural to me.[50]

In 1929, Avshalomov again feels drawn to the Middle Kingdom. In Peking, he literally absorbs every tone perceptible to the human ear: the cries of the wandering street sellers, the ringing of a bell in the numerous temples, as well as the sonorous tuba or percussion and reed instruments of musicians playing in funeral processions. If he is very lucky, he sometimes hears the bright, cheerful notes of a lonely flutist or the grating tones of an amateur musician playing an Erhu, a two-string knee violin. Inspired by these walking and listening strolls through the labyrinth of alleys in China's capital city, he finally manages in 1934 to compose a twelve-minute tone poem, the "Hutongs of Peking" (the famous old Beijing alleys).

The "Hutongs of Peking" was composed for a full Western orchestra, drawing on Chinese percussion instruments and a particular type of tuning fork, as Avshalomov called it. At that time, the Chinese barbers working on the streets usually announced their comings and goings with this instrument, which produced a continuous humming sound. "The purely Chinese character of this composition, the humor of the nation, the (feminine) contemplative melancholy, the ancient peacefulness are heard here in the themes and rhythms."[51] One result of the perception and association of specific ethnic, and in this case Northern Chinese, tones was that years after its premiere in Shanghai, Avshalomov's tone poem was compared in the West with Ottorino Respighi's "Pines of Rome" or Alexander Borodin's "In the Steppes of Central Asia."[52]

In the year of Hitler's rise to power, Avshalomov presents his first pantomime ballet, *The Soul of Ch'in [Qin]*, in Shanghai. He had composed the ballet during his brief stay in America in the mid-1920s. Above all, the

Western press of the metropolis praises the concert in the Grand Theatre, but a Chinese music critic also offers comments. He positively evaluates the work not only from a musical, but also from a historical viewpoint. Avshalomov has, he states, shown the Chinese the right path for the future of its independent music, and they are grateful to him for that. To be sure, he finds it regrettable, " . . . as it is we who ought to have accomplished this task and not Mr. Avshalomoff."[53] Avshalomov again agrees with him only to a point. To him it seems much more important that Chinese music take its own path independently of Western influences:

> The corruption in the form of Jazz and other banal Western music which has influenced the minds and emotions of the young will have to be fought against by widening the standard of musical appreciation among the masses, by directing their attention to the best Western music and to the appreciation of the folk music of China as well as the music of the Chinese theatre.[54]

At the start of the 1930s, the Shanghai Municipal Council appoints Avshalomov the Director of the Municipal Library, a position that not only bestows on him an improvement in his financial situation, but also puts him in contact with famous visitors to the Huangpu metropolis such as Somerset Maugham, Aldous Huxley, or Pearl Buck. Around 1935 Avshalomov composes a piano concerto with Chinese themes and rhythms inspired by a longer stay at West Lake in Hangzhou, where once centuries ago literati, with a fondness for art, and rich tradesmen set the tone and where even today, on the small islands, the pavilions, pleasure gardens, and ponds bedecked with lotus blossoms invite us to tarry. To be sure, Avshalomov's idyll does not last long: The threatening danger of war in the Far East affects him in psychological and financial regards. In 1938 he writes to his son Jacob, who has in the meantime moved to the United States, that his nerves are strained, he feels lost and has no energy to compose anything new. "It is terrible here, the town is crowded, speculation in every commodity, beggars, illness, gloom, bombs daily on the streets, suicides, crimes of every description . . . no place to go to take fresh air—there is none."[55]

Avshalomov finds his only consolation and spiritual relief in music: He composes the opera *The Twilight Hour of Yang Kuei Fei,* based on the history of the imperial concubine Yang Guifei, as well as the ballet *Buddha and the Five Deities.* In addition, contacts and discussions on musical topics with Jewish refugees from Europe, among them a few musicians, give Avshalomov a faint glimmer of light in his otherwise rather gloomy everyday life in Shanghai.

Called by his Chinese friends "Afu xiansheng" (Mr. Afu), Avshalomov reaches the summit of his musical career with his opera *The Great Wall,* also called *Meng Jiang Nü* in Chinese, which premiered in 1945 at the Shanghai

Lyceum Theatre. The opera is set in the Qin Dynasty (221–206 BC), at the time when China's first emperor, Qin Shi Huangdi, commands his subjects to build the Great Wall. Among them is also the husband of Meng Jiang Nü. After she has not heard from him for several years, the good wife sets out on an arduous search for her husband, but eventually learns that he has not survived the enormous physical exertions demanded by this project. The pain and suffering of Meng Jiang Nü are so great that as she weeps, the Great Wall collapses—an obvious symbol for the fall of tyranny.

In Avshalomov's view, the work is a financial failure, but most of the critics, both Western and Eastern, are deeply moved by the premiere. "Richly inspired, full of artistic distinction," notes the *Shanghai Herald*. "The Show is of considerable value," states the *Shanghai Evening Post*. "Avshalomov's *Great Wall* reaches the top of the music-drama world . . . and impresses our hearts deeply," writes a critic in the Nanking newspaper *New China Daily News*. A few Chinese reviewers object to *The Great Wall*, above all because they compare the work with classical Chinese drama. There was no single role for a star such as Mei Lanfang, which would have been in accord with tradition. Avshalomov's idea was, however, to assign each singer and actor his or her own important role. Likewise, the choice of orchestral instruments went far beyond the combination of a few simple instruments like the gong, drum, or erhu. The chief role, that of Meng Jiang Nü, embodies not merely the display of voice and gesture, as was previously usual, but additionally must be the bearer of an idea. Measured against the performance of a Pekinese opera, *The Great Wall* would inevitably seem false and third-rate. According to an anonymous Chinese critic, however, "If we wish to open wide the window for a new form of theatrical art . . . we should recognize that with all the shortcomings, *Mon Chang Nyu* [*Meng Jiang Nü*—author's note] is a worthwhile experiment in the direction of a re-construction of Chinese theatre on a national basis."[56]

Among those who attended the opera, which was performed several times in Shanghai and Nanking, were also a number of Chinese and foreign dignitaries, including Chiang Kai-shek and his wife, the American Generals Wedemeyer and Marshall, as well as Madame Sun Yat-sen. She later wrote to Avshalomov, "I have enjoyed it more than I can say, and I am very grateful to you for creating such a rare treat. I am hoping that it will be possible to arrange another performance very soon, for there must be many people who are eager to see this oeuvre where East and West blend so perfectly."[57]

Furthermore, Madame Sun expressed the hope that Avshalomov would soon take his theater group on a tour of the United States in order to bring the American public closer to China. But Avshalomov, a Jew of Russian origin, probably did not yet take into account that many questions would thereby be raised about his political views. Something else may well have given him, who has in the meantime become a Soviet citizen, greater cause for concern: the communist underground, which makes contact with him in the 1930s and insists on his cooperation. Was he not a friend of Nie Er, the revolutionary composer who wrote the music to "March of the Volunteers," which was later chosen as the national anthem of the PRC? Did not *The Great Wall* closely resemble the communist propaganda opera *The White-Haired Girl* (*Bai mao nü*), which was performed in distant Yan'an at about the same time?[58] One way or another, with the intensifying civil war, Avshalomov's situation, or respectively his prospects of obtaining a visa to leave the country for the United States, also worsens.

At least Avshalomov still has the support of Madame Sun, whose hand protects him from direct persecution by the Kuomintang. Nevertheless, the general assigned by Madame Chiang to "supervise" the artist does his utmost to block the tour of the United States so desired by Avshalomov. To be sure, the celebrated composer has in the meantime taken over the direction of the Shanghai Municipal Orchestra from Mario Paci, accused of collaborating with the Japanese, but Avshalomov feels inwardly at odds with himself: "I must be very careful when choosing between Madame Sun and Madame Chiang. What a life, Oh Boy. . . ."[59] The stay of many years in China has opened his heart and his soul to the country, above all to its music. It must have seemed all the more painful to him that he no longer had any future prospects. He does not want to accept the Chinese citizenship that is offered to him, in order not to be entirely at the mercy of the Kuomintang; for similar reasons he does not want to give up his Soviet citizenship.

Avshalomov increasingly senses that his time in China is nearing an end, without knowing how and where he can continue. The general assigned by Madame Chiang to "supervise" Avshalomov goes so far as to call on him to withdraw his name as the composer of *The Great Wall*. Both sides are literally disavowing the highly regarded artist. The Kuomintang accuses him of being close to the communists; and the latter do not conceal their displeasure at his contacts with Madame Chiang, who—at least outwardly—works to make possible a United States tour for the artist. In the end, the American authorities at the consulate, despite reservations, take pity on a man who had placed almost his entire life in the service of Chinese music and its renewal through Western forms and means. Avshalomov's aim in life—he passes away in New York in 1965—seems to have been to find a path according to Taoist principles. For Avshalomov, Chinese music represented a model for his creativity, which he had felt drawn to ever since his youth. He once even wrote from China:

> In the beginning, this ideal seemed within an easy reach. I will not say so now. On every turn of my musical road, I found new barriers to be overcome. Be as it may, I have arrived only now at the foot of the mountain on the summit of which there stands the magnificent Chinese Theatre, with its traditions rooted in antiquity.[60]

Benjamin Michael Levaco

In China, *Benjamin Michael Levaco,* born in Siberian Kainsk in 1911, pursues interests of an entirely different sort. His parents originally settle in Harbin. In Yokohama, his father had a successful business that is, however, destroyed by the great earthquake of 1923. The family then tries to make a new beginning in China, in Tianjin. Benjamin's father quickly becomes the owner of a first-class men's haberdashery, which enables him to send his sons to the British school. After completing school, Benjamin Michael Levaco works for an American company that, like so many others at the time in Northern China, has specialized in processing intestinal skins for sausages. Through this activity Levaco learns, as do only very few foreigners living in the treaty ports, about the everyday lives of the Chinese. As a chief buyer who is fluent in the Chinese language, he travels extensively in China's interior and even visits Mongolia several times.[61]

Levaco has nocturnal contacts with the banditry that the influential expert on Asian affairs Owen Lattimore referred to as "one of the greatest plagues of modern China."[62] On his trips he sleeps on kangs (heatable brick sleeping platforms) or in yurts, the round tents carpeted with felt blankets of Mongolia and Central Asia. Together with his business partners, he smokes opium pipes, eats culinary delicacies like bear's paws and lamb's eyes, amuses himself with sing-song girls (courtesans), or visits private bathhouses, "not my cup of tea by any means."[63] In 1926, Levaco experiences an adventure of a still more unconventional sort en route to the Temple of Heaven in Peking. He witnesses the horrifying spectacle of an execution, which certainly must have been especially terrifying in contrast to the Temple's majestic splendor. A year before the Sino-Japanese War, he moves to Shanghai, where he sets up a branch office of the American company. After the Second World War, Levaco opens his own factory in the Huangpu metropolis, from whose success he profits only until 1949. After that, like the majority of foreigners, he leaves the country that has been his second homeland for thirty years, commenting:

> As a nation they are tolerant, honest, hardworking and loyal as friends, and regardless of what the politics of the ruling body may be, I personally experienced

> that as individuals it is difficult to find a more friendly group and that my thirty-odd years in China were the most pleasant, carefree, productive and beneficial years of my life.[64]

Meyer Eliash Birman

Meyer Eliash Birman (Meir Birman), born in Lithuanian Ponevech in 1891, was also in the end glad to be able to leave China just ahead of the People's Liberation Army. "Mr. Birman had to escape from Shanghai where he had lived for many years because of the seizure of that city by the communists. He managed to escape on the last airplane that left Shanghai before the arrival of the communists. But for this good fortune, he would no doubt have been executed because of his reputation in Shanghai as spokesman for a democratic point of view."[65] But the path to the West is stony for Birman: Australia does not want to grant him a visa, despite his friendship with the General Secretary of the Australian Jewish Welfare Society; returning to the Soviet Union is out of the question for him. Finally, thanks to various recommendations by Jewish fellow citizens, he receives permission to leave the country for America, after the Americans originally turned him down because of the Latvian (!) quota.[66]

Birman had a distanced relationship with China, although he lived in the Middle Kingdom for more than 30 years. Equipped with only a basic education at a *cheder*, he studies—auto-didactically—the *Talmud* and its commentaries all the more diligently. In compliance with a 1915 Czarist decree, according to which the Jewish population was to be resettled in the Russian hinterland, he leaves Vilnius, the center of Jewish cultural, theological and political debates, for Southern Russia. After the next shock, the October Revolution, he continues his life journey toward the Far East. In Harbin, he becomes the business manager of the Jewish Central Information Bureau for Emigrants to the Far East (Daljewcib), a branch of HICEM, the Jewish emigrant aid organization.[67] In this function, he initially receives, among others, the task of finding ways of transit and emigration for "stranded" Jewish refugees in Siberia and Manchuria. Later, due to events in Germany, he works to inform Jewish organizations in Central Europe about the possibilities of emigration to Shanghai, as well as of transit emigration to overseas countries via Japan.

Birman's fields of activity also include sounding out the economic conditions across China for European refugees and job seekers. But he soon notices that the majority of them "do not adapt themselves to the specific requirements of the many-millioned Chinese consumer, and are being elbowed out by the new masters of the country" [i.e., the Japanese occupation troops in

Manchuria—author's note].[68] Birman knows about the occupational qualifications and preferences of his co-religionists, and it appears all the more difficult for him to aid Jews in building up new lives in the Far East, at least in the extreme North of China.

With the increasing flood of refugees from Nazi Germany, Birman, who in 1939 moves his offices to Shanghai, feels himself likewise forced to seek free corners and fields of activity in the vast empire for every sort of needy and job-seeking Jew. For the areas of China that have been under Japanese control since 1938, stateless persons and those whose German passports have a "J" stamp must obtain special authorization from the Japanese military authorities. This applies not only to all of Northern China, including Shandong Province, but also—with somewhat different legal regulations—to Manchukuo (the Japanese puppet state set up in Manchuria). Hankou in Central China is also out of the question for similar reasons, and in the Portuguese colony of Macao, Birman likewise sees no rosy prospects for Jewish businesses.

During the war years, Birman, who regularly gives his Chinese employees a little money to celebrate the New Year, maintains close contacts with other aid committees, as well as with the International Red Cross, which refers to him in a letter as a "gentleman of the highest integrity." In contrast to many other foreigners, he claims to have heard nothing of Chinese aggression against Westerners: "Here and there, there may have been smaller riots by bands of Nationalist soldiers, but one can not seriously speak of real plundering and unrest."[69] And, even regarding his intellectual opponents, Birman in the end has no harsh words about his stay in China: "Through complicated detours reports have often . . . reached us from other Chinese cities that all agreed that the foreigners have essentially been left in peace after the occupation by the Chinese communists."[70]

Yaacov Liberman

Born in Harbin in 1923, Yaacov Liberman represents a clear example of how attitudes toward China can change. The process of becoming an adult, as well as distance from the subject, creates a certain maturity that may find expression in an understanding reflection on the surrounding world. Liberman, a child of middle-class parents and raised by a "njanja," a typical Russian nanny, first realizes while growing up that he actually belongs to a privileged minority: "As I grew older, I often wondered what the Chinese population was doing while we continued to enjoy life in this city. . . . Hardly any Chinese youngsters shared our activities, and the grown-ups seemed to have moved out of sight in order to leave us, their guests, in total privacy."[71]

In Liberman's autobiographical summation, *My China*, much space is granted especially to the history, as well as the athletic, cultural, and political activities of his Jewish surroundings: *Beitar*, *bar mitzvah*, *Maccabean*, *Irgun*, and other Hebrew expressions established themselves in Liberman's memories. Beside them and of equal value is his attachment to Russian words, especially when it is a matter of culinary enjoyment: *pelmeni* (dumplings stuffed with meat), *bubliki* (ring-shaped pastry), *kuropatki* (a sort of small chicken from the Russian North), and so on. As so often, the Chinese were identified in the memory of the Westerners who grew up in China with not much more than mah jong, which Jewish women loved to play, not least of all in order to keep their boredom within limits. At any rate, thanks to various trips and stays in other places—Shanghai, Tientsin (Tianjin), and Tokyo, for example—Liberman is aware of differences among the Chinese people, a realization which is in itself something, given the Western stereotypification of the "Chinese mass": "Within China itself, one readily notices marked differences between the Chinese of Harbin and those of Shanghai. The Chinese in the North seem milder in character, less ambitious and obviously slower in the pursuit of life than their fellow citizens in the South."[72]

Like the majority of Westerners who once lived in the Middle Kingdom, Liberman has an astonishing life course behind him. The most noteworthy of the young man's simply endless travels is probably his stay in Pyongyang, Korea. In 1936, his parents send him there together with a friend to be educated in an American Protestant missionary school. Traveling on a comfortable night train, the trip via Mukden and Antung (Dandong) to the Chinese-Korean border lasts exactly fifteen hours: "Conquered by one and the same nation [Japan—author's note], the two peoples separated by this border at the Antung crossing were vastly different," he later explained. After his return to China, Liberman lives in Shanghai until, in 1947, two years before his departure for Israel, he is finally able to work briefly in Taiwan as a sales manager for the Hollywood Warner Brothers Company. Liberman needs life experience, distance, and a few years in order to be able to adequately express in words his mental state during his youth or respectively his position as a member of the "white race" among the Chinese. Thereby he is more honest than many others who boast of their relationships with their Chinese neighbors:

> China is not "mine," nor am I Chinese. . . . One can only become a Chinese citizen by having been born to a Chinese mother. . . . *My China*. . . . refers to a milieu rather than to an acquired second country, to a personal life rather than to an abstract national history. It must be remembered that at no time was there an attempt on our part to cross the illusory border of isolation and to become part of the Chinese colossus. . . . [To] those of us who were born in China, the

> everlasting memories we so zealously cherish are neither of the Chinese people nor of their life-style. "Our" China is an informal history of the way we lived and worked to achieve a full and healthy Jewish life in the Far East.[73]

Vic Schneierson

Vic Schneierson is one of the few Russian Jews who heed Stalin's siren calls and in 1947 depart for their former homeland—the "greatest mistake in his life," as he once told John William Powell, editor of the *China Weekly Review*. Like Anna Ginsbourg, who was ten years older, Schneierson earns a living in the circle of Shanghai journalists. Like her, he belongs to the free-lance staff of the *China Weekly Review*, albeit only after the Second World War. At the same time, he works as a reporter and later as a night editor for the *China Press* (chiefly responsible for sports events). Schneierson's biography reflects especially impressively the schisms of the twentieth century, the ideological and the revolutionary: He first saw the light of day in Vladivostok in 1921 as the son of a Latvian-Jewish merchant born in Dinaburg (Dvinsk, Daugavpils) and a mother stemming from Russian Tschelyabinsk. After the Soviets enter the city on the Sea of Japan in the course of the Russian Civil War, the family departs from Vladivostok, first for Harbin, later for Shanghai. They are not allowed to enjoy their freedom for very long: The police in the French Concession suspect his father of sympathizing with the communists, and in 1927, the year when Chiang betrays the Revolution, the family must once again set off on a journey: this time back to Europe via France to Czechoslovakia and finally to Germany. Two years later they return—via Moscow, which exerts a great influence on eight-year-old Vic—to the Far East, "to open-door free China," first to Mukden (Shenyang), then to Harbin and in 1934 finally to Shanghai. At Vic's insistence, as he himself later states, the Schneierson family obtains Soviet citizenship in 1940.

Vic Schneierson's young years in Shanghai are similar to those of other Russian Jews, at least initially. He attends the public, cosmopolitan Thomas Hanbury School, is a member of the Jewish Boy Scouts, as well as of Beitar, the Zionist youth organization. Vic is proud of his Jewish origins, although he is not religious. His interest in China is superficial: the Western culture of Shanghai fascinates him. At any rate, he enjoys taking part in rambles about the region to Chinese villages "where we were always cordially received." Schneierson's circle of friends is one of the reasons why he is increasingly critical of the Chinese Nationalists; at least his articles point to the effort to create and spread sympathy for Mao's cause. In an article under the title "UNRRA: A Cause Betrayed," Schneierson gives an account of the views of many Chinese who criticize the United Nations Relief and Rehabilitation

Administration for its one-sided support of the distressed population in the areas controlled by the Kuomintang.[74]

Likewise, the topic of Taiwan gives Schneierson occasion for critical reflection. In 1945, Japan returns the island to the Nationalist Chinese government, but the new masters prove unable to bring their power into harmony with the economic interests of the Taiwanese. Schneierson visits the island even before the infamous February 1947 massacre of native opponents of the Mainland's oppression policy by Kuomintang troops under the former military ruler of the province of Zhejiang. Almost prophetically he writes in his article "Taiwan: Prize or Province?" about the antagonism between Mainland China and the island, which he attributes to the nationalistic strivings of island residents: "No wonder then, that a national independence movement is taking root in Taiwan. There already are several independence parties, and according to one of my informants, Taiwanese youths are flocking to their banners."[75]

In 1947, Schneierson leaves China by sea for the Soviet Union. "I think the main reason for this was the heroic resistance and the ultimate victory of the USSR over one of the largest and most evil armies in the world," he said to explain his return to his former homeland.[76] Only in the 1980s does the Western public hear of him again, and then for translations of political texts from Russian into English. As well his stay in China forty years earlier comes full circle: Besides *Mao's Betrayal* (1979) and *Imperial China: Foreign-Policy Conceptions and Methods* (1985), Schneierson also completes an English-language translation of S.L. Tikhvinsky's *Chapters from the History of Russo-Chinese Relations: 17th–19th Centuries* (1985).

NOTES

1. See on the numerous minorities living in Shanghai: Ristaino, *Port of Last Resort* (2001).

2. Letter of March 4, 1940, by Michel Speelman, Chairman of the Committee for the Assistance of European Jewish Refugees in Shanghai, to M. C. Troper, Chairman of the AJDC (American Jewish Joint Distribution Committee) in New York, in: Kranzler Archive.

3. Cited in: *Peiping Chronicle*, February 28, 1940, n. pag., in: Kranzler Archive.

4. Letter to the editor by Dr. A. J. Kaufman, Chairman of the Jewish Community of Harbin, in an unidentified newspaper article from March 1940 (Kranzler Archive).

5. Jackson, *Sassoons* (1968), p. 238.

6. King, *Hongkong Bank* (1988a), p. 409.

7. King, *Hongkong Bank* (1988b), p. 252.

8. Meyer, *Sephardi Jewish Community* (1994), p. 141. In later years, the Kadoories compensated for this one-sidedness with generous support for the Jewish refugee community.

9. IM (Israel's Messenger), July 4, 1924, pp. 9. Huangpu is both a district and a river that flows through Shanghai.

10. Cited for example in: *The Wall Street Journal*, 2 March 1977, p. 1.

11. *Forbes Magazine*, December 19, 1983, p. 117.

12. Letter of July 31, 1990, by Lawrence Kadoorie to Rabbi Marvin Tokayer (Tokayer Archive).

13. Due to pressure from Arab customers, the HSBC saw itself forced to recommend that Lord Lawrence resign.

14. Sergeant, *Shanghai* (1990), p. 127. The British reported much the same about Sir Victor: "He was Jewish but one couldn't very well snub a man who played golf with the Prince of Wales." Ibid., p. 131.

15. See: Blackie, *The Kadoorie Agricultural Aid Association* (1972).

16. IM, July 4, 1924, p. 8.

17. Cited in: Betta, *Myth and Memory* (2000), p. 375.

18. The wedding ceremony was apparently performed according to Chinese and Jewish rites, although a Ketubah, a Jewish marriage contract, was never found. After Hardoon's death, this circumstance led to a bitter dispute on the part of his progeny over his inheritance. Only in 1928 did a civil marriage ceremony take place in the presence of the British General Consul in Shanghai.

19. Betta, *Hardoon* (1999), p. 220.

20. Betta, *Hardoon* (1997), pp. 132. Regarded as the most prominent example among the revolutionaries was Sun Yat-sen. In 1911 and 1912, as well as in the early 1920s, Hardoon briefly accommodated him in his home and also supported his movement financially.

21. Luo Jialing was regarded as a zealous Buddhist. Contrary to conjectures and rumors, however, her husband never converted to the Buddhist faith.

22. Betta, *Hardoon* (1997), pp. 187.

23. Ibid., p. 76.

24. IM, January 1, 1934, p. 17. In honor of his father, however, Hardoon had a beautiful synagogue, Beth Aaron, built for his Sephardic co-religionists in 1927; it was torn down in the 1980s.

25. An examination of Hardoon as a figure in Chinese literature and historiography is found in: Betta, *Myth and Memory* (2000), pp. 375–400.

26. IM, January 4, 1935, pp. 8.

27. IM, October 6, 1936, p. 12.

28. Ibid., pp. 12.

29. Krasno, *Strangers* (1992).

30. Recalled are, e.g., the Shanghai "Nascha Shisn" or the Harbin "Jewreiskaja Shisn."

31. Krasno, *Strangers* (1992), p. xiii.

32. This information is found in: NARA (National Archives and Records Administration), RG 263, SMP, File D 7088. The Shanghai Municipal Police was the Police Force of the Shanghai Municipal Council (SMC).

33. *The Shanghai Evening Post & Mercury*, November 11, 1935, n. pag.
34. CWR (China Weekly Review), February 13, 1937, p. 376.
35. CWR, March 28, 1936, p. 115.
36. Needham, *Within the Four Seas* (1969), p. 24.
37. Rudolph, *Shanghai—City of Refuge* (1940).
38. *Our Life*, July 9, 1943, p. 2.
39. Ben-Eliezer, *Shanghai Lost* (1985), p. 28.
40. In a letter to Judith Hasser, Sun Fo, Sun Yat-sen's son from his first marriage, several times Prime Minister under Chiang Kai-shek and after the Second World War for a short time acting Foreign Minister, supported "as a lover of democracy" his father's position on the founding of a Jewish homeland in Palestine. See: Ben-Eliezer, *Shanghai Lost* (1985), p. 348.
41. Ben-Eliezer, *Shanghai Lost* (1985), p. 380. In Israel, Hasser married the politician Ari Ben Eliezer from the Herut party.
42. Spunt, *A Place in Time* (1968), p. 24.
43. Ibid., p. 50.
44. Ibid., p. 72.
45. Ibid., pp. 262 and 265.
46. Letter from Georges Spunt to Ron Bulatoff of August 29, 1987, in: Hoover Archives, Spunt Collection, Box 1.
47. Spunt, *Chinese Cookbook* (1980).
48. Lunyu (Conversations), Book X, 7 respectively 8. The English translation stems from Arthur Waley (*The Analects of Confucius*, 1938).
49. Marshal Zhang Zuolin was the warlord of Manchuria from 1916 to 1928 and considered Japan's proxy until he was killed by a bomb planted by a Japanese militarist.
50. *The New York Times*, April 28, 1965, p. 45.
51. *Thoughts of a Chinese Music Critic*, loose-leaf collection, sine anno (Avshalomov Archive).
52. Avshalomov, *Winding Ways* (2001), p. 65.
53. *Thoughts of a Chinese Music Critic*; loose-leaf collection, sine anno (Avshalomov Archive).
54. Avshalomov, *Thoughts* (sino anno), n. pag. (Avshalomov Archive).
55. Avshalomov, *Winding Ways* (2001), p. 132.
56. Mon Chang Nyu and its critics; loose-leaf collection, sine anno (Avshalomov Archive).
57. Copy of letter from Madame Sun Yat-sen, who sponsored a performance of *The Great Wall* to aid Chinese Artists (Welfare Fund Committee), Shanghai 1946; loose-leaf collection (Avshalomov Archive).
58. Yan'an is a historical city located in Shaanxi Province, which is in the north of China on the border of Inner Mongolia. It was the center of the 1937–48 communist revolution.
59. Avshalomov, *Winding Ways* (2001), p. 227.

60. Avshalomov, *Thoughts* (sino anno), p. 1.

61. L.H. Goldman: Benjamin M. Levaco—A Brief Biographical Statement, p. 2 (1998), in: Hoover Archives, Ben Levaco Collection, Box 2.

62. Lattimore, *Manchuria* (1935), p. 224.

63. Benjamin M. Levaco: The Pros & Cons of Being 'The Honored Guest,' p. 3 (1991), in: Hoover Archives, Ben Levaco Collection, Box 2 (Adventures).

64. Levaco, *35 Years* (1979), p. 13 (Tokayer Archive).

65. Letter from Emanuel Muravchik (Jewish Labor Committee, New York) to Frederick Scheid of August 23, 1950, in: YIVO Institute, Birman Collection, RG 352 (Series 15.144).

66. YIVO Institute, Birman Collection, RG 352 (Series 15.147).

67. The HICEM had its headquarters in Paris and beginning in 1927 combined the emigrant aid organizations HIAS (Hebrew Immigrant Aid Society, New York), JCA (Jewish Colonization Association, Paris), and EMIDIRECT (United Committee for Jewish Emigration, Berlin).

68. Birman Report to HICEM, Paris, of February 28, 1935, in: YIVO Institute, Birman Collection, RG 352 (Series 15.144).

69. *Aufbau*, 20 May 1949, p. 5.

70. Ibid., pp. 5.

71. Liberman, *My China* (1997), p. 39.

72. Ibid., p. 68.

73. Ibid., p. 12

74. CWR, 3 May 1947, p. 266.

75. CWR, 28 September 1946, p. 108.

76. Letter from Vic Schneierson to the author, Moscow, 12 January 2004.

Chapter 2

Jewish Travelers: Temporarily and Voluntarily in China

I. JOURNALISTS

George Ephraim Sokolsky belonged to the practically endless stream of Western journalists whose professional field of activity centered in twentieth-century China. He was born in 1893 in New York, the son of a rabbi who had moved to America from Bialystok, which is now located in Northeastern Poland. The "Jewish Rasputin of China" (as Warren Cohen calls Sokolsky) was a typical product of his times and surroundings: He grew up on Manhattan's Lower East Side, attended school in Harlem and the Bronx and lacked any sort of social support. He saw himself as an outsider, in some cases even as an outcast. In 1917, the President of Columbia University expelled him, allegedly because he had made himself conspicuous through anti-war activities (according to other sources because of an improper sexual affair). In later years, he boasted in retrospect of his contacts with the Russian-born American anarchist Emma Goldman, as well as of his study of socialism.[1]

Sok, as friends later called him, made a stopover on his journey to the Far East in the city still called Petrograd (St. Petersburg) at the time of the February Revolution. In this period, more precisely during his daily commute to work at the Smolny Institute, he encountered among others Lenin, Stalin, and Trotsky, whereby the latter apparently made the most enduring impression on him. In March 1918, he was again on the move, this time on a train to China. It is not clear whether the Bolshevists expelled Sokolsky from the country, or whether he was simply traveling in search of new surroundings. We do know, however, that after his arrival in Shanghai, the Municipal Police thoroughly scrutinized his activities.

As a Jew and thus semi-Oriental, Sokolsky is also an outsider among the foreigners in the Huangpu metropolis, although he soon succeeds in establishing good, and in part close relationships with the American General Consulate. Despite his background, the Americans value Sokolsky's professional and personal ties with the Chinese as a source of information. Especially valuable are his contacts with the leaders of the student movement in the frame of the 1919 May Fourth Movement. He writes, among other things, articles for the *Shanghai Gazette*, a Kuomintang newspaper.

In the 1920s, Sokolsky has many employers: Besides the Kuomintang Bureau of Public Information, at least until 1923, he also works for the Bureau of Economic Information, an agency of the official Chinese government in Peking.[2] His direct supervisor is the Australian W. H. Donald, a former special advisor to Yuan Shikai and later advisor to Chiang Kai-shek.[3] Especially in the 1920s and 1930s, China serves for many as an experimental field for various freelance activities: journalistic, commercial, and political. Sokolsky is one of those who want to combine all three. He writes—in part under a pseudonym—above all political reports (initially against Japanese imperialism) for the columns of the *North China Daily News*, the *China Weekly Review* and the *Far Eastern Review*. His contributions also deal with the failure of the Chinese Revolution and the reasons why it failed. Through his marriage with a Chinese woman—Rosalind Phang, who was born in Jamaica—he succeeds to a certain extent in penetrating deeper into Chinese circles. His wife's contacts with Eugene Chen, a future foreign minister, and Soong Meiling, the future wife of Chiang Kai-shek, help Sok move closer to the political leadership of China, born in the South and educated in the West.

There are probably several reasons for Sok's special position among the foreigners. On the one hand, because of his relations with often-unpopular Chinese political groupings, many regard him as a puzzling outsider, but on the other hand, he also belongs to the Jewish religious community. He is the vice-president of the Shanghai-based Society for the Rescue of Chinese Jews and thereby interested in the history of the Jews in China. He even asks his friend Hu Shi, one of the great leaders of the revolutionary intellectuals, to help him with his research on this topic. Sok's book *We Jews* makes it clear that he felt like a misfit during his youth in the United States, although for him even Judaism did not mean much more than responsibility for the fates of the Jewish refugees from Soviet Russia.[4] In China, however, he could—at least when speaking to the natives—deny his Jewish identity: There, people did not know of such religious "marginalia."

For foreigners, the 1920s represented a very bad time to report positively about China. Too great are the differences between the prevailing reality in the country and the dreams of Sun Yat-sen. Nevertheless, at the start of his journalistic activity, Sok tries to create sympathy for China's desperate situation. Increasingly, however, he becomes indignant that the Chinese blame the West and the "unequal treaties" for every sort of evil. He criticizes the apathetic people and the growing decadence of the May Fourth Movement members. With this opinion, Sok is roughly in agreement with most foreigners in Shanghai, although as before he sympathizes with the Chinese people. In a letter to his former mentor and later opponent John B. Powell, he writes, "We cannot blame the Japanese or any other foreigner for what is happening in China today. The Chinese people are themselves entirely to blame."[5] Despite or precisely because of his relationships with Chinese Kuomintang politicians, Sok begins to harshly criticize their ways of working and viewpoints.

Sokolsky does not share Western fears, increasing since the 1920s, of the spread of communism in China. China was an agricultural country and therefore not susceptible to Bolshevist thinking, which intended industrial workers to form the leadership in the struggle for power. He also defends Sun Yat-sen, whom he criticizes in other places, against the charge of being a Bolshevist. Increasing Chinese xenophobia angers Sok, who does not understand why the Chinese are not more grateful to America, especially after the 1921/22 Washington Conference on the Limitation of Armament, which temporarily halted the naval race in the Pacific.

With regard to the inactivity and inability of the Chinese to undertake the organization of the country under their own power, Sok expresses resentment not only in numerous articles, but also in personal letters, for example to T. V. Soong, Chiang Kai-shek's brother-in-law and Finance Minister: "You cannot allow yourself to gain the reputation of being a bloodsucker, while he [Chiang Kai-shek—author's note] poses as a national hero."[6] He wants to open Soong's eyes: "A revolutionary government must give, at any rate, the impression of being clean. Nanking today is openly corrupt. . . . In a word, T. V., the job of the moment, war or no war, is to clean the house before the stink of corruption suffocates all of you."[7] Never one to express himself diplomatically, Sokolsky, despite his long stay in China, is apparently still insufficiently familiar with the Chinese mentality to be able to create trust with his openness. In somewhat patronizing letters to Soong, Sok shows himself to be the more embittered the longer his advice goes unheeded. He begins—combined with a proper portion of self-confidence—to lose his patience:

> It seems to me that my work is extremely valuable because no one has attempted to undo the harm that has been done to the Government and Party by extremely loose talk and by some careless thinking in China. . . . I have labored for China as no Chinese has ever worked, and I now know definitely how much can be done and how quickly it can be done if only there is a revision of manner in China.[8]

Figure 2.1
"Sok," as both the friends and the enemies of George Sokolsky called him alike, was described as a highly controversial figure with both a fascinating and a distasteful personality. Though his sharp comments on China certainly did not please everybody, his analyses of the communist movement possessed almost prophetic value.

Sok's lines to his former friend Soong emphasize his disappointment that the Finance Minister seemingly does not want to understand how negative the image of China is in the United States. China, according to Sok, is perceived in America as merely a country "where missionary women are murdered and where communists and bandits fight with an overwhelming army."[9] Perhaps it was his straightforwardness which must have been a slap in the face for the Chinese, if not even causing a loss of face. Certainly, the longer Sok speaks out, the more he emphasizes that China and Japan ought to negotiate their immediate problems without Western interference. To try to discredit him as pro-Japanese is certainly an unjust or at least superficial accusation in the light of the situation at that time.[10] The attacks bother Sok, and he complains to friends that the Chinese constantly leave old friends and advisors in the lurch. And as if to assuage his dissatisfaction somewhat, he adds in a typically Occidental, condescending, in those days common, Shanghai tone:

> I cannot hate the Chinese for anything they do, for were they not, at times, childish, immature, hysterical—were they full-grown and well-organized, we should all be facing an imperialistic menace such as mankind has not yet known. . . . The Chinese must learn that they cannot always be coddled children.[11]

In 1931 Sokolsky leaves China permanently, disappointed that nobody in the Chinese government wants his services and advice. He returns to the United States, to a country mired in a deep economic depression and having little or no interest in China's problems. Sokolsky even turns down an invitation from Ailing Kung, the sister of Madame Sun and wife of Industry Minister H. H. Kung, with the justification that he could not return to China, because he would have to take various incompatible positions there. In one of his "farewell letters" to his friend T. V. Soong, whom he had once almost idolized, he states, "I, at any rate, have never gained anything from your greatness and shall continue to love you even when you are no longer great." Sok thereby simultaneously expresses his regret about the quarrel with Soong, as well as his personal feeling for China's tragic situation:

> There has never been a moment when I have not deeply regretted the separation. . . . I do not believe that you [Chinese] can fight Japan and succeed. . . . I have never acted without realizing that irrespective of what any Chinese may think of me, my affection is for China and that if I were absolutely free to choose, I should want to live nowhere else.[12]

The Mukden Incident and the Japanese invasion of Manchuria in 1931 increase the demand in the West for people like Sokolsky who can use their knowledge and experience to competently explain the situation in the Far

East to the American public. For *The New York Times* Sok writes dozens of articles on historical, political, geographical, and cultural-historical topics, on the different *tempi* between East and West, on the role of loss of face, on Madame Sun, the Soong family, Chiang Kai-shek, Pu Yi, the last emperor, or the Yangtze River, China's lifeline. Sok's articles reveal his love for China, his nostalgic memories, linked with feelings of regret because he can no longer be there in person. In several letters to friends and acquaintances, he describes his almost unbearable sensitivity as a stranger in a strange land, for example, to the philosopher Hu Shi:

> I used to complain in China of the song of the singsong girl or the fearful noise of the Chinese flute as played by a neighboring tinker, but how melodious and harmonious were they compared with the tone of that motor-car civilization which you glorify. . . . God, Hu, if only I could sit on the Wing On building on Nanking Road and enjoy the peace of China's noisiest spot.[13]

The more time passes, the more Sokolsky suffers from the cumulative effects of being alone in the United States. No one in China seems to listen to him anymore, despite his intimate knowledge of the country. That is a hard blow for Sok, the somewhat patronizing advisor who believes he knows how to pull the Oriental cart out of the swamp. He sulks and blames the Chinese, sharing his misgivings and views equally with prominent Westerners in China and abroad. In a letter to John B. Powell in Shanghai he writes, for example, of a "terrible homesickness" that tortures him and of how afflicted he is, "because after all the Chinese people are the salt of the earth and they do get such a raw deal. . . . When I think of all the money that China has spent building up an army and all the time it has had to create a machine, and all the manpower and resources that it has, I can not but blame the Chinese themselves for getting into this mess."[14] As well, to a representative of the League of Nations, the Pole Ludwik Rajchman, whom he will years later accuse of being a communist agent, Sok expresses a very personal view:

> You and I have always differed. . . . You have always felt that the procedure of Chinese politicians is not essentially different from the procedure of politicians of other countries, and I have always insisted that the Chinese are unlike any other people. . . . Chinese politicians altogether ignore general considerations. . . . Politicians in China fight against each other as though they were fighting foreign countries, and they develop hatreds as though they were hating foreign nations. I sometimes fear that I am the last patriotic Chinese left in the world, and unfortunately I am not Chinese.[15]

If Sokolsky felt most closely tied to China over the preceding almost fourteen years, after his return to the West his attitude increasingly changes into a type of love-hate. Critics reproach him for harming the Middle Kingdom with his political views. In 1932, Sok publishes *The Tinder Box of Asia*, a collection of earlier articles written chiefly for *The New York Times*. He dedicates his book to his wife, who was to die just a year later. In the foreword, Sok seizes on the censure of his opponents, who accuse him of having become pro-Japanese:

> Actually, I seek understanding without bias. I have lived 13 years in China; I have married into the race. . . . To me China will ever be my home. To it I shall return even as the homing instinct brings the birds back to their mating grounds in the spring. It is only because I love China that I am moved, at times, to chastise her leaders. Too often they forget China to accomplish some small partisan gain. Yet China cannot be forgotten: she is too large, too permanent, too vital.[16]

Sok's Chinese friend T. V. Soong reacts in a slightly irritated tone: "I think that this book will do great harm to China, to the country which next to your own you and yours care for most."[17] It remains for Sok to rebut the assertion of the Chinese politician, who grew up in the West, and whom he had once regarded as a future political star.

Sokolsky's achievement in *The Tinder Box of Asia* was doubtlessly to present and explain various characteristics of Chinese society and its intellectual world to Western readers. Of particular interest are, for example, his explanations of cultural nationalism, on the basis of which the Chinese were entitled to lay claim to moral superiority over the spiritually underdeveloped West. Also Sok's analyses of the communist movement in China were at that time considered rich in insights, and they possessed almost prophetic value: He foresees the 1927 break between the Kuomintang and the communists and holds—in contrast to many other observers—to the conception that communism is quite compatible with China, which will likewise prove well-founded.[18] "Should a Communist government be established in China, Mao will probably be at the head of it," he writes seventeen years before this actually happens.[19] Sokolsky even quite accurately predicts the special character of the post-Mao era and concludes that the Chinese will do with communism what they have done with Christianity and Buddhism: They will simply Sinicize it.[20]

In the following years Sok turns chiefly to American politics and pleads for Western non-intervention in the long-term Sino-Japanese conflict, which understandably does not always meet with sympathy. In 1940, he starts his own newspaper column, "These Days," which thanks to simultaneous publication appears in three hundred important American newspapers. With regard to foreign policy, Sok urgently warns against a war between the United States and Japan and only changes his opinion after Pearl Harbor. After that, he once and for all claims the role of keeper and defender of American values.

As a member of the so-called China Lobby, Sok stands on the furthermost front of those who suspect a communist conspiracy within the American State Department and blame politicians (Dean Acheson, George Marshall), intellectuals (Owen Lattimore), and State Department officials (John Service, John Carter Vincent) for the "Loss of China." Sok fights vehemently against recognizing the PRC, proclaimed on October 1, 1949. If a few years earlier he still analyzed the development of Mao's party with insight, he now loses his sensitivity to and foresight about the decisive differences. In his contributions, he throws all communists, whether stemming from Moscow or Peking, into the same pot and thereby aids and abets Joseph McCarthy, one of the most notorious demagogues in American history. Warren Cohen underscores Sok's enormous contribution to the spread of McCarthyism in the United States and writes that it was perhaps even "greater than Joe McCarthy's."[21]

Sokolsky was certainly not free of contradictions. The only consistency in his life appears to have been his inconsistency. If, on the one side, he referred to the "Oriental" as the "power of darkness," on the other side, he noted in his autobiographical writings, "I liked China . . . because in the oriental countries I could live in freedom."[22] Nevertheless, Sok championed his principles where he saw them threatened and did so with an obstinacy that earned him the reproach that he made his own rules of argumentation, he "indicted, convicted, pardoned, paroled, and granted clemency according to his own rules of evidence."[23] Sok was convinced of himself and his worldview, and the latter was to a certain extent shaped during his stay in China.

Sokolsky was always a colorful figure, first in Shanghai, later in the United States. China was very near to him after 1949, even if he was never again to visit the Middle Kingdom. Up until his death, he writes personal letters to Madame Chiang Kai-shek in Taipei which she always answers with the greatest sincerity. Sometimes Sok seeks advice from Madame Chiang concerning historical facts, more often he argues about the political, for example the quarrel between Mao and Khrushchev. Meiling, as Sok called the Grand Old Lady in his Shanghai years, regularly sends him the Easter messages that she and the Generalissimo proclaim on the radio to their people in "Free China." For the Chiangs, Sok also occasionally serves as a ghostwriter; he already does this for Joseph McCarthy and former President Herbert Hoover. As if to free himself of his legacy and his helplessness, he projects his personal images of China onto Madame Chiang: On one of her U.S. goodwill tours, he attributes the statement "Perhaps the West will never quite understand China" to the former First Lady of China. In December 1962, just two months after Sok wrote to Madame Chiang that, "the morals in this country [United States] must be restored," he dies of a heart attack. It remains for Herbert Hoover to say that the death of George Sokolsky, whose independence was respected by "the tens of millions," was a great loss for the United States.[24]

Understandably, not everyone shared Hoover's views. *Nathaniel Peffer*, born in New York in 1890, allegedly called Sok a "son of a bitch."[25] Like Sok, Peffer, who studied at the University of Chicago, spent several years (1915–1921) in the Far East, first as an editorial assistant for *The China Press* in Shanghai, and later as a correspondent for *The New York Tribune* in Peking. Immediately after the decisive year of 1927, Peffer returns to the Middle Kingdom for two more years, this time with a fellowship from the John Simon Guggenheim Memorial Foundation. Unlike Sok, he maintains no personal relationships with Chinese politicians, which spares him the accusation of partisanship.

Peffer's words reflect the views of an observer who finds himself inwardly at an adequate distance from his research topic. The path to this value neutrality takes years if not decades. In a 1927 book entitled *The Chinese Philosophy of Life* he still defines precisely this "essentially Chinese" that he will criticize thirty years later as the dreamy illusions of the classic Old China Hands. As well, Peffer refers to this characteristic nature of the Chinese as something which then contemporary Westerners could grasp or understand only with great difficulty and weighs it against the well-known everyday and not very optimistic life view and attitude of Occidental people:

> Walk down any opulent street in New York or Chicago. Look carefully at the faces of the most opulent persons who pass. They are well-dressed, well fed, obviously in command of every material resource. Their faces are sombre and stolid, if not harried and oppressed. Go down, not an opulent street, but one of the poorer artisans' alleyways in Peking, Soochow or Canton. There are no opulent persons, none is well-dressed. None, indeed, is unpatched. To most of them even security is elusive. Yet the silversmith or the potter in his doorway and the itinerant barber or goldfish merchant in the road can laugh and does laugh—at you, as you walk by, at a neighbor . . . , at nothing at all, or at things in general, just at the sheer good humor of living. One is happy, that is all.[26]

Peffer's fine, masterful snapshots of Chinese life philosophy exude a breath of eternity. Of course, the newspaper correspondent, editor, and magazine writer is realistic and rational enough to point to the transitory nature of this apparent timelessness. He knows from his own experience the hard realities in the China of that period, the poverty of the masses, the flood victims, the horrible deaths of the hungry and sick. The modernization of the country alone seems to him to be no guarantee for the welfare of the population:

> Maybe it must [modernize—author's note]. Perhaps the drive of the age is irresistible. But I am not so sure as most foreigners who know China that in that direction lies advancement for China and happiness for the Chinese. I am not so sure that there alone is the path to human progress. But I am sure that if the

> Chinese way of life must go, as it must if China modernizes, much will be lost to the world that was precious. And the march of destiny may be irresistible; but one may mourn what it treads down.[27]

To Peffer, who during his stay in China met many native politicians (above all from Southern China) and discussed the country and its problems with them, it is clear that the "good old days," as they were accustomed to calling them, are past; the West possesses no means to prevent China from taking its own path over the longer-term. China, according to Peffer, is at the start of a new ascent that presupposes a transformation of not just the political system. "It must go to the bottom of one of the oldest and most deeply rooted civilizations in the world and change it at its roots. That cannot be accomplished in a generation. It may not be accomplished in two generations. There is no assurance that it will be successfully accomplished at all."[28]

In his first book, *The White Man's Dilemma* (1927), Peffer reminds the reader that Europeans were still cave dwellers at a time when China already possessed an advanced culture and was a world empire. As a product of his times, Peffer adopts the ideas of historicism, for which (world) history stands at the center of philosophizing. China represents for him more or less a litmus test for the entire imperialist system: Should the country "fall," Asia will be lost and imperialism thereby at an end. Thus, he holds that from a Western perspective it is imperative to take the reins as soon as possible, to the extent that this is still possible, after the West has wasted opportunities in all previous years: "We should make the grand gesture to China."[29]

What distinguishes Peffer conspicuously from other observers of Chinese realities at that time is his capacity for self-reflection and for confessing a distorted Western perspective of China. He regrets that in the popular mentality of Western peoples, China is solely associated with opium and chop suey (Chinese "za sui"—a Chinese meat and vegetable dish originating from Guangdong Province and brought to the U. S. by Chinese immigrants). In an imaginative contribution, *The Death of Chinese Civilization* (1930), Peffer anticipates the arguments with which almost fifty years later Edward Said will support his thesis in his famous study of "Orientalism."

Peffer disapproves of the superficiality of Western ideas of China, which arises from only reading newspaper texts and the "high-toned representations of experts." Therein the country with its civil wars and an almost complete lack of law and order—in the West generally perceived as chaos—looks bad each time. Of course, all these superficial manifestations of public life are familiar, "but knowing so much, we know nothing of what is essential in China; seeing so much, we see distortedly. . . . They are effects, not causes. The truth about China, about the whole East, is much more serious than we think it is . . ."[30]

In his second book, *China: The Collapse of a Civilization* (1930), Nathaniel Peffer, like Sokolsky (1946) and Huntington (1993), identifies the conflict between civilizations as a fateful essential characteristic of the twentieth century. In this book he acts as a bridge builder between East and West and one more time attempts to understand China for himself and American readers—an impossible task, as it turns out.

> The picture shifts too rapidly for focus. Perception is not sure enough; no concept can be fixed. No matter how long one has known China, how intently observed its progress or how intensively analyzed its affairs; one cannot grasp it. To attempt to do so is as one catching the surf. One clutches repeatedly, clutches feverishly, closes the hand on something—and the hand is empty.[31]

As if to circumvent the difficulty of ultimately being unable to understand China, Peffer's research interest shifts in the 1930s to the more global, open level and above all turns to Asian-American relationships and America's self-understanding in the changed world political situation. In 1935 he publishes *Must We Fight in Asia?* in 1942 *Basis for Peace in the Far East,* and again three years later *America's Place in the World.* After he becomes a professor of International Relations at Columbia University in New York, Peffer continues to be active as the author of articles published in noted American newspapers and journals. In articles for *The New York Times,* such as "Our Distorted View of China," Peffer—introduced as an "authority on Far Eastern affairs"—deplores the sentimental attitude toward the Chinese of many Americans who once lived in China. Doubtlessly, Madame Chiang Kai-shek's visit to the United States in 1943 contributed to this: "[O]n that occasion we rather made fools of ourselves."[32] The former Old China Hand attempts to serve as a mediator between those who idealize China and those who characterize the country as a fascist dictatorship, and does so by referring to the unsuitability of Western standards of comparison, as he often emphasized:

> Judged by our standards of governmental efficiency, China is no doubt messy. The exigencies of war bring out inefficiency in all countries. . . . But the main point is that there is no reason why the Chinese should be judged by our way of doing things. Chinese ways always seem perverse and incoherent on first observation. It is only after long experience there that one comes to see that on the whole the Chinese get about the same results as others with about the same effort, though the order of acts is different.[33]

In 1946, Peffer again journeys to China on behalf of the U.S. Department of State in order to spend a year as a visiting professor. Afterwards he also attempts in his assessments of the Civil War situation to maintain his distance with a neutral stance. However, he cannot avoid an evaluation of Mao's movement, which is that the Chinese communists were relatively independent of Moscow; there were signs that they would remain their own masters in the country.[34] Three years after the communist takeover of power, Peffer judges that the new regime is a stranger to Chinese structures: " . . . the Communist regime . . . is proving itself to be a surface, alien thing, artificially imposed on the ancient, authentic Chinese structure. And the history of China testifies that anything that does not rest on Chinese foundations cannot long endure."[35]

Then Peffer goes on to list all those "excesses" of the communist exercise of power that in his opinion are incompatible with Chinese thinking and feeling. These include the senseless demonstrations against class enemies, exploiters, or reactionaries, the total idolization of the communist leadership, or as well, the violence against those who think differently. For Peffer the end of the communist government is foreseeable, if not in the near future:

> . . . there is something new in Communist China, something new but so alien to the spirit of the people that sooner or later they will find it revolting. . . . They [the Chinese—author's note] have never been successfully regimented and in the long run will prove among the hardest to regiment. They are not doctrinaire nor given to thinking in formulae and flying to extremes of thought and action, except in momentary tensions of spasm. Beyond most people they can laugh at themselves, a fatal handicap to a Communist.[36]

In this insight or (depending on one's opinion) misjudgment, Peffer remains true to himself, for already twenty years before he had championed the view that it was very unlikely that China would ever become a communist state. Peffer rounds off his academic career with a 1958 book, *The Far East*, a sort of history of the Orient. Then he becomes less visible. A few more times he reaches for his pen with the self-descriptive phrase "A long time resident of the Orient" as the author of letters to the editor. In 1964, a few months before the Chinese detonate their first atom bomb, *The New York Times* reports: "Nathaniel Peffer of Columbia, Expert on the Far East, Dies."[37]

> I'd love to travel the world around,
> To be surrounded by foreign sound
> About strange peoples would I learn
> And see the Orientals, their incense burn.
> . . .
> With God's help and my own will,
> My ambition I hope to fulfill,
> Sure am I, that in some future day,

To these lands, I'll be on my way.[38]

Harold Robert Isaacs was in fact a world traveler. As a young adult, he learned more from "Orientals" than he could probably have dreamed of during his childhood. The drive to act, rather than the search for glory, was one of his life-long signature characteristics. We really could not call Harold Isaacs a poet, but more than anyone else in his discipline, the American-Jewish political scientist—who always referred to himself modestly as a "student of the political sciences"—was aware of the significance and simultaneous limits of the word:

I built a lifetime's work on words
The Truth is, a word on paper has meant
More to me than a thousand pictures,
Reaching for the beauty of lucid prose
Or the magic of love in a poem,
Worth all the trying, still even now,
When I have for so long known
That our best moments lie beyond words,
Moments beyond capture, like this one.[39]

To write about Isaacs' personality in less than an entire book is almost impossible. His life and the stations of his career point to his endless thirst for knowledge. The characterizations given to Isaacs in the course of his life offer some insight into the *conditio humana*—doubt and self-doubt, pride and malice, glory and downfall—put simply, human greatness and weakness. "You will have to give a thought, at least, also to whether association with Isaacs may not also put you outside the pale. . . . In general, I should say that by the official books I am a maverick, a premature anti-Stalinist, at best a dubious character."[40] Such self-assessments, fraught with negative connotations, make one sit up and take notice of a man who rose to become a professor of political science at MIT without ever having earned a doctorate.

But precisely his singularity, his personal evaluation (and certainly also those of others) during the individual stages of his life, literally on the margins of society and the norms it declares to be "correct," created in Isaacs' case an especially attentive observer of Chinese circumstances. Isaacs knows himself and his limits, he experiences more than just an identity crisis and reflects on object and subject in equal measure. Trained in Marxism, he knows how to think in clearly formulated, precise categories and combines this talent with a broadly developed intellectual creativity. In contrast to many who flirt with Marxist ideas, Isaacs possesses the gift of being able to reflect on his life.

Hri, as he respectively signs numerous heartfelt letters to his fiancée and later wife, Viola Robinson, is an engaged, but for that, no less qualified eyewitness of a period of the twentieth century that is fateful for China.

Isaacs is, however, not just an observer of a rupture of world-historical significance on Chinese territory. In the course of his life, he assumes many identities, sometimes also as an agitator in China, and tied to this also as a victim of persecution; at one point Isaacs' father even asks a member of the U.S. House of Representatives to help him persuade the U.S. State Department to protect his son.[41] In later years, Isaacs often thought about the difficulty or also the good fortune of being part of world history and at the same time active in its development. That he, the former zealot and admirer of Marx and Lenin, ended his professional career in capitalistic America is probably also connected to the fact that after an eventful life rich in experiences, Isaacs had to admit that the human factor, as opposed to class categories, plays a far more important role in shaping history than he once assumed.

Isaacs' path was surely the wisest, for otherwise the Communists (after 1934) and Nationalists (during the Second World War) would not have equally excommunicated him with their respective anathemas. In the judgment of his actions and accomplishments in China, it becomes especially clear how tenuous and sometimes daring a historian's evaluations can be in judging history. Looking backward, we could characterize Isaacs as naïve or reject his theses on the Chinese Revolution. We could call him a weather vane because of the hundred-and-eighty degree turnaround in his political attitudes, or praise him for this very reason as having a gift for deeper insight—entirely according to one's own political standpoint. But objectively seen, he remained true to himself and his markedly humanistic convictions until the end of his life: in his striving for justice, to relieve human distress, to end war and violence, as well as his later work for a better world order. A memorandum written immediately after his last visit to China in 1980 indicates that the search of this man of many qualities for the good, for the "eternal truth," was to a considerable extent shaped by his personal experiences there.

Born in 1910, Harold Isaacs grew up on the Upper West Side of Manhattan as the son of a wealthy real estate magnate of Lithuanian Jewish origins. Thanks to his multi-faceted education—at Columbia University he studied among other things French and philosophy—he succeeded in freeing himself from the Orthodox Jewish tradition that he saw as obvious fetters still tightly constraining his parents' feet. This process of disengagement from his roots did not mean, however, that Isaacs had no respect for the religious and intellectual (cultural) heritage of his co-religionists. To the contrary, as a lad, little Harold's thoughts already circled around the question of the relationship between man and God, and between man and the world. Already at the age of nine, he began to have doubts about the understanding of God in the Hebrew *Bible* as a stern, just, but of necessity, awe-inspiring master over humankind.

Starting at that point in time, philosophy begins to replace religion in the life of Harold Isaacs. Already as a seventeen-year-old he one day stands before the Church of the Nativity in Bethlehem and is aware that he has finally left Jewish teachings and rules behind him: "I replaced them with a great curiosity about religion as an experience of all kinds of men."[42] Isaacs sets out on a long quest for the meaning of life. He is outraged at the injustice and misery of this world, cuts himself off from the traditional values of his father and rejects "bourgeois society." Influenced by the works of the socialist politician and social reformer Norman Thomas, the historian and scholar of imperialism Parker T. Moon, and the China journalist Thomas F. Millard, he sets out on a journey to the Far East in 1930. As a twenty-year-old, he is concerned about ideas and attitudes such as the injustice of the capitalist system, an aversion to colonialism, the necessity of securing the territorial integrity of China, the Western betrayal of China at the Paris Peace Conference of 1919, and finally faith in the Chinese people.

In Shanghai, Isaacs begins journalistic work as an editorial assistant (together with Tilman Durdin) at the *China Press*, where Nathaniel Peffer was also active a few years earlier. His, in every regard, heartfelt letters to his fiancée, Viola Robinson, to a certain extent betray a thirst for adventure. His immediate superior is Hollington Tong, later the Deputy Information Minister of Chiang Kai-shek's government and the highest-ranking Chinese censor during the Second World War, with whom he has an ambivalent relationship for many years.

The young but unusually mature newspaperman Isaacs, who soon embarrasses his superior Tong with unflattering articles about Chiang Kai-shek's Nanking government, leaves the *China Press* and makes friends with like-minded persons. Among them are Agnes Smedley, a correspondent for the *Frankfurter Allgemeine Zeitung* and devotee of leftist ideas; Frank Glass, a founding member of the South African Communist Party; and other adherents of revolutionary ideas. Both Smedley and Glass greatly influence Isaacs' development and "ascent" in Shanghai. The resolute Smedley, who was decried by many Old China Hands as a Comintern agent, helped with her excellent contacts to Chinese authors like Lu Xun, Mao Dun, or Ding Ling.[43] Glass stood out with his great analytic talent for always putting everything in question.[44] Both belong to a group of Westerners in China who came to the Middle Kingdom not for economic or religious reasons, but for political ones. Thus, only a few weeks after his arrival in Shanghai, Isaacs unhesitatingly supports political-societal activities that chiefly serve the Chinese Communist Party (CCP) in its struggle against the Kuomintang. "I am being exposed to newer influences which are stirring something in me which may develop

. . . something of the dynamics that is Agnes Smedley has communicated itself to some part of my spirit not yet articulate," writes Isaacs to Viola shortly before the first great stage in his initiation to the status of a revolutionary.[45] This stage occurs on a journey taken by Isaacs into the interior of the country in the summer of 1931 in search of the true China—and to discover his own self. He travels together with Frank Glass.

The adventurous, almost three-month trip begins on a small launch on the Huangpu River, with which they travel downstream to its outlet in the Yangtze. Then they travel upstream toward Nanking (Nanjing), Wuhan, Yichang, and Chongqing (Chungking) and further overland to Chengdu and the jagged mountain landscape of Sichuan. "Shanghai going in a grey and unlovely light . . . as I'd always known it . . . grey and unlovely."[46] Like Shanghai, Nanking does not seem very attractive to Isaacs; he sees a couple of old Chinese gunboats, as well as a whole flotilla of Japanese, French, and American ships. It rains day and night: the mugginess and heat increase the closer they come to the "dead center of the Asiatic continent." "Hard to realize we are traveling into the middle of a war torn country. Stepping into the center of chaos. . . ."[47] Battles are raging; Chiang Kai-shek orders campaigns to wipe out bandits and respectively tries to smash the communist *rural soviets*. Glass and Isaacs also witness armies in motion:

> Long and irregular lines of unbelievably youthful and ill-equipped soldiers. Dozens of youngsters who could have been no more than ten or twelve years old, staggering under nondescript but heavy packs, slinging across their shoulders rifles nearly twice as long as they were high. . . . All were shod in grass sandals, many unshod. . . . These men, these lads are not soldiers, they are not fighters. Their dirt streaked faces and straggling figures carry nowhere in them the spark—or the suggestion of a spark—of morale.[48]

While his fiancée is starting out on a trip to the wealthy European cultural centers of London and Dresden, Isaacs encounters at every turn the misery and need of inland China. To be sure, in his emotionally tinged letters to his fiancée, Isaacs also offers atmospheric descriptions, but this is not in the foreground for the traveler searching for truth. What interests him is the inner constitution of the people and their socio-political interrelationships. In between times, he interviews a general from Sichuan, one of those "Japanese trained militarists of the sleek and ruthless sort." Having arrived in Chongqing, the explorer Isaacs becomes aware that the interior of China still does not provide the answers to the questions that bother him. Doubts surface about the meaning of his journey: "I'm traipsing farther into China. . . . I haven't in all honesty the vaguest idea of what the hell I'm about . . . and sometimes, to make it worse, I don't give too much of a damn."[49] Then suddenly in Chengdu Isaacs experiences his personal Eureka: "I believe, Viola, that I have reached an end of my aimlessness."[50] In his view, the impetus for this was the sight of human suffering ("a degraded mass of human beings living needlessly like animals"), long discussions with Frank Glass during the trip, and—a positive or negative contrast—talking with missionaries. "Ignoramuses mostly, among these missionaries, but one or two with a gleam of light . . ."[51] Isaacs' conversion comes about suddenly: "I can no longer bat about . . . do a lot of talking. . . . I MUST TURN MY HAND TO IT."[52] "It" means for Isaacs the revolution and support for the communists against the oppressive Chiang Kai-shek regime. "I must in other words—TAKE SIDES. I must cease being a neutral, a parasite, at the very best a parlor Red."

After this revelation, Isaacs feels irresistibly drawn back to Shanghai. There he soon notices that Western secret services are watching him.[53] This leaves him cold, as does the critique of journalist "colleagues" such as, for example, the British publisher of the *Shanghai Evening Post and Mercury*, H. G. W. Woodhead, a dogged advocate of imperialist views: "I never realized how much like bloodhounds these bastards are until now . . . and I'm enjoying the fun. . . . It's fun being 'Red' in Shanghai."[54] Isaacs pursues a single aim: not just to be a revolutionary, but also to act accordingly. He seldom participates in social events.

After a brief intermezzo as an initiate at Fenprecor, an offshoot of the International Press Correspondence news agency set up by the Comintern in the Far East, and after a basic reading of texts by communist theorists such as Marx, Engels, Plechanov, Bucharin, and Trotsky, Isaacs, together with Frank Glass, founds a newspaper, *The China Forum*. Agnes Smedley had introduced Isaacs to among others Soong Qingling, Sun Yat-sen's widow, at the latter's home on the Rue Molière (now Xiangshan Lu) in Shanghai. The idea for the paper first develops there, and it makes its debut on 13 January 1932 under the editorship of Isaacs and Glass. *The China Forum*—according to Isaacs—was not primarily the organ of a party or a group, but rather was conceived "as the vehicle for the publication of news and views now suppressed, ignored or distorted in the imperialist, bourgeois and Kuomintang press of China."[55] In deed and truth, the paper openly sympathizes with the Chinese Communist Party and thereby makes a significant contribution as a propaganda instrument. Thanks to Isaacs' exuberance and drive, Glass' and Smedley's good connections with the communist "underworld" and Madame Sun's contacts with Chinese authors, an East-West quartet functions to reach both Western and Chinese readers. For the first time, essays by Chinese writers appear in English translation, among others texts by the freethinking, non-dogmatic Lu Xun, China's Maxim Gorky, as well as the two literati Mao Dun and Ding Ling, who are closer to the Chinese Communist Party. They agree in their abhorrence of Chiang Kai-shek's terror and their will to pull

Figure 2.2
Harold Isaacs' travel on the Yangtze in 1931 changed his life: "I believe that I have reached an end of my aimlessness," he wrote in one of his letters to his fiancée. Isaacs was one of the first Westerners who unmasked the facts and *myths of the Chinese Revolution.*

China out of the morass of misery and need. Not a few workers for the *China Forum* are active in the underground, protected by the extraterritoriality that they in principle vehemently oppose. Isaacs condemns the cooperation by the Shanghai Municipal Police with Chiang's secret police, the Bureau for Public Security. With unparalleled audacity and persistence, he investigates and exposes the obscure intrigues of Shanghai's corruption and political exploitation.

Isaacs' sense of justice also finds expression in his ties to the China League for Civil Rights, founded in mid-1932. In that society, the young Isaacs profits from his acquaintanceship with Chinese intellectuals, as for example the philosopher Hu Shi, the writer Lin Yutang, or Cai Yuanpei, a former rector of the University of Peking—scholars who do not exactly have a reputation of holding an overly critical attitude toward Chiang Kai-shek. Yet also in this—significantly less communist tinged—world, Isaacs witnesses what happens to a loose association of Chinese intellectuals under Kuomintang rule. At the end of 1933, the League breaks up, in Smedley's opinion forced to its knees by terror.[56] Isaacs' work and accomplishments at the *China Forum* fascinate him, perhaps precisely because he sees his life task realized in China. "You ask if I plan to stay in China . . . for as long as I can, child, for many reasons . . . the major compulsions are the external interests . . . the fact that the Far East has claimed me . . . both objectively and subjectively . . . my field is here and here it shall remain . . . however precarious my own position is."[57] In fact, things do become precarious for Isaacs; his *China Forum* is not only a constant annoyance in the eyes of the Chinese police, but also increasingly for the Western police and secret services. Officials open letters, order office searches, and make threats. Even American General Consul Cunningham, under pressure from Shanghai's Mayor Wu, has enough of Isaacs' disruptive activities and wants to consider revoking the extraterritorial status of his rebellious compatriot. However, because this would set a dangerous precedent, the State Department declines to do so.

The end finally comes for the *China Forum*, not as one would expect after what had happened, but rather due to the movement that Isaacs had until then almost blindly trusted: communism. The twenty-two-year-old experiences at first hand the Japanese attack on the Chinese Zhabei quarter in the spring of 1932 and describes to Viola the outrages that occurred following an afternoon—"the evening curfew still applies"—of attending performances of Beethoven's "Eroica," Ravel, and Wagner at the symphony orchestra. Isaacs' first doubts surface as he compares the representation of the heroic struggle of the anti-Japanese resistance as published in the communist press with reality. In the same year, Kuomintang troops arrest Chen Duxiu, the first General Secretary of the Chinese Communist Party. He had incessantly warned against the Comintern's sinister politics and was expelled from the party in 1929 on the charge of an allegedly "opportunistic policy of betrayal." This was an accusation commonly leveled at the supporters of Leon Trotsky. The Chinese Communist Party asks Isaacs to publish a denunciatory article about Chen Duxiu in the *China Forum*—the American refuses. Thereby Isaacs has taken an important step away from the official party line forced by Stalin on the Chinese Communist Party. "They [the Chinese communists who cooperated with Stalin—author's note] supplied him [Isaacs—author's note] with false information defaming the Trotskyists, but the result was quite the opposite of what they had intended, and their squalid maneuvers merely succeeded in driving him into our camp."[58] The straw that finally broke the camel's back or respectively caused the estrangement between Isaacs and his "bosses" is his refusal to automatically join in the communists' obligatory adulation of the Great Leader Stalin. At the end of December 1933, Isaacs is on a mission of enquiry in Fujian, where there has been a revolt by soldiers of the Nineteenth Route Army against Chiang Kai-shek. The party orders Isaacs to spread the report that the "left opposition," thus the Trotskyists, was involved in this revolt. As an eyewitness observer, he knows better—and at a nightly meeting of the communist underground leadership, they ask him to travel to the Soviet Union for political reeducation. Isaacs refuses, with thanks. He has also heard of the first persecutions of dissidents in Moscow. In January 1934, the last issue of the *China Forum* appears, and with his wife Viola, Isaacs leaves the Huangpu metropolis for Peking. In a farewell communication to the Central Committee of the Chinese Communist Party, the "willing sympathizer" with communist ideas (an expression used by Isaacs himself) settles accounts with his former employers, who had for two years harnessed him for their purposes:

> Your blind adherence to false policies was once more demonstrative of your readiness to place your factional interests above the interests of the Chinese revolution. . . . Your only claim on me was my full-hearted loyalty to the Communist ideal and our common dedication to the struggle against a regime of hate and misery and oppression. In the end you forfeited this claim by ceasing any longer to be in my eyes honest or effective leaders of this struggle. . . . I had to refuse . . . to become a hack prostitute in the name of the revolution. . . . Only unswerving fidelity to our goal and active struggle toward this end with the weapons of a correct and tested political line will lift us from defeat to ultimate victory. To this struggle I shall continue to dedicate all my energy.[59]

Isaacs' estrangement from the Chinese Stalinists does not automatically mean a break with communist ideas. In his new home in one of the famous Peking hutongs, he devotes himself to the events that led up to the 1927 Chinese Revolution. In letters to Frank Glass, who has remained in Shanghai, he writes of his endeavors to find the "objective truth." Isaacs spends three hours a day reading the classical Marxist literature, as well as eight hours doing research and writing. His wife Viola helps him with this and in her free time practices the art of the Chinese sword dance. Occasionally they meet other Western foreigners, such as Owen Lattimore and his wife. Isaacs remains in continuous contact with Leon

Trotsky, the Russian revolutionary who is in the meantime living in Norway, with whose assessment of the Chinese situation he can fully identify. With the aid of a Chinese friend, Isaacs meticulously studies the records, working almost to the point of exhaustion. The results are, on the one side, exposés and revelations of Stalin's catastrophic China policy and the hypocritical policy of the Chinese Communist Party and, on the other side, his study *The Tragedy of the Chinese Revolution*.[60] In this book, which first appears in London in 1938, the still young American scholar and intellectual refutes the versions of the myth of the victorious communist path of revolution that the official PRC history books still uphold today. Reprinted several times, *The Tragedy of the Chinese Revolution* becomes the standard work for generations of students of Chinese history in the twentieth century.

After a five-year stay in China, in 1935 Isaacs and his wife leave Peking for America. Decades later he writes to a friend about the reasons for his return to the Western world: "I had been there five years and one of the feelings that was moving me to return to the U. S. was a weariness of being 'different' or 'conspicuous'—with the heavily-added element there of being conspicuously privileged as well. I could no longer abide it and wanted to get back home where . . . I would be again just a digit in the crowd."[61] We cannot call Isaacs a typical Old China Hand, not just because of his political convictions at the time, but also because of his rare ability to see the otherness in his own world. China taught the Western educated Isaacs precisely this insight.

Back in the United States, Isaacs works (besides completing his *Tragedy* manuscript) as a writer and editor for various news agencies, before returning to the Far East in 1943. As a *Newsweek* correspondent, he takes over the reportage on the China-Burma-India Theater of war. Just as during his first visit, "self examination" is his constant companion, which distinguishes him from other China reporters. In touching words to his still small son Ronny, Isaacs explains his credo for a better world:

> There was another question you asked, Ronny. You wanted to know why people shoot guns at other people. The reasons are not only too complicated for a boy like you to understand. . . . Your Daddy doesn't do any shooting. I am out here to help examine this sickness and to write about it on my typewriter. Perhaps if I am very lucky and very wise I can help a little to cure the sickness. That is what *I* am doing. And I hope son, I hope very much that when you grow up, no people will be shooting any other people anymore anywhere.[62]

From Chongqing, the father writes to his son that he is glad to be back in China: "You know Mummy and I used to live in China a long, long time ago, before you were born. And we liked it very much because we liked the people who live in China. As you know, they are called Chinese."[63]

That, in contrast, not all Chinese liked Isaacs is shown by the refusal of the Chinese leaders to let him return to the Middle Kingdom after a visit to the United States in 1945, the last year of the war. His commentaries are too critical, for example that the ordinary Chinese soldier had to take all the blows of the Japanese invasion as the price for the "criminal ignorance and greed of his superiors."[64] Isaacs simply denies the right to rule China to the corrupt leadership, the officials who live from theft. For Chinese tastes, that is too much criticism by a foreigner, although Isaacs does not refrain from calling the communists a totalitarian party made up of persons who "play with the notion of 'democracy' and 'people's power' just as unscrupulously as the KMT or Stalin does."[65] This statement again does not satisfy the American authorities enough to renew his passport in 1950 as they routinely did in the past. The influence of the so-called China Lobby appears to be too great, even though Isaacs has long since ceased to believe in communism. The former supporter of Marx and his teachings exchanges the role of an engaged intellectual for that of a respected, though still strong-willed, scholar. He becomes a Guggenheim Fellow (1950), a visiting lecturer at Harvard (1951), as well as at the New School for Social Research in New York (1951/52), and finally in 1953 a faculty member at the prestigious Massachusetts Institute of Technology.

Isaacs bases his ideas on how to interpret international political events and political change on his rich and varied experience and know-how in the Middle Kingdom. These are for him only understandable by recognizing and grasping the networks of historical, cultural, national, religious, and other complexities from the past that burden every society. Isaacs' writings attest to a passionate concern for the fate of humanity. One of his former students once commented, "I have never known a more empathic human being than Harold Isaacs."[66] Constantly putting in question old patterns of thought belongs to Isaacs' trademarks, just as much as examining his own fallibility or at least limitations: "The only thing we really know is our own lives, our own experience."[67] Besides Isaacs' experiences in China, the Jewish tradition, which ever since his childhood had seemed like a burden to him, probably also indirectly played a role in his scholarly work. When his father dies in 1953, Isaacs, "out of respect for his beliefs and practices," observes the prescribed Jewish mourning rites. He writes to his son Ronny in the following moving words: "Every person has his own way, and his own view of others, and the process of growing up seems to be the process of seeing more and more points of view. It is as though we live in a room of many mirrors of different sizes and shapes, and the image we see depends on who is looking and what mirror he is looking into."[68]

The Far East and especially China continue to be close to the American Jewish intellectual's heart. Isaacs defends the Indian freedom fighter Yusuf

Meherally, who dies in Bombay in July 1950, and that same year, in a letter to U.S. Secretary of State Dean Acheson, he spiritedly objects to American support for the French in Vietnam. He criticizes the inexperience of State Department officials, which was having catastrophic consequences in Asia, for "the trouble about Asia is that so much about it cannot be understood in the simplistic terms of the Cold War."[69] After *Tragedy*, his best-known work on China is *Scratches on Our Minds: American Images of China and India* (1958), an even today timely study that masterfully combines the techniques of journalism with those of the social sciences.[70] By means of evaluations of answers given on anonymously completed questionnaires by persons who in one way or another have something to do with China, Isaacs examines the form in which reportage from the Orient reaches American parlors, to what extent it is instrumental in implementing specific policies, and how perceptions change in the course of time. He shows the reader that "every observation remains subject to the awareness that the aspect of knowledge is constantly changing."[71]

In the frame of seminars held regularly by MIT and Harvard professors to discuss questions of world politics, Isaacs meets the most renowned political scientists in the country (Ezra Vogel, John Montgomery, Robert Weiner, Samuel Huntington), for example, shortly before the outbreak of the great Cultural Revolution in China in 1966. People listen to the opinions of the former *enfant terrible*—or "homme engagé," as others call Isaacs— for example, at Congressional hearings such as those of the Subcommittee on Asian and Pacific Affairs in 1972. Despite, or precisely because of, his individualism in thinking and research, Isaacs remains one of the most remarkable persons in his evaluation of the events occurring in China. "I must remind you that my views on the politics and history of the Chinese Revolution differ considerably from those of other people like Agnes Smedley or Edgar Snow. You must in no case confuse me with them," he writes to a Chinese student in Chongqing who wants to make a study of Isaacs' relationship with Lu Xun.[72]

In 1974 Isaacs' *Straw Sandals* comes on the Western market at a time when the mass campaign against Lin Biao and Confucius is reaching its peak in the midst of the Cultural Revolution.[73] A journey to the Middle Kingdom, which he so greatly yearns for, is still in the distant future. Of course in the meantime, in 1971, the PRC has been assigned Taiwan's former seat in the United Nations, yet the opening of diplomatic relations between China and the United States is still in the future (it finally occurs in January 1979). Letters to former friends often remain unanswered. Nevertheless, in March 1976, when Mao's death is already foreseeable, Isaacs receives mysterious mail from Peking: "Regarding . . . [here there is a gap in the original text, but Isaacs is meant—author's note] he very emphatically says the Traitor gave us so much trouble in Shanghai, stole the Party printing press etc. He should never be invited."[73] The news comes from Suzie, as Isaacs and other Western friends called Madame Sun during the time they spent in Shanghai, with no further commentary. She takes up his cause, and finally in October 1980 Isaacs and his wife receive permission to set foot again on Chinese soil.

A year before his death in 1986, Isaacs reports on his last visit to the Middle Kingdom in a book entitled *Re-Encounters in China.*[75] This autobiographical record is not an accounting of the conventional sort by an anti-communist hardliner, but rather more the melancholy memories of a today little-known eyewitness to Chinese history in the first half of the twentieth century. Isaacs understands the Chinese situation too well for his sophisticated thoughts to lead to a blanket critique of the communist system. It is much more an inexpressible pain that speaks from the sentences he sets down on paper subsequent to his meetings with former Chinese friends—Madame Sun, Ding Ling, Mao Dun, Chen Hansheng, and others.[76] Isaacs feels as though he were riding in a sort of time machine that carries him back to the Shanghai of the 1930s, whose wheels, however, jam and spin on their axles: The surrounding world, already sufficiently marked by anguish, has no interest in going along on this journey into the past. The once more or less profoundly present network of relationships between West and East is irrevocably destroyed, and Isaacs' sorrow over this loss can be felt by the reader in almost every chapter. Isaacs also realizes the impossibility of trying to understand the lives of the victims of their own system:

> Each one [of these persons who spent a certain period of their life in prison—author's note] had to settle somehow on his or her inner personal sense of the meaning of this experience, a difficult, delicate, and dangerous matter touching emotional depths they generally chose not to explore, as 'Marxist-Leninists' out of ideology, as Chinese out of deeply embedded cultural conditioning. But as 'Marxist-Leninists' and as Chinese, they were well-practiced at raising subjective difficulties to objective levels, in this case rather easily done, since the questions that made for inner crisis were closely related to the questions that dominated the political scene to which they had returned, all of them also difficult, delicate, and dangerous.[77]

While the Chinese Revolution is devouring its own children without much ado, Isaacs is slowly but surely approaching his own end: "As my claims on the world—and the world's on me—fall away . . . I feel the isolation, I feel more ending than beginning . . . nowhere I want to go, to be sure. But then, where is it I'm going?" His own childhood overtakes him, and his Jewish heritage has been "sacrificed" to other interests. Even what he strongly believes becomes alien: "I am looking again at all I abandoned for broader visions. I would go back to none of it. But there are no broader visions in its place now, only failure and bafflement and frustration."[78] In July 1986, Harold Isaacs dies after developing for the last time his own theory of the creation of values in various cultures.[79] Isaacs, today unfortunately almost completely forgotten, yet so current and topical, developed a sense of empathy to a high degree. No praise can better express Isaacs' ties to the life and intellectual world of China than that of his Chinese friend Chen Hansheng: "You know, we come from different places, we've had different lives, but we have the same kind of mind."[80] The success of his life work lies in his almost ideal combination of a historian's horizon with the acuity of an epochal critic.

Like almost no other event in *Theodore H. White's* life, the so-called "dinner of the pig" (as White himself called it) symbolizes his remarkable encounter with the "soul of China" and also the later Pulitzer Prize winner's occasionally intense examination of his own past. It is 1940, and Teddy, as all his friends call him, is a guest at a banquet hosted in Chongqing by Zhou Enlai, who later became Premier. After enjoying delicious appetizers, they are served bamboo shoots with chicken, then duck liver, and finally—as the main dish—a "golden-brown, crackle-skinned roast suckling pig." "Please, please," Teddy's host encourages him in a friendly manner to be the first to begin the feast. The latter, although he knows the imperatives of Chinese hospitality, summons up all his courage and declares to the flabbergasted gathering that as a Jew he cannot eat pork. After a moment of embarrassed silence, Zhou Enlai responds: "Teddy, . . . this is China. Look again. See. It looks to you like a pig. But in China, this is not a pig—this is a duck."[81] Thereby the ice is broken, and the way is cleared for White to liberate himself from the fetters of the past ("I hope my ancestors will forgive me") and cross the threshold to understanding others, to accept China as it presents itself to the Westerner. The path to a pork feast is difficult, and not just for an American Jew.

Despite this for observant Jews no doubt serious transgression, White—in contrast, for example, to Sokolsky or Isaacs—received an entry in the *Encyclopaedia Judaica.* There he is treated as "one of their own," even if he was later to break with the Jewish *Lebenswelt*, or at least yield to other "temptations." White first sees the light of day on May 6, 1915, in Dorchester, a then typical Boston immigrant quarter populated by newcomers from the Old World; White later calls his birthplace a "ghetto." They live on Erie Street, where gas lamps provide illumination at night, and a milkman in a horse-drawn wagon delivers milk to their doorstep. White's family is penniless; his father, who came from White-Russian Pinsk, gains admission to the American bar, but his clients are mainly poor people who have lost all the little money they had in the Great Depression of the late 1920s and 1930s. David White regards himself as a socialist who supports voting rights for women and opposes the oppression of workers under capitalism. After his arrival in the United States, he henceforth refuses to speak Yiddish. Very early, he strongly admonishes his son to never use derogatory phrases like "Chinkee, Chinkee, Chinaman." Teddy's maternal grandmother rounds out what his father teaches him as practical life experience: Herself raised in the orthodoxy of a small Jewish *shtetl* on the border between the Russian Empire and East Prussia, she places the greatest value on education according to strict Jewish rules. At a very early age, Teddy discovers very different ideas about life in his own family: During the Sabbath celebration they light white candles on the second floor of the house and serve sacramental wine and challah (the typical white, twisted Sabbath bread), while downstairs Teddy's father, the "unbeliever," reflects on religion as a source of all human superstition.[82]

It was hardly a miracle that someone who grew up in such a family would very early have become acutely aware of the conflicts between different cultures. This may also be the reason for White's belief that one should regard the other, the outsider, more leniently. Teddy attends Hebrew school, later Hebrew College in Boston, where he becomes acquainted with the epics of the Hebrew *Bible*, "Its themes and its stories are primitive—miracles; love; hate; killing; attack; sacrifice; wonder; above all, revenge!" The study of the *Torah* teaches him the melody of the language, the gift of imagination and the strength of the tradition. At school, he also learns to discipline his memory and to value the central significance of remembrance for Judaism. The contemplation of these young years leaves traces in his spirit that are in no way inferior to those in Isaacs' *Scratches on Our Minds*—naturally with different foci, but with similar results.

Another experience that left a deep trace on Teddy's memory occurred when he saw the Zeppelin circling over Boston on its flight to Lakehurst, New Jersey. "We hated the Zeppelin, because it was Hitler's and Hitler was bad for the Jews. . . . When we saw it coming, we gathered in a circle and danced the hora in defiance, dancing and singing until it passed from view overhead."[83] He was also to re-experience this "spectacle" in a similar way in China: The Japanese bombing of Chongqing that so graphically put the brutality of the occupation troops before his eyes causes him to experience the war as a personal call to resistance against every form of tyranny. "If Europe needs men to fight Hitler at that time, I feel that I must count myself as one. I've learned in China that men must fight for the things they believe are right; and with every well of feeling in me, I feel that Hitler must be licked."[84]

Before White enters Hebrew College in Boston, he attends the prestigious Boston Public Latin School, where he sits next to Irish, Italian, Protestant, and black students. This not only prompts him to think of society as a mixture of peoples—long before ethnicity became a political term—but also makes him aware of the "others." After his father's death, Teddy again faces poverty: He goes to work as a newspaper carrier on the streets of Boston in order to help his family survive. In 1934, he receives a scholarship that enables him to attend one of the most prestigious Ivy League schools. At Harvard University, the "adolescent socialist and Zionist" (as he refers to himself) studies alongside of classmates who later become prominent American politicians, entrepreneurs, and academics. Fate, or perhaps chance, is the reason that in his second year of study, while working every day in the library of the renowned Yenching Institute, he falls under the spell of a Chinese intellectual world that seems exotic to him:

> And if I was bleary with . . . the Reformation, or the Age of Imperialism, I could get up and pick Chinese volumes off the shelves—volumes on fine rice paper, blue-bound, bamboo-hooked volumes with strange characters, volumes with their own particular odor, an Oriental mustiness different from the mustiness of Western books. As I became more and more accustomed to the Oriental atmosphere, and my eyes rested on the scrolls of calligraphy on the walls, I began to feel at home.[85]

Teddy therefore enrolls in courses on the history and language of China. "And a more dangerous choice I never made," he comments years later on his decision. John K. Fairbank, one of the icons of modern American China studies, becomes for many years his teacher, mentor, and friend. From him he receives the philosophical instruments that were to make it easier for him to deal with the Middle Kingdom. "It is not possible to think well without making *distinctions* between this and that . . . . It is not possible to go very far in making distinctions without making use of *categories of thought* . . . . It is not possible to think with critical power without being *critical* of the categories with which one is thinking."[86] The conscious perception of the difference between the various images of reality and reality itself will help him during his China period to look behind the facades of "Potemkin villages." In September 1938, Theodore H. White embarks on a journey to the Far East made possible for the adventurous young man by a stipend and a degree "summa cum laude." Teddy believes he will later return to Harvard, perhaps as a professor of the history of the Orient. "But first I must satisfy curiosity, my absolute lust to see what was happening in the China I had studied. How *did* history actually happen?"[87]

Equipped with two identities—one Jewish and one molded by Harvard—Teddy makes several stopovers in foreign countries. There he has encounters that shape his thinking: in Palestine with a British officer ("You Jews are simply a bloody nuisance"), in Singapore with a European woman ("White people go to the head of the line"), and in Shanghai ("White, you're nothing but a goddamn Socialist and you ought to know it"). He senses that his own spirit has deceived him: Even before going abroad, he considered himself a revolutionary. In the meantime, he has become aware that in reality he is

Figure 2.3
Theodore White—the ex-newsboy who became a Pulitzer Prize-winning journalist. Teddy, as he was called by his friends, "was a lover. He was soft on the human race," words written for his eulogy.

merely a creation of different people and a different past. From this insight, it is only a small step to the question that will pursue him throughout his life: How can we best explain the origins of political ideas? In China, he sets out during the Civil War period to find the answer to this question. But it is first his experiences in Europe (Marshall Plan) and later in the United States during his travel and publication activity (in the frame of reportage on the American presidential elections) that help him to develop a clearer understanding:

> Identities in politics . . . were connected far more to ideas than to ego. . . . Whether it was Mao and Chou . . . or Kennedy and McNamara, or de Gaulle and Monnet, their identities came from the ideas that had been pumped into them, the ideas they chose in turn to pump out. . . . Most ordinary people lived their lives in boxes, as bees did in cells. It did not matter how the boxes were labelled: . . . the box shaped their identity. But the box was an idea.[88]

Arriving in April 1939 on a flight from Hong Kong, White lands on the Yangtze at Chongqing and is borne on a sedan chair into the old town, into a city that belongs to a different world. Within the city walls lies a China that was previously unknown to Teddy. "No one had ever told me how much the Chinese love flowers—but now in springtime, there were more flower stalls than in my native Boston."[89] He has luck; recommendations from Harvard (Fairbank) and Shanghai (Powell) help the twenty-four-year-old to obtain journalistic employment with the Kuomintang, and indeed as an intermediary between the Chinese Ministry of Information (Hollington Tong) and foreign correspondents ("In reality, I was employed to manipulate American public opinion"). In one of his first letters from Chongqing (to the Dean of his alma mater), Theodore White describes his new impressions of China and its people as follows:

> My work here in the office . . . has that peculiar Alice-in-Wonderland quality on which everyone who has worked for the Chinese government comments. The Chinese are different from us—and the observation and weighing of these differences is constantly interesting. The application of Chinese ideas to Western techniques and patterns produces frequently bizarre results. One can spend hours rocking with laughter at times at the end product of some of the projects of a Chinese bureaucrat; or hours in bristling indignation at the occasional stupidity; and again hours in admiration at some revealing stroke of their cleverness.[90]

Chongqing's alleys "offered a symphony of smells, fragrant and stinking at the same time—fragrant with the smell of food and spice, the aroma of flowers, roasting chestnuts, incense, the sweetness of opium, yet stinking of uncollected garbage and the urine that ran in the gutters. The noises were a symphony of another kind—of yelling men, screaming women, bawling babies, and squawking hens, which lived with the families in the huts."[91] He is concerned about the adverse living and working conditions in Chiang Kai-shek's capital, shocked by the filth and the misery on the streets, and deplores the Japanese bombing raids that bring death to many innocent victims. On the other side, he is proud to participate in a struggle that is part of a "world battle for some such vague thing as justice and the right."

For White, an excursion of several weeks to Shanxi, a province that nestles in a curve of the Yellow River, has the same significance as the Yangtze boat trip had for Harold Isaacs eight years earlier in the summer of 1931. It was then the only front on which the Chinese were actively fighting against Japanese troops. "For myself, it was the first real battlefront I had seen, and a giant step in education," notes White in his autobiographical recollections.[92]

Teddy's knowledge of Chinese improves with time, and he begins to understand at least some military phrases. "But I never did learn, even after six years in China, the vocabulary of motivation, personal history, political purpose, or how and why things come to be."[93] White's description of the front in the province of Shanxi, devastated by war and atrocity, earns the committed observer with an eye for the historical a job as a China correspondent for *Time,* the news magazine published by Henry Luce. While other journalists' psyches often weaken in the exhausting climate of Chongqing, and the one or the other finds relief from dreary everyday life in alcohol or in brothels, Teddy searches for the kernel in the husk of China:

> As for China: the longer one stays here the more confused one becomes. During the first month one is lost—one sees only the dirt and the filth, and wonders how the Hell this country is going to come through. During the second stage you accept the dirt and the filth and see the good, the heroic, the new striving to break through in the country. In the third stage, one sees behind the good and the heroic, to the corruption, graft, intrigue, administrative stupidity, cowardice, and greed of its officials. And one begins to doubt.[94]

Similar to Isaacs, White is a loner. He pays little heed to the staff of the American embassy and does not even inform them of his trip to Shanxi. In later years, he even censures a certain latent anti-Semitism in the diplomatic establishment.[95] For all his distance from his homeland, he remains tied to Judaism, writes to his friends that he could still sound the shofar and occasionally recalls poems by Hayim Nachman Bialik. Teddy develops a closer relationship to British Ambassador Archibald Clark Kerr, a diplomat of the old school who has already served the English Crown in Iraq and Turkey. Clark Kerr is regarded as a liberal of the first hour who does not even shy away from seeking contact with the Chinese communists.

In China, Teddy learns that being acquainted with influential personalities is "money in the bank" for reporters who think in terms of historical relationships: These not only play a role as references, they also aid in making further contacts. Their invitations result in new acquaintanceships that again also produce history: "For years, until 1963, my search for stories would be a search for names and personalities."[96] For the young man, who is extraordinarily enthusiastic about observation and discovery, interest in the individual stands at the center of his philosophy for the explanation of historical processes. The Chongqing of those years offers him enough possibilities to separate "the Chinese" from the masses, to individualize him, perhaps even to humanize him for Western readers. "I found all these people—government officials, scholars, soldiers, shopkeepers, restaurant men—historically romantic . . . in the beginning, it was inspiring to visit officials whose children played on the steps of their government offices, whose wives hung the wet wash from the dormitory buildings to the office buildings. . . "[97] Teddy's wish is to counteract the then dominant prejudices about China:

> I would like to write a chapter called Legends are Facts. . . . I would like to dissect the three legends of China: the legend of the treaty ports—to wit, that all Chinese are corrupt, stupid, and cowardly. The legend of the Chinese propagandists—to wit, that all Chinese are brave, death-defying, and solely concerned with defeating Japan. The legend of the Communists—that all Communists are pure, infallible, and innocently persecuted. There are dozens of legends that we have to recognize as politico-military facts.[98]

Does he manage in the frame of his journalistic activity to counteract this stereotype formation? He rightly points out that neither he nor any other American correspondent can read Chinese newspapers; the Western observer is thereby in some ways always influenced by his immediate political surroundings, by the Communists or the Nationalists. He sees the borders of objective perception, recognizes that the Kuomintang government is anxious to show Western correspondents the Western elements of Chinese life.[99] He tries to avoid mystification by government propaganda and does not shy away from airing his annoyance, once (1942) to T. V. Soong, and—extremely clearly and directly—in September 1943 to the Minister of Information.

> I must confess that the censorship of my dispatch [this was a report *nota bene* about India—author's note] has done more in a single day to alter my estimate of Chinese policy and wisdom in statecraft than all the petty criticism I had heard in years of journalistic experience. . . . I feel it only fair to put on record with you how bitterly I resent such political censorship as this; and to protest

> formally to you as Minister of Information of the Government of the Republic of China against your Ministry's policy of support in the suppression of truth.[100]

A few months before, he had already had experiences with censorship and the sloppiness of the Chinese central government, with disastrous results for the population: In the spring of 1943, hundreds of thousands of people die under the most appalling conditions in the province of Henan, which is stricken by a famine (the authorities do almost nothing to provide emergency aid). The authorities forbid newspapers to report on the catastrophe, but Teddy wants to see it with his own eyes and travels together with his British colleague Harrison Forman of the *London Times* to the areas plagued by hunger:

> Chinese children are beautiful in health; their hair glows then with the gloss of fine natural oil, and their almond eyes sparkle. But these shrunken scarecrows had pus-filled slits where eyes should be; malnutrition had made their hair dry and brittle; hunger had bloated their bellies; weather had chapped their skins. Their voices had withered into a thin whine that called only for food.[101]

After his Shanxi expedition in the fall of 1939, the Henan famine is a second key event which shapes Teddy's image of China. The experience of Henan brings about a change in his reportage on Kuomintang policy, which previously was more favorable. In his communication to Tilman Durdin, a reporter from *The New York Times*, he openly complains about Chiang Kai-shek's passivity, and after his return to the capital he tries to open the latter's eyes to the human catastrophe:

> The Gissimo was sitting there as he always does at the end of that long dark room where he receives foreigners and looking remarkably fit with his jowls just a bit heavy and well-fed. And I gave him the works; he denied my facts; and I said, 'Look at these pictures' and he looked and got sore and said 'where do these come from.' So then he listened while I told him what was going on up there. I don't know whether he was impressed or not. You know how completely impassive he is, how he sits there saying nothing but an occasional grunt, and stroking his chin with his hand always in silence. . . . I hope Madame gets back quickly to put the old boy on the beam. . . . Gissimo getting pettish as he grows old, losing temper more and more frequently . . . This place gets more and more Oriental as Time goes on.[102]

Teddy's relationship with Henry Luce, who had in the meantime assigned him to report as a *Time* correspondent on the China-Burma-India Theater of war, worsens due to his increasing critique of China's deplorable state of affairs. Madame Chiang Kai-shek becomes outraged about White's Henan reports. She thinks that these disclosures have destroyed the positive image of China that she and her friend Luce had so skillfully built up for the American public, in the manner of Potemkin villages: a loss of face for the whole country. During her United States visit in the winter of 1942/43, she consequently demands that Luce dismiss White. She allegedly calls him "that little Jew."[103] Luce still hesitates, however, to comply with the wishes of China's first lady, but the differences of opinion between him and Teddy become greater—and his manner of expression becomes even more pointed:

> I know it too well in fact. My writing about China has grown sharper and more incisive and people dislike me for the things I say. I have a great affection for this country and it hurts like hell to see it throttled by blockade and rotted with inflation—but what I see I must write down. The Chinese are suffering too bitterly now to enjoy keen and biting writing; they want praise and flattery to soothe their wounds.[104]

One of the last touches of color in White's six-year China stay is the visit of the Harvard protégé to the city of Yan'an (Yenan) in October 1944. Obtaining authorization is one of the sleights of hand that only a few other journalists accomplish in those months: Chiang Kai-shek wants under all circumstances to prevent more Westerners from meeting the "people in the promised land" (Isaacs). General Patrick Hurley, Roosevelt's special envoy, personally turns down Isaacs' request; White to the contrary is lucky, because he had asked for permission months earlier. He is also irresistibly captivated by the almost friendly atmosphere and charm of the communist revolutionaries: "Yenan [Yan'an] . . . embraced us as allies and friends. . . . All seemed to chuckle with a joviality that, even now, I cannot conceive as feigned. . . . I wonder if they themselves can recall the days when they were young and made puns and danced. Perhaps power changed them before they knew they were changing. . . ."[105] Teddy recalls the ping-pong games between Zhou Enlai and his translator, the jokes of Zhu De, Peng Dehuai, or Lin Biao, the Red Army's best battlefield commanders. The evening dances remind him of "old-fashioned Jewish marriages." Here in the loess region of Yan'an he learns from experience that intellectuals make revolutions. He avails himself of the opportunity to talk for hours in this think tank with precisely these giants of the communist movement. Of all the numerous interviews, one with Mao Zedong was to be fateful for him, perhaps even the reason why after the former guerrillas take power he has to wait more than twenty years before he can once again visit his beloved China.

On November 7, 1944, General Patrick Hurley lands, unannounced and without any pomp, on the little runway of Yan'an. He has flown here in order to mediate once more between Mao and Chiang. Teddy, who has been here for several days, wants—with positive intentions—to inform the man from Oklahoma about his talks with the communist greats. He informs Hurley that Mao has told him there was no possibility to achieve agreement without American recognition of the communist government's de facto existence. Hurley later interpreted this (and passed it on to the State Department) to mean that White "was definitely against the mission with which I am charged."[106] For him this means not only a loss of confidence on the American side, but also a loss of trust on that of his Chinese friends: "In the only open yelling argument I ever had with a Chinese Communist, I was accosted by Mao's interpreter, a young Chinese named Huang Hua, now Foreign Minister of China. Furiously he denounced me for repeating to Hurley what Mao had said to me. 'Mao trusted you; we thought you were a friend.'"[107]

After his return to Chongqing, a reporting trip to Japan following the Emperor's capitulation and a final "farewell visit" to the Middle Kingdom, Teddy's years in China end in the fall of 1945. In that year, Teddy—for political reasons—must likewise refrain from composing overly political contributions for *Time* or *Life*. Journalists who express even a little sympathy for the communists find themselves avoided or even denounced. "Guys like you and Edgar Snow, who talk about the Communist guerrillas and their areas—you guys are what makes their strength. They aren't there, I tell you; they exist only on paper."[108] Teddy knows that this is not true. Together with Annalee Jacoby (the widow of his best correspondent friend in Chongqing), Theodore White pieces together the disparate interconnected pieces of China's history since the Japanese aggression of 1937, until the book *Thunder Out of China* appears a year later and even wins a Book-of-the-Month Club prize as a bestseller. White's book is an uncensored, meticulously documented and engaged reportage that explains the collapse of the Kuomintang regime three years later and the rise of the communist movement linked with it.

With *Thunder Out of China,* Teddy takes leave as well of *Time* and his former boss Henry Luce. With his prize of $80,000, Teddy can live well without the position at *Time*, even if he faces denunciations as a communist sympathizer during the McCarthy era and consequently can find no work as a foreign correspondent for any large media firm. He occasionally writes for smaller papers and for a relatively unknown news agency in Paris. Now he devotes his talent and his future to a historically based journalism that largely neglects historically informed current actualities. In general, historiography assumes that the more remote events are in time, the better we can understand them. Teddy, to the contrary, attempts to soften this theory with an approach that George Kennan later referred to as the "history of the present," for as a historically thinking eyewitness, he tries to understand currently ongoing processes and actions. In his engagement, he thereby finds himself in—as Timothy Garton Ash fittingly termed it—"a Three Country Corner between journalism, history, and literature."[109] Teddy, who as a boy once had to sell newspapers in Boston in order to alleviate his family's misery, becomes the author of political bestsellers like *Fire in the Ashes* (1953).

In all the years after his return to the West, the Middle Kingdom never lets go of his innermost heart. He hopes in vain, as a journalist and friend of China, to find a loophole in the strict American and Chinese visa requirements. But even Harvard cannot help him to visit the Middle Kingdom as a "Fellow of the Harvard Center for International Studies." The State Department turns down White's application. In a communication, he turns to Premier Zhou Enlai personally:

> As you know from the days when we used to see each other in Chongqing, my eyes are American eyes and my loyalties are American. In those days you respected those loyalties as much as I respected yours. It seems to me that it would serve the interest of both our countries if someone with the background of China's past, someone who saw China suffer as I did then, and who can measure what has been achieved against the background of the war, could come to China and report on it again.[110]

The letter goes unanswered, as do Teddy's numerous attempts to reach China's Premier through other contacts. The American State Department shows no inclination to aid him; it is, to the contrary, rather uncooperative: "I would like to point out, however, that even if you were to obtain permission from Chou En-lai to enter Communist China, we would not be disposed to alter our existing policy to authorize your travel to that area."[111] Teddy's goal to visit "his" China continues to be more remote than he thinks. He cannot resign himself to the fact that the Middle Kingdom has turned away from the West: "I find myself intellectually, morally, politically, emotionally uncomfortable to live in a world in which so vast a portion of the human race is sealed off from American study and analysis. The very lack of knowledge we have of China, we who once knew so much about it, makes our political thinking a nightmare unreality."[112] In desperation, he finally even turns to Mao Zedong and tries to remind him of their days together in Yan'an. Teddy deplores the anti-Chinese propaganda of certain American circles; he offers himself to the Chairman of the Central Committee of the Chinese Communist Party as a so-to-speak objective reporter. Despite the different conceptions of both countries, he wants to avoid conflicts. "Thus, I should like to come to visit Peking, to travel in the new China, for a few weeks or a few months, and to report to my own people and my own government where and how our purposes can be made to meet in harmony."[113] But Peking remains silent—the country is too occupied in that year with Lin Biao's mass campaign in the army to bother with the personal concerns of a Western correspondent.

Only the rapprochement of America with China in the early 1970s opens a small window for Teddy to look behind the Red Chinese bamboo curtain: He is a member of the press entourage during President Nixon's historic visit to China in February 1972. His encounter with China is in many regards a shock for him. Whereas earlier he could hear a symphony of noises on the streets of Peking, calm prevails now. He perceives the Bund (Shanghai's famous waterfront promenade) as declining. The language, like the mind of the people, has been rewired. A personally tragic moment for Teddy is his reunion with Zhou Enlai, the "youthful Robin Hood of revolution." To be sure, the Premier recalls his former guest at the 1940 "banquet of the pig," but his attitude is rather stiff and no longer consistent with that of a friend, as Teddy had hoped. "We were friends many years ago—or so I thought."[114] White recalls that already in the old days Zhou Enlai held the view that Westerners could not understand China and should therefore likewise not interfere in internal Chinese affairs. The farewell at West Lake in Hangzhou—"Maybe it's both our faults"—helps him, he who since his Harvard years had so much wanted to understand China and its intellectual world, to get over his sadness a bit.[115]

After this short official visit in China, Teddy still does not stop pressing for a "personal" visit. He wants to employ his theory, according to which the course of history and politics is primarily dependent on the human intellect and ideas. A trip to China would allow him to test this hypothesis there as well. Thus, his overriding goal is to speak with the men who created the "new China" about their lives and thereby to find out what ideas motivated them in Yan'an or still earlier on the Long March. In a letter to Zhou Enlai, who is already seriously ill, Teddy writes:

> I want to explain what happened, what the revolution achieved, and how its great leaders transformed the past and what they see of the future ahead. You had a vision then when last I left China; that vision became real. . . . To explain your thinking and the new China seems to me more important for long range American thinking than simple journalistic reporting and articles. We all grow older. More and more I seek to understand the history we have both seen and lived through. In the years of vigor that remain to me I want to write some large work of explanation of our times.[116]

Teddy again receives no answer and never sees China's Premier again: The latter dies on January 8, 1976. Jimmy Carter's National Security Advisor, Zbigniew Brzezinski, asks Teddy to provide the American President with China-specific diplomatically well-formulated information for Deng Xiaoping's official visit to the United States in the spring of 1979. Teddy's most important message to Jimmy Carter is that, as balsam for the soul of the Middle Kingdom, he should address China's humiliation by the West in the previous century. Concretely, he advises the President to offer the Chinese food aid: "Modern China has simply never been able to feed itself. . . . If we can offer anything at all to China, it is our ability to produce the good things of life for ordinary people—food, medicine, health services, etc."[117] While the two countries normalize their diplomatic relationships during Deng's visit, Teddy continues working to achieve his personal wish to return to the Middle Kingdom as a private visitor and to make China understandable to the West. In the spring of 1983, his luck finally changes—White receives permission to return on a trip into the past as a representative of two American magazines.

His *tour d'horizon* through the "history of the present" begins in Peking, more precisely in the "Fragrant Mountains" (Xiangshan), which Mao Zedong and his loyalists first reached in 1949 on the march to Peking ("Like Moses and the Israelites, they had been wandering the arid northlands"). Teddy examines the propaganda slogans lit up with neon lights—"Long live Chairman Mao"—and thinks about Western conceptions of events in the Middle Kingdom: "We could sense shapes, forms and fears, almost touch them. But we could not see through the membrane, or define or measure what it was we really wanted to know."[118] He has to admit that even his presence on site adds little to his understanding of China. In Chongqing, for example, he misses the familiar smells of opium, urine, flowers, and oranges or the blind beggars. Even friends of the past are not necessarily friends of the present. In a conversation with Peng Zhen, mayor of Beijing for fifteen years before the Cultural Revolution and one of the last survivors of the Long March, Teddy hopes to accomplish more.

But his disappointment is great when the meeting does not go as he had expected, "I had expected a jovial reunion. But . . . he was lecturing me" [on the relationship of the United States with Taiwan—author's note].[119] Culture-specific cases or universal human paradoxes? The question remains open: "The Chinese are still a 'struggle' people. . . . The transition regime in Beijing . . . chooses to go its own way. . . . So one returns from China, as one first arrived there long ago, fearful, yet hopeful."[120]

In 1985, Theodore White visits China for the last time, hoping to complete the circle of his personal striving to understand the events happening in the Middle Kingdom. In reality, however, even he senses that he is as far as ever from solving the Chinese riddle. "This was a new China with its own hidden turmoil of sufferings which I would understand only after time had passed."[121] History he learns, especially while engaging with China, is a stage full of dark objects: Depending on the angle of illumination, they assume different contours. Even during the war, White stated in a handwritten note that China's problem was not its politics, but rather its history. His great service is to have made a few Eastern images and *Lebenswelten* from this history familiar in the West, in a manner characteristic for this American Jewish reporter. On May 15, 1986, Theodore H. White passes away, the former newspaper boy and Pulitzer Prize winner who, as *The New York Times* states, "as reporter, historian and storyteller" wrote "books of lasting value."[122]

"*Emily Hahn* is here too," writes Teddy to his mother from Chongqing in January 1940, "a superb mad woman. Brilliant, beautiful, Jewish, extraordinarily clever, smokes cigars, talks Chinese, writes like a saint, has every man in love with her, lives with a Chinese poet."[123] White was probably not the only one who suddenly felt reverent, or rather a certain "ah and oh" sentiment whenever the name Emily Hahn was mentioned. Others also remembered strong-willed, capricious Mickey, as her friends always called her, who was born in St. Louis, Missouri, in 1905. The British author and world traveler Sir Harold Acton met Emily Hahn during his Shanghai stay in the 1930s at one of those famous parties in honor of a Chinese musician—"Emily Hahn, like a voluptuous figure from a Moroccan *mellah*" (the name for a Jewish ghetto in Muslim countries).[124]

Emily Hahn was in fact a headstrong, self-confident, and at times eccentric woman. Her parents stemmed from German-Jewish families, but wanted to have nothing more to do with the faith of their ancestors. Isaac, Mickey's father, frankly called himself an atheist. In St. Louis, where the winters are cold, and the summers are hot and sultry, Mickey spends a happy childhood in the circle of her five siblings. Already at that time, she was most interested in books, and she liked most of all to page through a large *Webster's Dictionary*. Emily's biographer, Ken Cuthbertson, points to the competition among the Hahn children that is thought to have resulted in Mickey's tendency to define herself more in terms of who she was *not* rather than of who she was.[125] In 1920, the family moves to Chicago, Al Capone's city and the home of the world's first skyscraper. Thereby a world of unusual possibilities opens up for Mickey, which immediately fascinates her: As the first woman to attend the University of Wisconsin in Madison, she studies "mining technology" and graduates with a Bachelors degree in 1926. She begins her years of wandering through the United States, Europe, and finally the Belgian Congo, where she works for the Red Cross at the start of the 1930s.

In 1935, Mickey, along with her sister Helen, embarks on a ship for Asia, first to Yokohama and three weeks later to Shanghai. The two dissimilar sisters set out in hopes of getting over casual affairs; the destination of their journey plays no role thereby: "'I don't really care for the Far East at all,' I was saying to myself. . . . I don't know and I don't care who these Chinese persons may be, but everybody is aware that the Japanese are the only *subtle* Orientals. China is garish. China is red and gold and big, everything I don't like. Pooh."[126] International politics is also foreign to Mickey: She seems not to have ever heard of the Japanese invasion of Manchuria.

That Emily Hahn's engagement with China, despite her initial ignorance regarding the situation there, once fascinated millions of readers, chiefly in the United States, is largely due to her ability to describe selected persons and their manners in the then trendy Shanghai scene with dedication and human warmth and sympathy—whether their character is good or bad. She has the good fortune that she can put to use her journalistic gifts as a temporary reporter for the *North-China Daily News*. Mickey begins, after Helen has returned to her homeland, to cultivate a lifestyle that she could not have afforded at home. On Kiangse Road (Jiangxi Lu) she rents an apartment with a direct view of one of the most famous Shanghai entertainment districts. Through an acquaintance, she meets Sir Victor Sassoon, with whom she enters into a relationship that is to last for years. To be sure, it is not the Sephardic tycoon, but rather a Chinese man of letters who ultimately introduces Mickey to the Eastern *Lebenswelten* of Shanghai and stands at her side (at least in the early years) as a cultural and political guide to China. This step in the life of the thirty-year-old is one reason why practically overnight she becomes conversational topic number one in the foreign community. Even her closest friends warn her against overstepping with a Chinese lover the

Figure 2.4
Emily Hahn, a reporter for The New Yorker *and gifted writer, was always driven by curiosity and energy. "She went there and did that, and then wrote about it without fuss." Cover of the First Edition of Emily Hahn's book "*China to Me,*" New York, 1944.*

boundary lines of what Western society could tolerate. That he was in addition already married makes the static about Mickey's private life all the louder.

The Chinese intellectual was Zau Sinmay, in today's orthography Shao Xunmei, who in 1928, together with the poet Xu Zhimo (an admirer of Rabindranath Tagore), especially highly valued by China's youth, and the famous Hu Shi, founds the so-called Crescent Bookstore. The latter is able in March of the same year to publish the first issue of *The Crescent Monthly*, a journal in which scholars find a voice who among other things campaign for the modernization of classical Chinese literature. Zau Sinmay's grandfather served as the Qing Dynasty's envoy to the court of the Russian Czar, while his father appears to have been the governor of Taiwan before becoming the mayor of Shanghai.[127] One evening after an extended restaurant visit, Mickey violates racial taboos and thereby entangles herself in this exotic world. To be sure, she continues to occasionally lunch with Sir Victor (although the latter perhaps somewhat jealously comments: "You are getting too damned Chinese") or hangs around with girlfriends in the Cathay Hotel's bar, yet she spends more and more time with Zau Sinmay and his Chinese friends. She helps him edit his articles for the monthly magazine *T'ien Hsia*, to whose editorial committee Lin Yutang also belonged in later years. The not merely physical nearness to Zau sharpens her awareness of China's problems and its people. She even tries smoking opium, knowing all too well that according to then current laws, inhaling the "great smoke" is illegal.

It is always possible to sell opium smoking as a moment of experience for a Western woman in the Orient to the American public in the form of an exotic story: *The New Yorker* hires Emily Hahn to send ongoing reportage from distant Shanghai to America. Not without pride is she extolled by the culturally oriented and socially critical journal as a China Coast correspondent. Writing for *The New Yorker,* Mickey can optimally relate her own personality to her colorful surroundings: "Though I had always wanted to be an opium addict, I can't claim that as the reason I went to China. . . . It had become clear to me the first day in China that I was going to stay forever."[128] It is Mickey who can make a journalistic contribution out of almost anything and is constantly searching, and with great curiosity studies people, and their concerns, fears, and thoughts. She does not shy away from placing herself in a story, so that readers have no reason to complain about a lack of glimpses into her private sphere.

Polygamy, which was then legal in China, always represented a source of disagreement for the majority of Western visitors. Emily Hahn is one of the few who see more than just the negative aspects of the concubine system (for example the non-existence of illegitimate children). She must have known: After mulling it over for a long time, she enters into such a marriage with Zau

Sinmay, as his concubine (whereby his wife seems to have nothing against this). In her short story "Mr. Pan," she describes this life for her readers.[129] Pan Heh-ven is her lover Zau Sinmay, whom she describes as she sees and believes she understands him, not always quite correctly from a Chinese viewpoint, as Zau once complains to her ("You portray me as an idiot"). In this personal portrayal, her surprise, and occasionally even helplessness, comes to expression in view of the ambivalence of his character. In contrast to many other Western authors, Mickey avoids generalizations; she observes and describes what she sees without offering much background information, but with an eye and a heart for detail, for the individuality of the "Chinese soul."

In the meantime, Mickey has acquired another "partner," the legendary, mischievous "Mr. Mills," a gibbon (short, tailless ape with a round head and very long arms), and this—not surprisingly—further increases Emily Hahn's reputation as an indeed rather unconventional Western woman. She makes appearances with Mr. Mills at the bar in the Cathay Hotel or in the Chocolate Shop, sometimes frequented by Agnes Smedley and Edgar Snow. Besides her extremely productive journalistic activity, she wants to open a business to sell Chinese silk underwear. She meets Mei Lanfang, China's most famous opera performer, Western entrepreneurs, and diplomats. One weekend she decides—despite her friends' warnings of possible Japanese attacks—to take a train to Nanking. The intrepid young woman refuses to be dissuaded, and writes about the experience in the short story "A Round Trip to Nanking," with the first sentence "Nobody said not to go," which sixty years later Ken Cuthbertson chose as the title of his Emily Hahn biography. As Japanese troops move ever closer to the Western concession territories, and more and more Jewish refugees from Europe flood into the city on the Huangpu, the moment has come for Mickey to reconsider her situation. In a letter to her sister Helen, it is obvious that despite the desperate situation she still does not want to leave the Middle Kingdom: While she feels she cannot get rooted in Shanghai, she still loves China.[130] Finally it is her old friend John Gunther (the famous world traveler and author of the "Inside" series), who helps her decide "What now?" He suggests that she write a book about the Soong sisters (Ailing, who married H. H. Kung, heir to a banking fortune and Chinese finance minister (1933–44); Qingling, the wife of Sun Yat-sen; and Meiling, the wife of Chiang Kai-shek).

"In any case, the book on the Soongs is the stabilizing, gravitational force in the nine-year Chinese adventure," concludes *The New York Times* a year after its appearance.[131] Before she can write it, however, Mickey has to clear a few hurdles: She must overcome her opium addiction (or she has no chance of reaching Chongqing), make contact with the Soong sisters, and finally manage the journey into the interior of China. A German refugee doctor cures her addiction using hypnotherapy. Zau Sinmay's relationship with Madame Kung (Soong Ailing) facilitates meetings with the Soong sisters. In Hong Kong, Mickey first meets Soong Ailing, who immediately questions whether a foreigner is capable of understanding Chinese affairs. Having overcome all the impediments, in December 1939 Emily Hahn finally boards a Douglas DC3 headed for China's war capital: "Chungking. What does the name evoke in my mind? Air raids. Oranges. Szechuan food, good, full of strong pepper, probably to warm up the blood on the cold, wet, muddy days that come so often. Air always so moist as almost to drip."[132]

Just as in Shanghai, in the exhibitionism-oriented Western "community" of "Free China" Mickey is an attraction, as she once described herself. She soon meets Tilman Durdin, Teddy White, Reverend James Endicott and his wife (even though Mickey cannot stand missionaries), and also Chiang Kai-shek's Australian advisor W. H. Donald, who arranges for her to meet Madame Chiang (Soong Meiling). There she chances to meet—while she is interviewing China's First Lady—the Generalissimo in his house slippers, which probably annoys him more than it does the young American woman from St. Louis. Mickey remains in the war capital for ten weeks and accompanies the First Lady on official occasions.

The biggest hurdle for Emily Hahn's plan to write a biography of the Soong sisters proves to be Soong Qingling. Mickey returns to Hong Kong without having spoken with Sun Yat-sen's widow. She wants to continue on to Shanghai, but Madame Kung personally dissuades her from this idea for fear of provoking the Japanese. As an alternative suggestion she invites Mickey to fly back to Chongqing with all three Soong sisters in order to so-to-speak collect the material for the final chapter (in the form of a demonstration of solidarity among all the Soong sisters in the struggle against Japan). Mickey later recalls this conversation with Madame Kung as follows: "I don't want you to be exploited by China. . . . If this happens . . . you will end by hating us all. Yet, I think you will. I know China and I know America. You will go away from China without complaining, but you will feel bitter. Isn't it true?"[133] Mickey agrees and returns a second time to Chongqing, where she completes *The Soong Sisters* in summer 1940.

Her return to Hong Kong is very much under the influence of her affair with Charles Boxer, the top British spy in the Crown Colony, to whom she bears a child before his arrest by Japanese troops following the attack on Pearl Harbor. While Boxer—like almost all Western prisoners—is detained in the Stanley Internment Camp, Mickey tries to get by as well as possible (protected by a marriage of expediency with a Chinese, she is not harassed). In 1943, after a stay of eight years, she leaves the Chinese mainland on a prisoner transport (the MS Gripsholm) in an exchange for Japanese POWs. This is possible because the American State Department has intervened on her behalf in response to her friends' entreaties.

Back in the United States, Emily Hahn writes her 1944 book *China to Me,* describing her experiences and mental states in the Middle Kingdom. Since she seldom thinks and writes in terms of political relationships, no one suspects her of harboring pro-communist inclinations, as they do Teddy White and many others. To the contrary: The Congressional Representative and "China Lobby" supporter Walter Judd invites her to honor the list of the so-called "Defend China Committee" with her signature. In subsequent years, Mickey publishes countless books about China, such as the beautifully illustrated children's book *China A to Z,* in which she lovingly explains Chinese concepts to Western children by going through the entire alphabet with short verses.[134] A further work on China appears in 1955: an unauthorized biography of Chiang Kai-shek, who lost the Chinese Civil War.[135] In 1968, Emily Hahn publishes—after she has long since turned to other topics for her creative work—her last book entirely dedicated to China and thereby demonstrates her versatility: *The Cooking of China.*[136] In her foreword, she frankly admits that initially her ignorance of the Chinese matched her ignorance of Chinese cuisine.

In all the years following her China adventure, she maintains contact with the persons together with whom she had witnessed the decline of Western supremacy in the Middle Kingdom. Among them is Sir Victor Sassoon, who regularly bombards her with personal letters from London, Rio, or the Bahamas, and with whom she ponders about "how the sinologues who have never been to China manage to get the taste and smell of the place in their writing."[137] Another is Colonel David Barrett, whom she asks to put in a good word for her with Chiang Kai-shek concerning her planned biography. There is also Pearl Buck, whom she accuses of having spread false rumors about her during a lecture; Vicky Baum, who suggests she put "Mr. Pan" on stage; or Randall Gould, the famous United Press correspondent in Chongqing and editor of the *Shanghai Evening Post & Mercury.*

There is also the one or the other exchange of letters with Edgar Snow. The latter is the only journalist who manages to remain politically respected after the victory of the People's Liberation Army not only by the new leadership in Peking, but also by the "China Lobby" in the United States. In a noteworthy 1956 letter to Mickey, he writes about his understanding of events in China:

> I was looking through my small library the other day and the thought occurred to me that only half a dozen books in it were worth reading from the viewpoint of understanding what is happening in China or Asia generally today; all or nearly all this past comment is irrelevant; it was written from minor elevations now all

wiped out. I speak of books on social, economic and political matters. It is less true of books of personal experience, like your own.[138]

It is hard to imagine greater praise and recognition for Emily Hahn's accomplishments in regard to China, if one considers Edgar Snow's conclusion that her essays on China might turn out to be much more valuable in the future than all the political speculations of others. Snow's evaluation applies in any event to the Western perception of China in the twentieth century. In 1997, at the advanced age of ninety-two, Mickey, who in the course of her rich life wrote more than fifty books in every literary genre and dozens of articles, passes away in New York. Following her death, *The New Yorker*, "her" magazine, writes: "She was, in truth, something rare: a woman deeply, almost domestically, at home in the world. Driven by curiosity and energy, she went there and did that, and then wrote about it without fuss."[139]

In contrast to Emily Hahn, *Gunther Stein* (or Günther Stein) was not an apolitical author. Indeed, his personal political engagement proved disastrous for him after his return from China. Even Mickey, who often picked people to pieces but avoided slander, could not refrain from calling Stein an opportunist, one of those "gullible journalists" who contributed to "losing" China.[140] Even more serious accusations are made against him; he is one of the most "complicated cases," as the publisher of the *Christian Science Monitor* once remarked. According to the *Biographical Handbook of German-speaking Emigration after 1933*, Günther Stein was born in Berlin in 1900.[141] We have no information about his childhood and young years. He studies economics at the university in Berlin and earns his living as a journalist for the *Berliner Tageblatt*. At the start of the 1930s he journeys to the East for the first time, reports in 1932 from Moscow and in the years of Hitler's rise to power emigrates to England. A year later, he visits Japan as a foreign correspondent for British and American papers (among others the *Manchester Guardian* and the *Christian Science Monitor* in Boston) and reports on the rise of the military empire. He writes two well-researched books illuminating the societal context of the Asiatic countries in that period: *Made in Japan* in 1935 and *Far East in Ferment* a year later. In Japan, he becomes acquainted with China and its dismal political situation. He interviews the Generalissimo, who at that time grants very few interviews to foreign journalists. From the very start, Stein appears fascinated by Chiang Kai-shek, whom he describes as a counter-pole to the "average Chinese":

Everything about Chiang Kai-shek impressed me as a conscious protest . . . against the characteristics of the average run of Chinese people; a protest against their often soft, undisciplined and slovenly appearance, and their careless and easy-going manners; against the waste of time . . . and conventional politeness in their speech; against everything that an efficient, modern general and states-

> man must regard as a shortcoming, even though it sometimes contains so much grace and charm, so much that is human and that helps to make life bearable.[142]

Stein, whose works display a talent for making sensitive, detailed observations of subjects without generalization, settles in Hong Kong in 1938 in order to follow the Sino-Japanese war from a different perspective. He resides in the British Crown Colony for two years, and from there he undertakes various trips to many provinces of the fragmented Middle Kingdom, whose territorial and ethnic diversity he has already recognized as a characteristic of China in *Far East Ferment*. In 1940, he makes Chongqing the base of his journalistic activity. As a war correspondent for the *Christian Science Monitor,* he travels the Burma Road and writes—like all his colleagues—about the wretched conditions of the soldiers "trained" by the Nationalist government.[143] In the spring of 1944, he is one of a very few journalists who receive permission to visit the "liberated areas" in Yan'an, for half a year. In 1945, he describes the experiences of this trip in *The Challenge of Red China*.[144] Nathaniel Peffer praises the book in the *China Weekly Review* as the most detailed report on Communist China since Edgar Snow's visit ten years before.[145] A few years later, it was referred to as a model example of the naiveté or even conscious distortion of facts by pro-communist journalists with the aim of spreading falsehoods about the true intentions of China's rising new rulers.

The Challenge of Red China, interspersed with illustrations of the socialist-realist woodcut artistry that flourished in the 1930s, created by teachers and students at the Yan'an Art Academy, portrays the, in Stein's view, completely utopian life of the people in Shaanxi Province. Stein observes the Chinese at work, at political assemblies, in hostels, lyceums, or in evening entertainment. Like other journalists before and after him, he carries on endless conversations with the communist leaders, one twelve hours long, for example, with Mao Zedong. His original reservations about the communists become fewer and fewer. Stein—in contrast to Harold Isaacs—knows nothing about the background of the murder of Ding Ling's husband when he sits across from the author of *Miss Sophie's Diary*.[146] Nor does he know (or only superficially) that with the Rectification Movement (1942–44) Mao gave an example of the limits of intellectual inquiry. Consequently, his questions are tame and the answers no less trivial. Stein's investigation of the accusation repeatedly made by the Kuomintang in Chongqing that the communists supported opium cultivation likewise produces no results, in contrast to, for example, the research by Tass representative Pyotr Vladimirov.

Despite his, from a contemporary viewpoint, propagandistic historiography, Gunther Stein is able to write an article about "The Other China" for the October 1945 issue of *Foreign Affairs*, which also includes an article by John

Foster Dulles, later American Secretary of State and declared opponent of accommodation with Red China. However, Stein's predictions—in contrast to those of Dulles—proved correct regarding the future communist takeover of power: " . . . I contend that the Chinese Communist movement is now so strong, and has its roots so well embedded in economic and political realities in China, that it could not be destroyed even in a civil war."[147] In the June 1946 issue of the *Yale Review,* Stein urgently pleads for not judging China in terms of current events; we cannot understand the country and its characteristics using Western concepts like "president," "nationalist," or "communist." "Behind that bewildering foreground are the real actors, of whom we hear little, the people of China,"[148] he explains. Western politicians, chiefly American, ignore Stein's warnings. At a December 1948 podium event on China, in which China specialists including Gunther Stein participate, he points out that even without assistance from the outside world, the Chinese communists could rebuild the country after their victory in the Civil War: China is not an orphan begging for alms.[149]

As the end of the Civil War nears, the dark clouds that have already appeared on the horizon also cast their shadow over Stein: *The New York Times* links him with Richard Sorge, a German-born major Soviet spy, and the journalist Agnes Smedley.[150] The newspaper claims that Stein was a member of the Sorge spy ring (which, for example, informed the Soviets of the planned German invasion of Russia, and also knew about the Japanese attack on Pearl Harbor) and therefore indirectly worked for the communists. Consequently, it regards him as an enemy of America. He prefers to leave the country as quickly as possible to return to Europe, since the accusations have made it impossible for him to continue his work as a journalist.

In *Shanghai Conspiracy*, a collection of documents by Major General Charles A. Willoughby, the Chief of Intelligence under General MacArthur from 1941–51, concerning alleged activities of the Sorge ring and its offshoots, among others in Shanghai,[151] Willoughby accuses the German Jew Stein of being a Soviet spy and important member of the Sorge ring.[152] Willoughby's pro-fascist attitude becomes clearly apparent in later years. After retirement, he lives in Franco's Spain, which he praises greatly. His book is obviously grist for the mill of Joe McCarthy, who cannot pass up the chance to use his "revelations" for his own purposes and to launch an attack on Stein and the *Christian Science Monitor.*[153] The editor of the *Christian Science Monitor* comes to Stein's defense as a correspondent of his paper and attests to his objective reportage for the *Monitor*. He also points out that even Hollington Tong, the former Deputy Minister of Information and later ambassador of the Nationalist government to the United States, mentions

Stein favorably in his book *Dateline China* (1950).[154] To be sure, he himself disputes each of Willoughby's accusations from his London exile, but no one ever completely clarified how things really stood with the former Berlin journalist and refugee from Hitler's terror. The *Biographical Handbook of German-Speaking Emigration after 1933* merely notes that after his return to Europe, he works as a correspondent for the *Hindustan Times,* India's leading newspaper, and dies on January 22, 1961. Many interesting aspects of his life will remain shadowy unless new documents are found.

II. COURIERS, EMISSARIES, AND ADVISORS

Couriers and emissaries served entirely different functions in the twentieth-century network of East-West relations than did journalists. Dispatched by Western organizations or governments to the Far East for the most varied of reasons, they were primarily there to fulfill assignments: political, economic, humanitarian, and sometimes to work for a secret service. Many of these envoys from the West could not always resist the allure of China; in China their sympathy or antipathy was at any given time great enough to prevent them from entirely withdrawing from this sometimes mysterious foreign land.

Israel Cohen, born in Manchester in 1879, is such an emissary, although his employer was not a state, but rather an organization, namely the World Zionist Organization (WZO), founded in 1897. His encounter with China is limited in time and equivalent to that of a transient visitor. His 1920/21 assignment does not consist in learning as much about China and its population as possible, but rather in seeking out Jewish communities in the Far East and making close contacts with his fellow Jews. In addition, he offers interesting observations about the sometimes-foreign Jewish *Lebenswelten* before the background of exotic Chinese surroundings, which he adds to his travel report, *The Journal of a Jewish Traveller* (1925).

The Balfour Declaration was not yet four years old when the WZO decided to send its Director of Publicity and Propaganda to South East Asia to explain the significance of this very important twentieth-century document. If possible, he was to obtain the urgently needed financial means to realize the dream of a Jewish state.[155] In his baggage, Cohen carries references and tracts by the great representatives of the Zionist idea: Chaim Weizmann, Nahum Sokolov, and Max Nordau. The mission leads him in May 1920 from London via Egypt and Australia to Hong Kong, and from there he visits Jewish communities in Japan (Yokohama and Kobe), Manchuria, Peking, and Shanghai, before he begins his return trip to Europe, a year later, via India.

In Shanghai, Cohen learns of a group of Chinese with "Jewish" features in the area of Nanking, a strange story that does not appear in the literature.[156] Orthodox Jews confront him with the open question of whether or not the use of a rickshaw is permissible on the Sabbath. Cohen sees the Chinese in Shanghai merely as waiters in "spotless white." In the house of Edward Ezra (not to be confused with the publisher N. E. B. Ezra), he meets a Russian Jew, "the son of a rabbi, who was in the service of the Chinese Government and always wore Chinese garb at home."[157] At the YMCA, he attends a performance of *Das Opfer Isaacs* (The Sacrifice of Isaac), an opera by the Yiddish dramatist Abraham Goldfaden, whereby paradoxically the stage set is decorated with a Chinese temple and garden. Via Mukden (now called Shenyang), the former Manchurian capital, and Changchun, whose railway station "could compete in smell, dirt and disorder with any railway station in Poland," Cohen then travels to Harbin, where he observes the activities in the parts of the city where the most varied ethnic groups live. The Chinese police catch his attention when he sees policemen in the middle of the street, more an impediment than a means to directing traffic. Or he sees Chinese women with children bound on their backs or a baby at their breast, waiting for hours on a bridge over the Sungari River in hopes of receiving alms.

In Harbin, Cohen's attention is attracted to his fellow Jews, the "most accessible Russo-Jewish community in the world."[158] Their "spiritual vitality" especially impresses the WZO emissary. Meetings with a former, mentally stricken prisoner of war from Galicia, a former Czech student from the University of Vienna, and an unemployed Hungarian Jew make an impression on Cohen. Still, in the midst of all the misery he also hopes that here in the Far East he will be able to recruit settlers for Palestine. At a conference dedicated to this topic, he speaks in Hebrew, which a Chinese police officer forbids (Harbin was in the meantime formally under Chinese sovereignty). The situation, embarrassing for all sides, is resolved in an Oriental manner, "when the Chinaman returned with a smile."

Peking is the last stop of the trip by the Zionist emissary to the Far East. There he again encounters a concentrated charge of "foreignness": Here are "rare porcelain, ivory figures, cups of jade and lamps of red-lacquered wood, and there a row of unsavoury stalls, where slaughtered cats and fried rats and divers undistinguishable pieces of meat were offered for sale, and little fat cakes of dubious ingredients were frizzled in spluttering pans." He feels great admiration for the native architecture, especially the majestic Temple of Heaven. With L. S. Regine, the owner of the first English-speaking newspaper in Peking, the *Peking Post*, he shares reverence and respect for what lies behind the facade of direct human perception: "I [L. S. Regine—author's note] don't know whether I shall ever see *Erez Israel*, but there is nothing that

I would so much wish as that our Temple should be as beautiful and majestic as the Temple of Heaven."[159]

Neither Zionist ideals nor religious sentiments were involved in *Hans Shippe's* engagement in China. The challenges of the Chinese Revolution and later the fate of the Middle Kingdom, threatened by Japanese aggression, were close to his heart (he used numerous pseudonyms: originally Mojze Grzyb; then also Heinz Möller, Heinz Grzyb, "Asiaticus," and many others). Shippe was born in 1896 or 1897 (depending on the source) in Galician Tarnov (now part of the Ukraine), the son of a building contractor, Isaak Grzyb. He belongs to that category of Western visitors who were active beginning in the 1920s in the service of the Chinese Revolution. This is not to say that it would never have happened without the foreigners, but at every moment in its course, progressively oriented foreigners like Shippe gave it substantial impulses. This was due to the historical situation in Europe: The First World War had destroyed the foundations of the old world; the upper classes' aristocratic lifestyles were outdated. Many young people saw the Russian Revolution as a signal for the dawn of a new age. In Western Europe people also wanted to take things into their own hands, cast off the fetters of their parents' inflexible ideas. Not a few saw in socialism a possibility to overcome the misery of the world and liberate humankind. Knowledge of Marxist-Leninist ideology played—for example for Shippe—an important role in the striving to serve as a cog in the wheel of the Chinese Revolution.

Much of Shippe's biography remains shrouded in mystery. For a long time no one even knew who was writing under the pseudonym "Asiaticus."[160] It is certain that Shippe, who served in the Austrian Army during the First World War, was linked to the communist movement and arrested as a pacifist. After his move to Germany, he joins the German Communist Party (KPD) in 1918/19. With a study of philosophy and national economics, he acquires excellent tools for his later work as a journalist, and he already starts writing articles under various names about the revolutionary situation in Europe. For an editorial on the fifth anniversary of the Russian October Revolution, Shippe is expelled to the Soviet Union as an "undesirable alien." Back in Germany in 1923, he writes for the KPD organ the *Rote Fahne* (Red Flag). In disputes within the KPD over the "correct" policy toward Social Democracy, Shippe bets on the wrong horse (namely the United Front) and is consequently barred from working for the KPD. He leaves Europe, now apparently "on probation," in the direction of China. There he witnesses the memorable 30th of May 1925 in Shanghai and as a reporter takes part in the Kuomintang troops' Northern Expedition. He earns his living writing reports for the *People's Tribune* (the mouthpiece of the "leftist" Kuomintang) in Wuhan in 1926/27, but also as a political propagandist for National Revolutionary

Army publications. Back in Germany, his book *Von Kanton bis Schanghai 1926–27* (From Canton to Shanghai 1926–27) appears under the pseudonym "Asiaticus." It is a collection of contributions written in China and is intended to show how Chiang Kai-shek betrayed the Revolution with the Western powers' aid.[161]

Once again, Shippe entangles himself in trench warfare within the KPD. This time (1928) it is a matter of the demand for democracy within the party, with which Shippe also sides. Like others, the party expels him and replaces him as chief editor of the Chemnitz newspaper *Der Kämpfer* (The Fighter). He retreats into "inner emigration" and seeks his own special niche: In leftist newspapers, among others Carl von Ossietzky's pacifistic *Weltbühne* (World Stage), for which Tucholsky also writes, Shippe publishes articles on China's economic problems, on personalities like Sun Yat-sen, the "Christian General" Feng Yuxiang, or relations between the Soviet Union and China. In 1932 the Galician Jew and ardent Marxist undertakes another journey to the Far East. A few months later, his wife Trude Rosenberg follows him to Shanghai. There he works in a small chemical factory and she as a nurse, typical jobs for many Jewish "Shanghaiers." Shippe manages to obtain a higher profile in the still relatively small group of revolutionary-minded foreigners by organizing political circles, in which he also offers guidance to interested natives and foreigners in the study of communist theorists from Marx and Engels to Lenin and Stalin.

On one such discussion evening, there is a memorable meeting between Shippe and Karl August Wittfogel, a German emigrant, academic, and KPD member. After Hitler takes power in 1933 (and after being held in a concentration camp), Wittfogel leaves his homeland for England and later America. Between 1935 and 1939, Wittfogel, who during his studies had already analyzed China's political system and historical development, regularly travels to the Middle Kingdom to do additional research. Shippe disagrees with an idea that Wittfogel discusses in his monumental 1931 *Wirtschaft und Gesellschaft Chinas* (China's Economy and Society). Starting with the Marxist concept of the Asiatic means of production, Wittfogel develops his theory of a "hydraulic society." According to this theory, the spatial expansion of Chinese public projects for regulating the water supply (dikes, irrigation, canalization) has led to a concentration of power over the centuries. This, in turn, gave rise to a bureaucratic elite that in equal measure rules man and nature and makes change very difficult. Shippe, to the contrary, regards the existence of an exploitive land-owning class as the key reason for feudalism and thereby revolution-prone conditions in Chinese society.[162]

Shippe links the debate over communist theory with what he sees everyday on the streets of Shanghai. He publishes his insights in articles in the international media, thus for example in the Soviet *Izvestia*, the Shanghai *Voice of China*, *The New Yorker*, *China Today*, published by the Friends of the Chinese People, or *Pacific Affairs*, published by the renowned Institute of Pacific Relations (Honolulu), whose special correspondent he becomes in 1936. In his contributions, he devotes himself chiefly to economic and political topics. His critique of Edgar Snow's *Red Star Over China* acquires particular significance.[163] In this review, Shippe does, it is true, praise Snow's work as an excellent and well-documented report, but he also accuses him of holding Trotskyite views. This accusation was then common in domestic Chinese debates on the "correct" policy of the Chinese Communist Party, but irrelevant in Snow's case. Shippe recommends strict compliance with the China policy promulgated by the Comintern, in other words, the United Front between the Kuomintang and the Communist Party. Furthermore, he takes exception to Snow's critical attitude toward the Soviet Union, which the latter accuses of failing to provide the Chinese communists with sufficient support. The debate with Snow has consequences: Mao supposedly reacts with annoyance to Shippe's censuring Snow, whereas the communist party in the United States (which follows a markedly pro-Stalinist line) subsequently bans Snow's book from its bookstores.

Whether or not Shippe ever worked for the Soviet secret service has never been determined. It is certain that the Comintern was one of Shippe's bosses. Shippe also has good contacts with Tass, the Soviet press agency, which at the time had the reputation of occupying itself with more than just journalism. His conspiratorial activity attracts the attention of the German Embassy in Nanking, at the latest after the outbreak of the Sino-Japanese War in 1937. Shippe provokes great displeasure, especially with his article in the *China Weekly Review*, "Nazi-Nippon Alliance Most Dangerous Threat to China's Sovereignty," in which he analyzes the so-called anti-Comintern pact of 1937 between Berlin and Tokyo from a Chinese perspective.[164] The German Ambassador regards the article to be anti-German. His ties to German and Austrian anti-fascists, primarily Jews, as well as his contacts with leading representatives of the Chinese CP, create a public image of a Westerner for whom the struggle against Japanese militarism is more important than the quest for luxury and personal esteem. This is rare in Shanghai. For Shippe it is time to leave the pavements of Shanghai, which have become too hot, and not just for him.

With a few followers, among them Agnes Smedley and the physician Shen Qizhen (later vice-president of the Chinese Academy of Medical Sciences), who secretly works for the Chinese CP, he sets out for the first time in the spring of 1939 for the headquarters of the communist New Fourth Army in the south of Anhui Province.[165] On his meetings with the leading military and political figures of the revolutionary movement in the war years, he reports in detail for the American magazine *Amerasia*. The controversy over this, by contemporary standards left-leaning, magazine was to provide a starting point for the postwar debate on who in the American government was to blame for the "loss of China."[166] In the following months—the United Front between the Kuomintang and the Chinese CP breaks up as a result of the attack by Nationalist armed forces on the New Fourth Army in January 1941—Shippe travels back and forth between the "two liberated areas," mostly through territory occupied by the Japanese. In September 1941, he manages, accompanied by soldiers of the New Fourth Army, to reach Shandong, the theater of action of the Eighth Route Army, where he witnesses Japanese war atrocities first hand. In one of them Shippe loses his life on November 30, 1941.[167] Over a period of fifteen years, this Galician Jew, whose Chinese adventure can only be understood in terms of Hitler's rise in Germany, succeeds during important periods of Chinese revolutionary history in visiting areas that remained inaccessible to the majority of Westerners in the Middle Kingdom.

When *Max Granich* comes into the world on March 19, 1896, no one could imagine that he would someday guard the house of Madame Sun in Shanghai and in later years serve as the chauffeur of American Communist Party leader Earl Browder. To be sure, Granich will thereby never achieve a very high level of name recognition, but his stay in China is no less strongly marked by revolutionary zeal than that of Hans Shippe, born at almost the same time in Galicia. Manny, as his friends always called him, is simultaneously both a typical and a rare product of the Lower East Side, the New York immigrant quarter and center of leftist political activities around the turn of the century: His mother stems from Hungary, his father from Romania. Although the latter is not very religious, this does not protect them from anti-Semitic attacks. After the mandatory schooling, Manny, who if nothing else speaks Yiddish, must find work. The not very rosy economic situation necessitates this. He earns his daily bread as a delivery boy, pawnshop employee, and office assistant at an insurance company. At the same time, in the politically seething environment of the Lower East Side, he inhales his first breaths of leftist-oriented prescriptions for world improvement.

In May 1917, the United States having declared war against Germany a month earlier, the U.S. Congress passes a conscription law in order to raise an army for the European conflict. Manny decides to leave New York for the West. In the following years, he moves from job to job as a transient laborer, among others on cattle ranches and in orchards. Back in New York (1923), he works as a taxi driver and finally as an employee for various industrial equipment manufacturing companies in the Northeastern United States. Even then, he appears to be interested in the Russian October Revolution, although he does not claim to be a communist. A later interview, however, makes obvious his youthful enthusiasm for Lenin and the latter's presumed qualities.[168] In the wake of the Great Depression, he loses his job and returns to New York almost penniless. He makes friends with members of the American Communist Party, among them his future wife, Grace Maul, who works as a secretary for Earl Browder. Through her influence, he gets a chance to observe the communist "workers' paradise" with his own eyes for more than a year: From December 1931 to May 1933, he works in Leningrad, in the Ukraine and in Siberia, first for the Ford Motor Company, later on mechanical engineering projects and for the railroad. It is the time of the great famine, when millions of Ukrainians die of starvation. The idealistic utopian theory is nowhere in evidence amidst the terrifying reality, and yet back in the United States, via London and Berlin, where he experiences incidents with Nazis, he himself becomes a member of the Stalinist CPUSA.

In December 1935, the time comes unexpectedly for Manny and Grace to fulfill their internationally oriented yearning in the Far East. After the "failure" of Harold Isaacs' *China Forum* in 1934, it is once more incumbent upon Agnes Smedley to seek new "fuel" for the revolutionary movement. She energetically encourages Earl Browder to dispatch someone to Shanghai to give the Chinese communists more publicity. It is almost by chance that Grace and Manny Granich are chosen. Sailing on the S.S. President Taft, the couple arrives in Shanghai at the end of January 1936. They reside on the Rue Paul Henry (today Xinle Lu) in the French Concession, not far from the villa of drug boss Du Yuesheng. Thanks to the very energetic Agnes Smedley, they soon meet the revolutionary group around Madame Sun, among them also the Western members of this East-West community of fate. These include, for example, the New Zealander Rewy Alley, who, himself on assignment from the Shanghai Municipal Council (SMC) as an inspector, investigates the inhumane working conditions in factories, or the Viennese Ruth Weiss, a journalist and educator who received Chinese citizenship in 1955 (see below). However, before they begin work on their actual assignment, the publication of a journal, Agnes Smedley again aids the American couple to catch a breath of Chinese air on a rail trip to Peking. "Peiping was like a realization of all my dreams. . . . I wanted to visit it [the Temple of Heaven—author's note] in the moonlight, and we planned to do this, but like so many other plans and dreams about China, this one was not fulfilled."[169] Thanks to Agnes Smedley's efforts, the Granichs spend much of their Peking visit with Edgar Snow and his wife, Helen Foster (who publishes articles on China under the pseudonym Nym Wales). They have their own cottage with a garden and trees not far from the site of the Qings' former summer residence, the Old Summer Palace (Yuanmingyuan). Snow's political orientation was then already a bit more to the left than that of his colleagues Thomas Franklin Millard (major journalist specialized in China, founder of the *China Weekly Review*) or John William Powell from the Missouri School of Journalism. No wonder he personally experiences boycotts, student protests, and arrests. It was just before Snow's visit to Mao in Shaanxi and the "liberated areas."

Back in Shanghai, the Granichs immediately start to carry out their assignment. With Smedley's support, they found the *Voice of China*, initially a bimonthly magazine registered with the American General Consulate. While Grace is responsible for the editorial work, Manny occupies himself with the practical affairs, a no less arduous task. Both Chinese and foreigners write for the magazine, openly and—if necessary—under a pseudonym.

One selling point is that the *Voice of China* is the only English language magazine that prints unadulterated news on the Chinese people and its liberation struggle against Japanese aggression. In fact, the magazine is more emphatically anti-Japanese than pro-communist. Even the State Department in Washington admits this in a communication to the American General Consulate in Shanghai.[170] By contrast, Clarence Gauss, the American General Consul, judges the Granichs' activities less leniently. Similar to Isaacs, in the coming months Manny grapples with Shanghai Municipal Council authorities, with Gauss and even with the Chinese powers that be, but with only moderate success. As in Shippe's case, the German General Consulate is also outraged about a report in the *Voice of China* by Rewy Alley (pseudonym: Han Su-mei), "Visitors from Naziland" (February 15, 1937). For the *Voice of China*, which since February 1937 has included a Chinese-language supplement, the end comes when the Chinese printer that has until then brought the *Voice* on the market is forced to give up this work. The Japanese attack on Shanghai in autumn 1937 is rapidly approaching: "The second bomb hit beyond at the point of the park [meant is Huangpu Park—author's note], . . . into the water. Splashed us and we crawled out. There was no place for a good Yiddish people [sic], and we moved."[171]

In December 1937, the Granichs leave Shanghai by ship for Marseilles, ending two years of intensively struggling with the social problems of Chinese society, which are not noticed by the majority of the Old China Hands during significantly longer stays in the Middle Kingdom. In December 1936, during the Xi'an Incident, the Granichs still spend days and nights with Madame Sun in order to shield her with their presence from armed Kuomintang sharpshooters, who have posted themselves around her house on the Rue Molière.[172] (Forty-five years later, Max Granich stands at the deathbed of Madame Sun: As one of the few foreigners, he belongs to the funeral committee that pays Madame Sun its last respects at her funeral in Peking in 1981.) Immediately after their return to New York, the Granichs begin devoting all their energy to the Chinese cause as editors of *China Today*, a magazine founded in 1933 by the American Friends of the Chinese People (chiefly members of the CPUSA), an organization committed to supporting China's resistance struggle against Japan. In the May 1938 edition, Manny writes that for the Chinese, despite their trials and tribulations, despite the destruction of their cities and regions, the days of humiliation are numbered.[173] After Pearl Harbor, the Granichs discontinue *China Today,* because most of the other media have begun to offer similarly anti-Japanese reportage. After the end of the Chinese Civil War, both are negatively affected by the McCarthy era hysteria (although they are not members of organizations that support the recognition of the PRC). However, the hearings by the House Un-American Activities Committee do not lead to charges, despite their ties to the CPUSA, which the couple breaks in the mid-1950s. Then the two fade from public view: After working to help the children of people persecuted in the McCarthy era, the couple withdraws from political life. In 1971, Grace dies in an automobile accident, and Manny, who in the final years of his life is still active for the US-China Friendship Association and as a travel guide for group excursions to the PRC, lives until 1987.

Hans Shippe and the Granichs are by no means the only communists, and definitely not those with the highest profile, who are active in the service of world revolution in the Middle Kingdom. In the 1920s and 1930s not only the Comintern, but also the Soviet government sends numerous agents and party members to China with precisely defined assignments. These include not only journalists such as, for example, Hans Shippe, KPD members such as Heinz Neumann, or the later SED (the governing party of the German Democractic Republic) member Wilhelm Zaisser, who were active in the underground, but also a long line of emigrants from the Nazi dictatorship who sympathized with revolutionary, humanistic ideas. Among them was *Ruth Werner*, born in Berlin on May 15, 1907, the daughter of the respected Jewish economist René Robert Kuczynski. Only in the 1970s does a larger circle in the West become aware of her as the East German author of a book, *Sonjas Rapport* (English: *Sonya's Report,* 1991), which describes her remarkable life.[174] This autobiography illuminates her life only in part, but she gives names and specific dates that are unusual in the report of a noted spy.

At a very early age, Ruth Werner becomes aware of what economists today call the gap between the rich and the poor. The Kuczynski family lives in a large villa, but with a simple standard of living. Ruth, or better Ursula, her real name, takes an early interest in socially critical literature and is confronted everyday on the way to her job at a bookstore by the poverty of unemployed people reduced to begging. In 1926, she becomes a member of the German Communist Party (KPD) and consequently loses her job at the

Ullstein publishing house. Two years later, she marries an architect, whose relationship with a friend living in Shanghai prompts the couple to leave Germany and travel via Siberia in the direction of Dalian (Dairen) and later by boat to the Huangpu metropolis. "Upon arriving in the harbor I was horrified by the extent of the exploitation and the poverty, such as I had never before experienced."[175] Ruth Werner's husband finds a good job; they can afford "boys," coolies, cooks, can go to parties and attend cultural events, and live just like the Old China Hands. We can well imagine that this greatly displeased Ursula Hamburger (the name she bore then): "Besides the heat, the boredom and my difficulties with Shanghai 'society' tortured me so that I found no relationship with the Chinese people in the first weeks. The filth, poverty and cruelty repelled me."[176]

Ruth Werner takes her life in her own hands, reads books—Gorky, Ehrenburg, Kästner, Maurois, etc.—and takes Chinese language instruction: "Imperceptibly I accustomed myself to the country, saw the qualities of its people, the beauties of the surroundings and enjoyed the culture. Above all, however, I tried to understand the political processes and win a more complete insight."[177] Many friends help her. Among them are Agnes Smedley, Irene Wiedemeyer (who had studied in Moscow and manages the leftist Zeitgeist Bookstore on Bubbling Well Road in Shanghai), the military tactician Otto Braun (who was soon to become the only Western foreigner to take part in the Long March), the professional revolutionary and convinced Stalinist Manfred Stern (who became famous in the Spanish Civil War as General Kleber), and other like-minded foreigners. Willoughby's *Shanghai Conspiracy* refers to most of these names. In addition, she benefits from her acquaintanceship with Madame Sun and the authors Ding Ling and Lu Xun. With Ruth Werner's aid, Lu Xun publishes a volume containing pictures by the German graphic artist and sculptor Käthe Kollwitz. The art of woodcutting is regarded at the time by many, especially progressively thinking Chinese artists, as a relatively simple technique and excellent possibility to make direct contact with ordinary, unlettered people.

Ruth Werner also visits a few other attractions in China, for example, the Beidaihe seaside resort or the retreat idyll of Westerners in Kuling (Lushan) that, because of its altitude, she only reaches by means of sedans strenuously transported by coolies—who cheat on the payment. "These are the reasons why many people complain about the Chinese. Often people are terribly angry, but what should one expect from under-paid, over-strained coolies?"[178] In Kuling, she encounters the wives of missionaries, "sweetly smiling, dried-out hussies." She not only visits such islands of Western civilization but is also intent on discovering the other China outside of Shanghai, as she writes to her parents in enthusiastic tones:

> Otherwise I occupied myself with enjoying China. I stay outside of Shanghai as much as possible. There are such wonderful villages and grave mounds and temples, and the streets and the people! I believe, if I stay here a few years more, it will swallow me up, and then I will no longer want to leave. Especially now it is a consolation that I have so much sympathy for this country. I ought to bring you here![179]

If the Kuczynskis had actually visited China, Ruth Werner would probably also have shown them the factories for processing silk, where mothers plucked silk cocoons out of scalding hot water with their bare hands. Or the miserable clay huts of Pudong (then the village of Pootung, today *the* commercial center of Shanghai), where adults wandered about half naked, wrapped in a few rags, and lived in shabby huts built of scraps of old tin cans. At any rate, Ruth Werner is certainly not merely an ordinary visitor to the Chinese scene, but also—for somewhat more than a year—a co-worker of Richard Sorge, the major communist spy. She makes her house in the French Concession available for the meetings of Sorge's collaborators, as well as for hiding weapons and documents. During a short stay in Moscow in 1933, she learns both broadcasting and how to set up and operate a radio station. A year later, Ruth Werner is sent as a radio operator to Mukden (Shenyang) in Manchuria, shortly before the Japanese annexation. Again a year later (in the summer of 1935) she leaves China for her own safety. At least she has enough time before her hurried departure to spend a few weeks in Peking: "Peking is magnificent. Here you could spend your life. This city is incredibly beautiful—such as I have never seen before. . . . What I know of Italy, Germany, America or other countries does not match it."[180]

Leaving China is hard for Ruth Werner. In the coming fifteen years, she continues to work for the GRU, the Soviet military espionage organization, first in Moscow, then in Poland: "Warsaw is not bad, but Europe is boring compared to China."[181] Her further secret-service activities lead her to Switzerland (1938) and then to England (1940): In 1950, she moves to East Germany (GDR). There she has difficulties in orienting herself, because after 1959 relations between the GDR and China must be subordinated to the intellectual scheme of the Soviet-Chinese conflict. She begins to write and refers to her five-year stay in China as "one of the greatest joys of my life." In a letter to a friend, she laments, "Will I ever lose the longing for this country?"[182] In summer 2000, *The New York Times* reports the death of Ruth Werner, the "colorful and daring Soviet spy."[183]

Ludwik Rajchman, born in Warsaw in 1881, was a Polish Jew who in the 1930s likewise finds himself on a mission in China, for the "good of mankind," as is stated in Marta Balinska's biography of the Polish statesman.[184] Rajchman, like Werner, is a completely assimilated Jew—and we now know a few more details of his life. However, in Rajchman's case the Cold War and its black-and-white mentality have made it impossible to achieve a greater degree of name-recognition and the necessary shading in the assessment. Who could hold this against a historian, in view of Rajchman's objectively incompatible professional positions—first as an advisor in the service of the Chinese Nationalists and later as a civil servant of the People's Republic of Poland?

Rajchman's professional career is in a certain sense similar to that of George Sokolsky, a model example of the role played by networks of personal relationships on the Chinese political stage in the first half of the twentieth century. At a young age, Ludwik becomes accustomed to meeting celebrities, especially from the intellectual and artistic worlds. His parents carry on the tradition of Polish patriotism, which despite massive pressure from foreign occupiers has survived since the division of the country at the end of the eighteenth century. In 1863, there is a revolt of Poles and Jews against Czarist rule that ends in a national catastrophe. In 1881—the year Rajchman is born—a Polish assassin murders Czar Alexander II. It is not long before repression begins, and many Poles, insofar as they do not emigrate, withdraw into the private sphere. Ludwik's parents—they both work as journalists—engage in social and cultural activities, take part in discussion groups in literary salons, and finally form their own theater agency, the predecessor of the later Warsaw Philharmonic.

At the age of seventeen, he joins the Union of Young Socialists, a political association that engages above all in distributing illegal publications attacking the Czar. He wants to study law, a choice his parents reject. Instead, in 1900 he starts to study medicine in Cracow and graduates five years later—specializing in bacteriology. Because of the poor conditions of health and hygiene in Europe, he rapidly climbs the career ladder in this important field. First he serves as an assistant at the Pasteur Institute in Paris, then as the chief bacteriologist at the Royal Institute of Public Health in London and finally, in 1913/14, as a research fellow at King's College in Cambridge. Immediately after the First World War, he founds the Central Institute for Epidemiology in Warsaw, serving as its Director until 1931. In this capacity, he contributes decisively to controlling typhus and cholera in Poland. During this period, he also establishes contact with the Epidemic Commission of the League of Nations, which assigns him to organize aid for the plague-stricken areas of Russia.

In 1921, Ludwik Rajchman is chosen as the Director of the League of Nations' newly founded Health Organization, the predecessor of the WHO (a post that he will hold for eighteen years). He sets as his goals limiting and controlling epidemics worldwide, and also developing programs to prevent

Figure 2.5
Ludwik Rajchman, "a servant of any government which requires his services," as he once said of himself, was also described as a "medical statesman," "founder of the China Lobby," and a "Jew, Free Mason and agent of the USA."

diseases and protect children. In 1925/26, the League of Nations sends him on an investigative trip to China and Japan to clarify the hygienic and medical situation there. His report recommends that the League of Nations conduct a comprehensive program in the areas of the health system, economy, state finances, and public transport system.

As a representative of an international organization, Rajchman meets a wide range of influential politicians, among them Jean Monnet, later known as the "father of Europe," who becomes a lifelong friend. Rajchman has long since left the medical orientation of his activity behind him and has ventured into political fields. After the Chinese Nationalist government establishes its power base in Nanking following the Northern Expedition of 1928, the newly appointed Health Minister, who is not a medical doctor, seeks advisors—and among others finds Ludwik Rajchman. He receives an invitation to come to China as soon as possible. Along with this, similar to Sokolsky, Rajchman makes friends with T. V. Soong, the Generalissimo's brother-in-law and influential Finance Minister, and bets almost blindly on the T. V. card, which is to prove not very advantageous.

In the years from 1929 to 1939, Rajchman visits the Middle Kingdom on the most varied missions. First, he travels to Shanghai, then to Peking, Nanking, and Canton (Guangzhou). He champions the founding of a National Institute for the Health System in the Huangpu metropolis. With his activism he provokes both the French and the British, who are critical of greater involvement by the League of Nations in "their" concession areas. Rajchman's aim is to persuade the League to give China more generous economic and development aid. He puts his trust in T. V., but also in Chiang Kai-shek, although he already suspects that the Chinese people are not happy with the Kuomintang: "As for the people, it is difficult to say what they think. If they could follow their instincts, they would probably go over to Communism."[185] Rajchman—"a servant of any government which requires his services," as he once said of himself—does not listen to his own intuition any longer. His work absorbs all his energy, not least of all in view of the vast Yangtze floods of the summer of 1931 and the ensuing epidemics. Shortly later, politics catch up with him again: In response to Japan's aggression against Manchuria, he suggests that his Chinese friends appeal to the League of Nations for aid, and thereby use exactly the means the Japanese most vehemently oppose. The Japanese press consequently portrays him as anti-Japanese. China's Foreign Minister, Eugene Chen, refers to him as the "real minister of foreign affairs for the Nationalist government."[186]

After Japan withdraws from the League of Nations, Rajchman receives another mission to China, not least of all because he enjoys the complete confidence of the Nationalist government. This time he is to sound out projects for technical and economic cooperation between the League of Nations and China. His aim is to encourage Western entrepreneurs to invest in China. He wants to bring his friend Jean Monnet to the Middle Kingdom in order to create a development plan. The latter is helpful between 1934 and 1936 in reorganizing the Chinese railroad system and finances, a task that demands much of him, including mastering the art of managing the negotiations: "I needed much time in order to understand that in China one should not ask for an answer, but rather should infer it."[187] Monnet notes in his memoirs that Rajchman was "literally enchanted." Others accuse him of following a markedly pro-China policy. The French chargé d'affaires in Peking objects to his "almost blind Sinophilism." The Germans call Rajchman "Soong's Polish Jew."[188] He comes under fire from all sides, because he has interfered too strongly in China's domestic politics or respectively in the Sino-Japanese conflict. In 1934, the League of Nations withdraws his mandate for China, whereupon he reluctantly returns to its headquarters in Geneva.

Three years later, as the world moves with rapid steps toward the Second World War, Rajchman is on a secret mission in Hong Kong. He regards China as the first victim of fascism and wants to aid the country as much as possible. The issue is French weapons shipments from Indochina via Yunnan Province (in Southwestern China) to the Middle Kingdom, an awkward matter after the Japanese have put pressure on Paris. Rajchman mobilizes all his skill and attempts to gather support from all his connections in Europe and America, but without success. "Plan Mandel," named for French Colonial Minister Georges Mandel, fails. As well in this case, his enemies suspect a conspiracy of the "Jew Mandel" and the large Jewish banks.[189] Rajchman, who for three months in the summer of 1939 waits in damp, sultry Chongqing for a response to his proposal, must finally give up. Back in the United States, he continues to support China. Thanks to his contacts with the inner circle of power around President Roosevelt, he soon learns of the projects of the so-called Lend-Lease Act, according to which countries, including China, that are allied with the United States would not have to pay for the U.S. war materials they received. Together with T.V. Soong, Rajchman strongly urges Treasury Secretary Henry Morgenthau to grant a loan of five-hundred million dollars to China. The Soong-Rajchman team functions until the fall of 1943, when Soong, the "most unembarrassed and untiring lobbyist of his time" (as Barbara Tuchman states), calls for the dismissal of General Stilwell, thereby making a serious mistake. Rajchman takes this dismissal as grounds to end his work for China and dedicates his energies to European concerns:

> For fifteen years, I helped T.V. lay the foundations of a Chinese New Deal. I am confident he will triumph after the war. But no foreigner can be useful in

> China if he does not act 'through' a Chinese politician or political activist. . . . That's life. It is not the first time that with my eyes wide open, I have devoted myself to an undertaking strewn with adventures. Otherwise, life would be too easy—and boring.[190]

After the Second World War, Rajchman works for communist Poland, a choice he apparently makes only after a long struggle with his conscience. He serves as a representative to the UNRRA, before completely committing himself in 1946 to founding UNICEF, the UN organization to aid children, and is elected to be its first chairman. When the Soviet Union boycotts the UN following the non-recognition of Peking in 1950, this also affects Rajchman, just when a vote is held on whether to replace the Nationalist Chinese representative at UNICEF with a Red Chinese.[191] After the "defeat" of this proposal (it is still a secret whether Rajchman decided according to his heart or to Moscow's wishes), he leaves his post and withdraws to France, where he dedicates himself to a new task, the founding of the International Children's Center. Still in the same year (1950), the Polish government revokes his diplomatic passport, a move that hurts him especially as a bridge-builder between East and West. In 1957, he visits the United States briefly to attend a UNICEF session and thereby becomes another target of the Red Scare: He does not respond to a written summons to appear at a hearing before an investigative committee of the American Congress and instead returns at once to Europe. The United States accuses him of having headed a Soviet espionage ring in Washington during the Second World War. Many areas of Cold War history remain shrouded in mystery, as does Rajchman's biography: The "medical statesman" (according to his biographer), the "Founder of the China Lobby" (*New York Herald Tribune*), a "Jew, Free Mason and agent of the USA" (according to the Polish government) dies on July 13, 1965.[192]

Considered to be China's most famous, even if not most successful, Western advisor in the twentieth century is *Michael Borodin,* who was born in 1884 in the Russian Pale of Settlement (Vitebsk District, today part of Byelorussia). The connection of his life story to China is therefore of great significance, because his work is linked with the most important event in Chinese history in the twentieth century, the takeover of China by the Communist Party. We know little about Borodin's childhood. His biographer, Dan Jacobs, reports that his family—his original name was Michael Markowitsch Gruzenberg—moved to Latvia when he was three years old. Even if we do not know whether Borodin ever visited a synagogue or even a cheder, his homeland was the Jewish shtetl, the Yiddish language and Jewish "*Lebenswelten*." At sixteen he joined the "Allgemeyne Yidische Arbeiter Bund in Lite, Poly und Rusland" (General Jewish Labour Bund in Lithuania, Poland,

and Russia), the first Jewish socialist party, founded in Vilnius in 1897. Three years later, he changes horses and bets on the Russian Social-Democratic Workers' Party and thereby on Lenin's fraction of the Bolshevists. Thus, his journeyman years begin and ultimately lead him to Canton in the fall of 1923 as a revolutionary and communist agent.

But back to his youth: In 1904 the twenty-year-old travels on assignment to Lenin in Switzerland and helps him set up a communist party in Latvia, even before the "Bloody Sunday" of 1905 forces him to leave his homeland for the West. Before he turns his back on it, however, he meets Joseph Stalin at a party congress in Stockholm, a very fateful meeting, as it later proved to be. Borodin is not a typical Russian Jew who emigrates because of pogroms or economic misery. Rather, he wants to gain further training as a revolutionary in the West in order, when the time is ripe, to overthrow the moribund Czarist Empire from within. He spends the following years in Chicago, which then has the reputation of being the center of socialism in the United States. He marries the Lithuanian-Jewish immigrant Fanya (Fanny) Orluk and enrolls at Valparaiso University in Indiana for a short period of study. Later he founds (under the name of Berg) a small school for immigrant children and at the same time increases his knowledge of the rising urban working class. The encounter with America certainly influences him. Despite a meeting in 1915 with Alexandra Kollontai, a Russian revolutionary and ambassador sent by Lenin to the United States as a "fundraiser," he toys with the ideas of the Mensheviks: In the important year of 1917, he even briefly supports the provisional Kerensky government. Only when news of the storming of the Winter Palace reaches America in November of the same year does he recall his intellectual affinity to Lenin. Back in Russia, he is granted an audience with the revolutionary leader himself. This opens up the possibility of a career as a diamond smuggler, Communist agent, and, later, professional revolutionary. And all this for a man from the same district that also brought forth a Marc Chagall. Assignments from the Moscow headquarters of world revolution send him to Scandinavia, Mexico, Holland, Germany, and England.

In contemporary historiography, there are various views as to the Comintern's influence on the founding of the Chinese Communist Party (in 1921 in Shanghai). Some historians regard it as certain that communism took hold in China thanks to the direct spread of Bolshevist theories by Moscow's emissaries. On the other side, there are those who emphasize the Sinicization of Marxism and point out that even in distant Sichuan, communist tendencies are discernible in the early 1920s, without any prior contact with Chen Duxiu and Li Dazhao, the founding fathers of the movement in China. The sometimes close links between the Kuomintang and Comintern representatives in China are well documented. After the Sun-Ioffe agreement of January 1923, which includes the support of Soviet Russia for Sun Yat-sen and his party, another eight months pass before Michael Borodin sets foot on the Canton stage. As stated in a communication of Deputy Soviet Foreign Minister Karachan to Sun Yat-sen, he is to be treated "not only as a representative of the government, but also as my personal representative, with whom you can speak as cordially as with me."[193]

Borodin's most important and at the same time most complicated assignment at the start of his career as a professional revolutionary in Canton lies in implementing a policy that his boss, the Comintern, has in mind. First, the Kuomintang must become a national party structured according to a Bolshevist pattern so that someday after the country's unification it would be in the position to drive the imperialist powers out of China. Second, in terms of membership, the relatively small CCP must be strengthened so that as soon as possible it can transform the nationalist revolution begun by the Kuomintang into a socialist one. No wonder Borodin has enemies in all camps. The communists are dissatisfied with the United Front slapped together with the Kuomintang because of its domination by the bourgeoisie. Right-wing Kuomintang supporters find the communists too radical. Finally, the Western powers also come to see Borodin as a representative of expansionist Soviet power in Southern China. Given these circumstances, Borodin keeps as low a profile as possible at the start of his advisory work and tries to convince the Western powers, in the guise of a correspondent, of his "political innocence."

Not exactly conflict-free is Borodin's relationship with Sun Yat-sen, whom Western representatives, on the one side, ignore, and on the other side, warn against Soviet agents. Sun often advises Borodin against proceeding all too forcefully against his old friends, the Kuomintang members, who think little of communism. Already in October 1923, Sun Yat-sen appoints Borodin an official advisor and instructor for the reorganization of the Kuomintang. Borodin is rather critical of the so-called Three People's Principles, today known under the name *Sunyatsenism*, Sun's conception according to which China's path and salvation consists in the combination of nationalism, democracy and the welfare of the people:

> He [Sun—author's note] is still the leader of the Kuomintang precisely because he did not demand anything in either an intellectual or an organizational regard from the Kuomintang people. Precisely because he applied a simple formula to the Kuomintang, who resemble a brightly speckled ball of wool—Nationalism, Democratism [sic!] and Socialism—and left it up to each to decide for himself how he understood it. From this it follows that a really revolutionary, closed, disciplined party of the Kuomintang under the leadership of just that Sun, as I

found him then, and as he is even now still described to me, is at present not yet possible. But neither can I imagine a reorganization of the party without Sun.[194]

Borodin's work in Canton includes among other things organizing strikes, building up labor unions, courting the agricultural community and coining political slogans like "Down with Imperialism" and "Unite with farmers and workers." He lives a sort of double life: He has a passion for riding and playing chess; together with his family, he lives in a spacious two-story, albeit drab and poorly furnished house—with a view of the Canton parade ground and the Kuomintang headquarters.

A few weeks after his arrival, one of Borodin's most important jobs consists in organizing and holding the first Kuomintang National Congress in January 1924 in Canton, where among other things they are to negotiate on the relationship between the Kuomintang and the CCP. The most important achievement thereby is an agreement that communists have to join the Kuomintang individually and not *en bloc*. When it becomes known in the middle of the congress that Lenin has died in Moscow, Sun reads his famous speech on the founder of a new state who will forever find his place in the memories of all "oppressed" peoples. We do not know whether Borodin composed Sun's funeral oration and eulogy, but the former hints at this possibility in his notes. "If I say to him [Sun—author's note], taking into consideration his way of thinking, that Lenin's legacy to oppressed peoples is sacred for us whatever happens, I thereby tell him things that he still does not understand at all and probably also will not understand. . . ."[195] There are similar doubts concerning the authorship of Sun's testament, which is made known after his death in March 1925. It proclaims to the world that the Soviet Union is China's best friend and predicts the future victories of oppressed nations in cooperation with Moscow.[196]

After Sun's death, Borodin is the most important person in Canton. On the one side, to be sure, he does not succeed in managing Sun's successor, Chiang Kai-shek, in the same way that he had influenced the founding father of the Chinese Republic, or in dispelling his fear of an all-too aggressive intervention by Moscow. On the other side, he makes it clear to Chen Duxiu, the leader of the CCP, that at the time his party is only in the position to "do coolie services for the Kuomintang." Moreover, he apparently thinks little of the "leftist" Kuomintang people. It is no wonder that also Chiang must remain mistrustful, even without knowing the contents of Borodin's reports to Moscow. Not without reason does he fear a further leftist radicalization of the Kuomintang, perhaps worsening his troubled relations with the leftists in Canton, and so he takes the offensive: In a March 1926 incident involving a gunboat (the Zhongshan) commanded by a communist officer, he has all the Russian advisors in Canton arrested, about thirty in all. After his return to Canton, it is again necessary for Borodin, who is staying in Peking for secret negotiations on Comintern strategy, to work out a compromise with Chiang, which stipulates among other things that Kuomintang members may no longer join the Chinese Communist Party. Shortly after this agreement, which the Comintern wants to downplay as much as possible, partly because of Stalin's power struggle with Trotsky, Chiang decides for the Northern Expedition. Borodin initially opposes this, but later supports it under pressure—and merely plays second violin. During this large-scale national unification operation that is organized by Soviet military advisors and General Blücher (Vasily Blücher or Blyukher, 1889–1938, was a Soviet military commander and a prominent victim of Stalin's Great Purge), the breakdown of the Chinese society becomes inevitable: The "rightist" Kuomintang, with Chiang Kai-shek as its leader, sets up its headquarters in Nanchang (capital of Jiangxi Province in Northeastern China), while the "leftist" Kuomintang under the leadership of Wang Jingwei establishes both communists and leftist fellow-travelers (among others Soong Qingling) in the working class city of Wuhan (Hubei Province).

Borodin himself reaches the "Red City" in December 1926 and immediately begins from his headquarters in the former German Concession to found labor unions and promulgate new slogans: "The masses of peasants and workers are the chief forces of the national revolution" and "Destroy the counter-revolutionary groups." For native merchants and former supporters of the Kuomintang, such slogans decidedly go too far, and so they move to Shanghai and Peking. The Western residents of the Hankou concessions (Hankou is one of the three cities that later merged into modern-day Wuhan and the place where the Westerners resided) also become fearful of the growing revolutionary fever, massive demonstrations against foreigners, and violent riots. Borodin, who at the start would like to prevent this unorganized outbreak of violence by the Chinese masses, clearly loses influence. Nevertheless, he remains for Western journalists, authors, and leftist fellow travelers a living landmark in the "new Jerusalem," a sort of cult figure and magnetic point of attraction.

> Mikhail M. Borodin was a great big, handsome and impressive man, standing more than six feet in his stocking feet. In his early forties at the time that I worked with him in Hankou, Borodin's dark and glossy hair and walrus mustache showed no threads of silver. His skin was fair. There was nothing of the conspirator in the direct, friendly gaze of his brown eyes. . . . Borodin was calm, he was benign . . . he could be moody, melodramatic, witty . . . and he had the gift of gab. He had a remarkable memory for names and for faces, and he liked

Figure 2.6
Michael Borodin, originally from a Russian-Jewish shtetl, later became Stalin's envoy to China. He was a man "with the natural dignity of a lion or a panther, had the special quality of being in, but above, the battle. He seemed to take 'the long view' by nature, by an almost physical superiority of vision." In the background staring into the camera stands Morris Abraham Cohen.

> people, especially Americans. He was a man to capture the imagination and the heart as well. . . . Borodin was a dreamer, an intellectual, an original . . . and somehow, he always managed to look like an actor. He walked into a room with that lumbering, awkward kind of grace, and presto, the situation was his. . . . A lover of conservative music, Borodin had a preference for Tchaikovsky, Borodin, and Meyerbeer. . . . Borodin was abstemious. As with most such people, he had no taste for alcoholic beverages.[197]

In these weeks and months during the turn of the years 1926/1927, Borodin becomes *the* symbol of the supposedly imminent world revolution, though he probably already suspects that it is too early for one in China. In China and Moscow, political-strategic factors finally lead to the end of Borodin's work in the Middle Kingdom: In April 1927, Chiang Kai-shek suddenly ceases to be a revolutionary and orders his supporters in Shanghai to crush the communist underground movement in the city. Thousands fall victim to this terror. The report of the suppression of the revolution in Shanghai also prompts persistent questions for Borodin and the leftist Kuomintang leadership in Wuhan/Hankou. But Stalin and the Comintern insist stubbornly, to the horror of Borodin and their Chinese "friends," on the alliance of the CCP with the leftist Kuomintang and that the property of the military power-holders sympathetic to the Kuomintang should not be touched—an utter mockery, in view of the just suppressed peasant movement. For Borodin the situation becomes increasingly precarious; he sees no way to bring China's complicated realities into harmony with the simple guidelines of the Comintern. One of his last attempts to in some way rescue the presence of the Soviet Union in the Chinese chaos consists in taking up contact with the "Christian General" Feng Yuxiang. When this attempt also fails, he has no choice but to leave China in summer 1927.

> If the Chinese leaders who have been my friends and fellow workers for four long years believe that the moment has come when they can continue the fight without my help, then I shall submit, for I have played my part and given my advice. I have no intention of fighting for communism in China—the time is not yet ripe. . . I came to China to fight for an idea. The dream of accomplishing world revolution by freeing the people of the East brought me here. But China itself, with its age-old history, its countless millions, its great social problems, its infinite capacities, astounded and overwhelmed me, and my thoughts of world revolution gradually sank in the background. The revolution and the fight for freedom in China became an end in itself, and no longer a means to an end. My task was to grasp the situation, to start the great wheel moving, and as time has passed, it has carried me along with it. I myself have become only a cog in the great machine.[198]

Borodin's assessment is noteworthy when we consider his revolutionary-dogmatic career. His re-examination of previous conceptions and his readiness to measure China according to Chinese standards seem astonishing for "Stalin's man" in China. They reveal a personal flexibility in thinking that had become necessary, as well as—entirely in the Marxian sense—the ability to accept given conditions that human hands can hardly influence. His departure from China also fits into this context. True to the Leninist maxim, he does not trust Chiang's assurances of safe-conduct. Though shaken by fits of malaria and without his wife, who a few weeks before was kidnapped by Zhang Zuolin's henchmen, he sets off on the difficult three thousand kilometer long return trek from Wuhan via Xi'an, Gansu, Ningxia, and Mongolia to the Soviet Union.[199] They travel at first by railroad, then in a convoy of motor vehicles with originally five autos and five trucks, among them Borodin's Buick. Accompanying him on the "retreat to the North," besides Russian comrades, bodyguards, mechanics, a cook, and other helpers, are the journalist and activist Anna Louise Strong and the two sons of Eugene Chen (Chen Youren), the Foreign Minister of the Wuhan government. In Ulan-Ude, east of Lake Baikal, he boards the Trans-Siberian Railway and in October, after almost two months of travel, reaches the Soviet capital. While still on Chinese soil, he is honored everywhere; the farewell in Wuhan with Wang Jingwei and T. V. Soong is in its own way solemn and even General Feng Yuxiang prepares an almost statesmanlike reception for him in Zhengzhou (Henan Province).

Immediately after Borodin's arrival in Moscow, he reports at a general meeting of the old Bolshevists' All Unions Society—in those days, he even spoke quite candidly—on his experiences in China. "To be sure our knowledge of China is still full of gaps, but the fact that already a vast literature on China is nascent is evidence that we will sooner or later understand China. But in the old days we knew very little about China. Nevertheless we have started the work and in the process of working have become familiar with China."[200] To the last, he defends Stalin's policy of supporting the United Front, but admits that they should have dropped Chiang Kai-shek after the April events of 1927 in Shanghai. On certain questions—such as whether or not imperialism hindered the industrialization of China—Borodin's views resemble those advanced by Harold Isaacs in his *Tragedy of the Chinese Revolution*. In that period, no one in Stalin's empire dares to clarify the backgrounds of historical events and processes in more depth. In December 1927, the Fifteenth CPSU Party Congress is held, and more urgently than ever Stalin wants a final victory in China—and over his perennial rival Trotsky. At the Soviet leader's behest, the Comintern orders the Chinese communists to stage a hopeless revolt in Canton, which is ruthlessly crushed. The Comintern blames the CCP for its defeat. This is supposed to prove the correctness of Stalin's line. The Chinese Revolution has thereby suffered a final defeat, and Borodin's career is over. The committed revolutionary, who only carried out Moscow's orders, ultimately pays for Stalin's errors, the latter not being known for admitting his own mistakes.

Once again, because of a scholarly event on the historical background of Chen Duxiu's ideas, Borodin receives a summons in January 1929—and is thereby severely criticized for his misinterpretation of Chinese revolutionary history.[201] Despite all the ill will, he almost miraculously manages to escape the maelstrom of Stalin's campaigns against the so-called leftist and later rightist opposition. The former hero, the legend of the Wuhan revolutionary experiment, accustomed to fame and power, leaves the boulevard of world revolution and finds himself in the dark alleys and impenetrable labyrinths of drab everyday Soviet Russian life. He even criticizes himself at a few party meetings. Apart from that, he refuses to answer questions about his past and about China. As the publisher and chief editor of an English-language newspaper (*Moscow News*, later *Moscow Daily News*) published in Moscow, he at least finds a niche. Politically oriented friends, among them Ruth Werner, encounter a man who speaks only privately and reluctantly about his stay in China; otherwise, however, aside from meetings with Eugene Chen's sons, who regularly visit him, or with Chiang Kai-shek's son Chiang Ching-kuo, who is studying in Moscow, he wants nothing more to do with the Middle Kingdom. In the years 1934–36, Klaus Mehnert, a German author and prolific journalist, repeatedly encounters a "melancholy, introspective man" who "seemed to me like a scrapped, slowly rusting locomotive. It was Grusenberg, alias Borodin, who lived here in disgrace on Stalin's charity."[202]

In 1948, Anna Louise Strong returns to Moscow from a longer stay in China, where she among other things visited Mao in Yan'an. The author, known for her independent mind, would like to publish her manuscript about Chinese communism and Mao's theories at an extremely unpropitious point in time for the paranoid Stalin. A gloomy Borodin informs Strong that the Kremlin is unhappy with the text. They demand changes from her; the grande dame of world revolution refuses. She would like to return to China, but cannot obtain permission to leave the country. Instead, together with Borodin she is arrested in early 1949. After a few days, Strong is released from the Lubyanka and flown to Poland.[203] Borodin's fate remains uncertain. Half a year after Stalin's death (in March 1953), *The New York Times* reports the death of the "red agent" Michael Borodin.[204] The star of Wuhan, once cheered by thousands of Chinese in the workers' city on the Yangtze—like hundreds of thousands before him—died in a labor camp in Siberian Yakutsk on May 29, 1951.

III. ADVENTURERS AND LONE WOLVES

"One man has saved me and that is the biggest man in China today, the high advisor, Borodin. . . . He has impressed me more than any person I have met in a long time, as a mind, a personality, a social force." The, at the time, somewhat more than thirty-year-old *Rayna Prohme* confides these impressions to a girlfriend in a letter written in Hankou during the revolutionary months of 1927.[205] Rayna Prohme belongs to the category of foreigners who sought out the Middle Kingdom because of a thirst for adventure, a desire to find their own identity, or for other personal motives. In this group there were Westerners who wanted to dedicate their lives to the Chinese Revolution; initially they were politically moderate activists, but in later years for obvious reasons persons came who were more left-leaning. Similar to those who acted covertly (Shippe) or openly (Borodin) in the service of the Soviet Union, this loose collection of persons interested in China's fate consisted mostly of young people who plunged into the Chinese world unprepared and without much previous knowledge.

Rayna Prohme was born in Chicago on 23 January 1894 into the family of a wealthy Jewish broker named Simons.[206] Her childhood and young years are carefree, and Rayna becomes a very independent and open-minded person. Her first love is for Samson Raphaelson, a Jew from New York's Lower East Side who would later become a successful Broadway writer. Together with Raph, as everyone calls him, Rayna enrolls at the University of Illinois. One of Rayna's best girlfriends in her college days was Dorothy Day, then regarded as a leftist, but in later years a champion of the Catholic workers' movement. She describes her personality as impressive, always interested in others and ready to discuss everything: "Whatever she did she did with her whole heart. If she read, she read. If she was with you, all her attention was for you. She was single-minded, one of the pure of heart, and her interest in life was as intense as her interest in books."[207] Dorothy Day probably confronted Rayna with her socialist ideas, but the latter was too independent to let herself be seduced, not even by Michael Gold (Irwin Granich), Max Granich's brother, and later the author of a socially critical novel, *Jews without Money* (1930).

After her marriage to Raph in 1918, the couple decides to move to Berkeley. There she meets William Prohme, who becomes her second husband after she separates from Raph in late 1922. At the University of California in Berkeley she attends lectures on literature, philosophy, religious studies, and anthropology. Probably it is the closeness to San Francisco, the most important gateway of the sea route to the Far East, along with the intellectual climate of Berkeley, in which they discuss the fate of China, that awaken Rayna's curiosity about the Middle Kingdom. In 1922 or 1923 (reports differ) she sets out for China in hopes of being able to work there as a journalist and at the same time collect material for a dissertation. Eventually, she finds a job as a secretary at Peking Union Medical College and works as an English teacher at a girls' school. "I'm in China. There are strange noises and strange speech and strange things going on down in the streets and strange clothes and strange things to eat, and I watch it all in a rather detached way and haven't yet come out of the stage of wondering what the devil it is all about."[208] A few months later, she returns to California with the intention of coming back to China for a longer stay:

> I am going to stay five years in China. I want to see for myself what happens to a people when their friendly familiar world suddenly becomes strange and bewildering. When their age-old social customs are being overthrown, when their religions are being challenged, their houses, their cities, their language, their clothes, their very thoughts are being transformed. I want to see what happens to them—and help, if I can, in the task of keeping the new forces under control, of preventing the changes from coming too fast.[209]

In the summer of 1925 Rayna and Bill Prohme travel together to the Far East, first to Peking, where the two work as reporters before being hired by Eugene Chen as journalists in the Nationalist cause. Bill, who despite reading Hegel, Marx, and Lenin, is not much more radical than Rayna in his political views, becomes Chen's private secretary, and both subsequently work for the Chinese-American News Agency, as well as for the English-language *People's Tribune*, also a Kuomintang paper. With this step, Rayna Prohme is inevitably drawn into the Chinese Revolution. The couple is regarded as "radical" by Western foreigners in Peking, who in those times make no distinction between Communists and Nationalists, but this certainly does not apply to Rayna: One of her friends recalls that she longed for the rescue of the Chinese people from the darkness and poverty of "medieval Asia."[210]

Besides editorial work, the Prohmes also begin hiding prominent communists in their apartment and claiming them as house servants to protect them from Zhang Zuolin's henchmen. Officials search their offices several times and confiscate press material, whereupon they shift their work to their apartment. The couple refuses to be intimidated. Rayna asks herself what significance the events in China might have for America: "Absolutely nothing, I'm sure, for we see the American papers and also remember how unimportant changes in China seemed to us a few years ago. But . . . it is exciting here now."[211] For Rayna the intellectual pivot of their work is Li Dazhao, a cofounder of the Chinese Communist Party and one of the chief organizers of the May Fourth Movement: "I visit him every day to get news, etc., etc. He is a fine middle-aged man, with the most beautiful hands I have ever seen. And with a patience that puts me to shame."[212] In October 1926, together with Eugene Chen, the Prohmes, travel to Shanghai and continue their trip by boat to Canton, where Borodin is arriving from the USSR at about the same time. She is glad that she can leave Peking: "The servants formed habits and Chinese habits are almost unbreakable."[213] In Shanghai, she becomes aware for the first time of the difference between the Western concessions and Chinese territory: "No wonder the Chinese get mad, even while they use the district to save their skins. The Chinese city is a crowded, dirty, vile hole."[214] To be sure, she finds Canton interesting, but the "worst city for any joy in the world." "Much of Chinese hour by hour life is not beautiful. No Spitting Allowed, promulgated and enforced, would help a little. But no one would think of such a thing."[215] Her description of Canton shows that she feels herself simultaneously attracted to and repelled by China:

> Everything is open to the eye. Women fixing dinners in the streets, peddlers cutting fish, butchers, fruit merchants, weaving, a thousand kinds of shops, long pieces of cloth being dyed, washing clothes, and of course all the eating, nursing and latrine operations that are always open in China. It's hard to decide between withdrawal from the dirt and going on and on through fascination.[216]

She decides for the latter, although she enjoys working for the *Canton Gazette;* it demands so much that she works almost to the point of exhaustion every day, in exchange for which she is a witness to history: "I wish I weren't so interested in China. I miss . . . Berkeley terribly."[217] In February 1927 she travels upstream to Hankou to a "most exciting world, and a most exacting one." In this milieu, she realizes that Westerners will never completely understand the Chinese. She says of herself: "Often I think that I'm so buried in Chinese events that I have the perspective of an ostrich."[218] Of course, conversations with people like Chen ("a great man"), Borodin ("the greatest man"), or Madame Sun ("a marvelous person") help her to better cope with the daily revolutionary life and the work at the *People's Tribune*, which in the meantime appears in Hankou. She serves as the chief editor of this paper, which on March 12, 1927, celebrates its reappearance in the "Red City." In an editorial in the first edition she describes the newspaper as pro-nationalist, anti-imperialist, but not anti-foreign. Its editorial offices are located in the same building where Borodin also lives and works, and the exchanges with the Soviet revolutionary are therefore especially close. It is incumbent on Rayna Prohme, among other things, to schedule the access of Western visitors to Borodin. It is thanks to one of them, Vincent Sheean, that Rayna Prohme has not been entirely forgotten. In his biography, *Personal History*, he creates an incomparable monument to her, "most unlike my idea of

Figure 2.7
Rayna Prohme from Chicago longed for the rescue of the Chinese people from the darkness and poverty of "medieval Asia." She belonged to a rare group of people who commit their lives to a cause, "regardless of the consequences, self-sacrificing and full-hearted."

a 'wild Bolshevik'": "It must have taken a peculiarly insatiable cause-hunger to bring a girl like this into the exact middle of the Chinese Revolution."[219] After the daily revolutionary work, the East-West community of fate—including Madame Sun, Sun Fo, Eugen Chen, the Prohmes, Milly Bennett, and Borodin—meets to close the day with political discussions, dancing, watching films, and singing. It is a matter, according to a visitor, more of an excited group of first-graders than of truly revolutionary work.[220]

With Chiang's betrayal of the Revolution in April 1927, Rayna Prohme's time in Hankou also nears its end. On the 12th of the month, the *People's Tribune* publishes the editorial "Expelled!"—referring to the end of the cooperation between the left-wing of the Kuomintang and Chiang Kai-shek.[221] Then everything starts to happen quickly: The strived-for alliance of Borodin with the "Christian General" Feng Yuxiang falls through in negotiations in Zhengzhou, at which among others Rayna and Anna Louise Strong are also present. The Russian exodus begins, and on July 18, 1927, the *People's Tribune* publishes, so-to-speak Rayna's momentous last act, Madame Sun's "Declaration to the Chinese People," in which she openly names her reasons for her break with the Kuomintang. Among others, it has betrayed the principles of Sun Yat-sen.[222] Abandoning Hankou, Rayna and Madame Sun set off under a veil of secrecy for Shanghai, almost a thousand kilometers away.[223] Back in "Western Civilization" (on the Rue Molière), she writes to her first husband about the satisfaction she has experienced in her life over the past two years: "Despite the collapse of the Revolution here, I am on top of the world, above all because I have made contacts that are more stimulating than I have ever experienced."[224] But her days in Shanghai are also numbered: In mid-August the former Wuhan community (without Borodin, who has started his journey through the desert, and without William Prohme, who at Chen's behest must remain in Shanghai)—to avoid Chiang Kai-shek's guards—sails by ship from Shanghai to Vladivostok on a secret mission. From there the journey continues on the luxurious Trans-Siberian Railway to Moscow, which they reach on September 7, 1927.

In Moscow Rayna Prohme first realizes that for political reasons her odyssey to the USSR must finally end. To be sure her arrival at the Soviet capital's railroad station is still ceremonial (with a welcoming committee ranging from Karachan to the later Foreign Minister Litvinov), and they spend the first days together with Madame Sun in a charming government guesthouse that is placed at the disposal of selected visitors. However, she soon has to look for a place to stay, especially as it turns out that the former Wuhan government, the once "leftist" Kuomintang, will not be able to set up an exile government in the frosty climate there.

The more time passes, the more Rayna Prohme feels deserted by the group of former Chinese revolutionaries. "In the jumble of impressions, two are clear, one that I feel relieved at being away from China for a while and the other that I feel lost here."[225] In addition, various factors come together, the tension and uncertainty of the situation, the new climate, the foreignness of the place and language. She does occasionally attend theater and opera performances, but her joy in life palpably declines, which does not change with Borodin's arrival in Moscow. Likewise, Anna Louise Strong contributes little to improving her state of mind—to the contrary: Because she accompanied Borodin on his return trip, she holds herself solely entitled to report on the failed Chinese Revolution. Vincent Sheean, who followed Rayna to Moscow (by a different route), writes that she was thinking of joining the Communist Party of the Soviet Union.[226] At the start of November, she attends the anniversary celebration of the October Revolution, an event of a sort she has never seen before. Her last public appearance is at a meeting of the Congress of the Friends of the USSR. On November 21, 1927, she succumbs to meningitis in the Moscow Savoy Hotel. Six days later, in the midst of a snowstorm she is borne along the streets of Moscow to her final resting place. Almost the entire Wuhan community of fate (without Borodin), Chinese student representatives of Sun Yat-sen University, and Russian friends take part in the funeral procession.

Thus ended the life of the still young, impetuous and easygoing, some believed naïve woman who, according to one of her friends, Milly Bennett, was obsessed with the idea of: "A free China. An enlightened, democratic Republic of China."[227] *The New York Times* compares Rayna Prohme with John Reed, a young American reporter who witnessed the October Revolution of 1917, and writes that she belonged to a rare group of people who commit their lives to a cause, "regardless of the consequences, self-sacrificing and full-hearted."[228]

Milly Bennett, Rayna's friend and assistant in China, who was mentioned above, was born Mildred Jacqueline Bremler in San Francisco on May 2, 1897.[229] Her life did not progress along a single unbroken path, but instead it was punctuated by many adventures; she took part in societal upheavals, and personal blows of fate struck her. Like Rayna Prohme, she has nothing to do with the faith of her Jewish ancestors. Her mother stems from a well-to-do German-Jewish family, her father is from Poznan (now in Poland).[230] Already at seventeen, she dreams of writing as a career: "I would be a reporter, a writer, an international figure. A newspaperwoman, I would tear around the world. A war here. A coronation there. A flood, a famine, a revolution or two. All in the day's work. A writer, I would hobnob with the famous, the rich, the beautiful. The great books would run out of my pores."[231] The last-named dream is not realized; she succeeds in part with other ideas, for example, the wish to be an eyewitness of upheavals and wars: She is present in China (1927), in the Soviet Union (1931–1936), and then in Spain (1936–38) when history is written by professional revolutionaries.

At the age of twenty, Milly works for the *San Francisco Daily;* a year later she moves on to Hawaii, where she marries Mike Mitchell. There she also meets Rayna Prohme, whom she follows to China in the summer of 1926, knowing almost nothing about the country where she is to spend a year serving the Revolution. The heat in Shanghai nearly makes her ill; there is as well the noise and tempo of a large city: "Bang. Bang. Bang. That can only be the brass section of a Chinese orchestra. Bang. Bang. Bang. That is the smashing sound that is as restless and ferocious, that is as formless and demanding as the great China itself."[232] Her description of the Huangpu metropolis is not very flattering: "Take the foulest, the stinkingest tenement district that you ever saw in your life and spread it indiscriminately over the byways and alleys of an enormous, sprawling city. That is Shanghai." Milly can palpably sense that the end of Western luxury in the midst of Chinese misery is drawing near. "Oh, the whole giddy, reckless, sycophantic, leeching life . . . going on there . . . the old China Hands reeling their heels to the funeral music that was their own."[233] Her stay in Shanghai is brief, work summons her in Peking: She is to replace the Prohmes, who are transferred by Eugen Chen to Canton to take charge of working with the Chinese-American News Agency.

Initially, Milly Bennett is completely helpless in a city then ruled by the warlord Zhang Zuolin. But like the Prohmes before her, she also finds a variety of supporters of the Chinese Revolution, Chinese and Westerners who aid the still young woman in carrying out her assignment. These include a certain Farstan T. Sung, chairman of the Chinese-American News Agency's administrative board; Li Dazhao, who has in the meantime found refuge in the Soviet Embassy; Joseph (Joe) Mussin, the Tass correspondent; James (Jimmy) Dolsen, a U.S. journalist who covertly works for Soviet organizations; and the less suspect newspapermen Randall Gould and Wilbur Burton.

Milly Bennett spends her Peking days attending press conferences at the Soviet, American, and Japanese embassies, as well as occasional meetings in the Grand Hôtel des Wagon Lits. She realizes that the Japanese are better informed on the Chinese situation than are the Chinese themselves, and likewise better than the Americans. The Russians are also less prone to distance themselves from the natives than are people from other Western countries. At the start, Milly lives in a so-called "siheyuan," a typical Peking residence with ground-level houses built around a rectangular court. Only as the situation worsens in the wake of the Nationalists' successful Northern Expedition do things become unpleasant for Milly, prompting her to move into the

Hôtel du Nord, operated by a Swiss couple in the embassy quarter. Besides her work, she enjoys the strange, exotic surroundings, and takes strolls in the city of "the dreams of her youth." She sees camel caravans arriving from the Gobi Desert that enter Peking through the Hademen Gate (formerly a gate in the city walls). And there are the overwhelming city walls, a few strips of farmland, the *hutongs* waiting placidly in the mist, the confused alleys of the city that is still the capital, the slowly trotting donkeys pulling carts, or the sapphire blue lake with the dome of the Lama Temple.

The idyll ends for her when her activities in the service of the Revolution finally become too colorful for Zhang Zuolin's troops. The representatives of the Western powers, above all the American Embassy, have also had enough of Milly Bennett's activities: In spring 1927, after Milly did not, like other Western press representatives, blame the plundering of Western diplomatic missions and the murder of five foreigners solely on the Nationalists, she must leave Peking in great haste. On a detour via Tianjin, Mukden (Shenyang), and Dalian, she finally manages to return—by ship—to Shanghai. On the train to Mukden in southern Manchuria, she again finds time to think about the Middle Kingdom and the Chinese people:

> China. China. Aching, breaking, frightful, starving, stinking, lousy China. Those rude, dismal creatures in their wilted grey uniforms on the seat, on the floor all around me were human beings. They were people. They were men. What chance did they have for love, for work, for hope? Where was China and who was God that He had forgotten them?[234]

Milly's stay in Shanghai is brief; she wants to travel on to Rayna Prohme in Hankou. There she serves as Rayna's right hand, and she brings a much-needed element of humor which lights up the atmosphere. As well, like many observers of those events, Borodin's personality captivates her, but unlike others, she also notes his weaknesses: "[H]e was not fitted for the post to which he was assigned in China. I see in Borodin . . . a vain fellow of good looks and great charm, a great deal of the actor, witty, imaginative, civilized, adaptable. Also, soft, romantic, and erratic. He is scatterbrained. He is entirely lacking in organizational ability."[235] Milly's experiences in China end with the final victory of Chiang Kai-shek over the "leftist" Kuomintang. For the still young American it is an encounter with a revolution that represented for her the beginning of the upheavals that shook the Middle Kingdom throughout the twentieth century: "You've got a long row to hoe, Citizen Liu [Liu Shaoqi, China's later President—author's note]. Let me predict in this land of the unpredictable and the surprise packages that your first hundred years are going to be the hardest."[236]

After the fall of Wuhan/Hankou, Milly Bennett returns to the United States, where she works for various news agencies and composes a number of reports on China. In 1931, she visits Moscow, perhaps out of boredom after her Chinese adventure, at the invitation of Anna Louise Strong. Returning to the no longer very revolutionary world of the exiled Wuhan society does not seem very hard for her. At the *Moscow Daily News,* she renews her contacts with Borodin and the sons of Eugene Chen, who work for him and his newspaper. In the Soviet capital, she marries her second husband (1932), the ballet dancer Evgeny Vasilievich Konstantinov. Milly seems to like Moscow, a rare "mix between Orient and Occident." She attends operas, travels around the country and observes the new political stage. A few months pass, and she becomes aware that revolutions do not abolish classes, but rather merely regroup them. Although Milly sees many faults, much filth, and misery in the workers and peasants' paradise, she loves the country and its people: "I love Russia and the Russians. I have often wondered why the German Jews consider themselves better than the Russian Jews. . . . Some of the smartest men in the government are Russian Jews, and believe me, that is a magnificent government that has defied the world fourteen years long."[237] Besides her reportage for the *Moscow Daily News,* she also works freelance for foreign newspapers such as *The New York Times*. In 1936, Milly Bennett leaves the Soviet Union to rejoin her lover in Spain. However, the latter dies in combat while fighting with a volunteer international brigade. She marries her third husband, an American named Hansford Amlie, who tragically dies in a farming accident in 1949. Marked by loss and pain, and after a stay of several years in a psychiatric clinic, the journey through life and suffering of this extraordinary woman, who was almost unknown in her homeland let alone in Europe, ends on November 6, 1960.[238]

"Ignatius Timothy Trebitsch alias Trebitsch Lincoln alias Timothy Lincoln alias Jackson James Lamprecht Trautwein alias Tandler alias Keehan Patrick alias Lohmand Theodore Tolnai Ludwig alias Hermann Ruh alias Anagarica F[P]ukkosaty. . . ." Thus begins one of the dozens of memoranda of the Shanghai Municipal Police on *Ignácz Trebitsch,* born in Hungarian Paks on the Danube on April 4, 1879 (one of the fourteen or sixteen children of a pious Jewish businessman, Nathan Trebitsch).[239] Despite extensive research by his biographer, Bernard Wasserstein, numerous stations of his mysterious life have never betrayed their secrets. Moreover, posterity must accept that although Trebitsch-Lincoln wrote two autobiographies, both should be read *cum grano salis*.[240] Trebitsch himself: "Before I practised Buddhism I was the most accomplished liar in the world, but since accepting the doctrines of Buddha, it is absolutely impossible for me to lie."[241]

Trebitsch-Lincoln would never have imagined in his young years that he would one day find his eternal rest in the Middle Kingdom. Nor that in the course of his life thousands of files would be compiled on him by a variety of different governments, embassies, police organizations, and secret services: with notes on his exotic travel goals, diverse undertakings, and suspicious contacts with other, no less dubious persons. Like his brothers, Ignácz receives an orthodox religious education. In the Pressburg (now Bratislava) of the time, he learns German before he begins school in Budapest. Because of a stolen gold watch, the not yet twenty-year-old leaves the European continent for England. A year later he returns to Hungary, tries his luck as a journalist, and ends up a thief once again. This time his flight leads to Germany and to estrangement from his faith. The year 1899 sees his conversion to Presbyterianism in Hamburg. He then spends a brief interlude with the Lutherans before he sails for Canada. There his task is to convert the souls of Jewish immigrants from Eastern Europe to Christianity. Not very successful in this endeavor, he comes up with the brilliant inspiration that the London Anglican Society should take over the Presbyterian Mission in Montreal.

The unrealized dream of a bonanza brings the still not yet twenty-five-year-old back to Europe; first to Germany, then to England. The death of his father-in-law and the resulting inheritance enables him to break his ties with the church and return to a bourgeois life, and here he likewise swims like a fish in water. He meets the Quaker and philanthropist Benjamin Seebohm Rowntree, whose father had founded a well-known candy company. As Rowntree's private secretary and assistant, he travels all over Europe and in the years 1906–1909 gains insights into the world of the rich and famous. In 1910, aided by endorsements from Lloyd George and Winston Churchill, he unexpectedly and just barely wins a seat as a Liberal MP in the British Parliament. His career as a parliamentarian does not last long, but he makes himself heard with a few, for his time progressive, words in the *House of Commons* on 13 June 1910. Thereby he is talking of the British colonial administration in Egypt, which a conservative member of parliament defends with a reference to the "superior white race." Trebitsch replies:

> I submit that if the white man cannot rule races which we call inferior races save by resort to arms, then his prestige is already gone. I speak, I confess, as an Oriental myself. I have Oriental blood in my veins, and I cannot but laugh at the doctrine of hon. Members opposite that Orientals must receive treatment in some way different from that given to other peoples.[242]

At least for a short period Trebitsch's interlude as a politician brings him publicity, the satisfaction of one of his greatest cravings. After that he tries his luck in business dealings involving Galician oil pipelines and oil drilling in Romania. The First World War upsets his plans. His financial situation is dire, and he works as a spy and later even as a double agent (for Germany and England). England requests his arrest and extradition for fraud, but not—which deflates Trebitsch's vanity—for treason. Even before he disembarks, his 1916 book *Revelations of an International Spy* appears. From 1916 to 1919, he sits out his punishment in England, loses his citizenship, and is expelled from the country. At first the English understandably consider sending him back to his former homeland, Hungary, where Béla Kun's brief Soviet Republic has just been proclaimed (March 1919), but Scotland Yard thinks better of this, probably not incorrectly assessing Trebitsch-Lincoln's psyche. "Lincoln is probably of superior ability to any member of the Communist Government and he might easily become a sort of Lenin of Central Europe."[243]

Finally, Trebitsch-Lincoln gets a foothold in Germany and that none too subtly: He becomes involved in right-wing circles, above all with Colonel Max Bauer, a collaborator of General Ludendorff. His avowed aim is to restore the monarchy and place former Crown Prince Wilhelm (Kaiser Wilhelm II's eldest son, who returned to Germany after the war on the promise not to participate in politics) on the now vacant Imperial Throne. Trebitsch also has a hand in the failed Kapp Putsch of March 1920. He leaves Berlin for Bavaria to join the White International, an organization of militarists and reactionaries who suffer from hurt pride. Conspiratorial visits to Vienna and Budapest round out the stations of his European odyssey, which ends when he finally, after he hears of a conspiracy to murder him, betrays the White International to the Czech intelligence service (his stolen documents later prove to be forgeries). Subsequently there are more arrests, trials, and expulsions, first in Vienna, later in the United States. In 1922, Trebitsch begins his odyssey to the Far East, where he finds a new field of activity in China: "It was madness on my part to make the journey to China with a miserable six hundred dollars in my pocket. And I could not speak a word of Chinese, nor had I any connections there."[244]

It has never been satisfactorily explained why Trebitsch-Lincoln was attracted to the Middle Kingdom. Perhaps it was easier to pursue his underhanded dealings there in a nearly total legal vacuum that protected him from an ever-growing number of enemies. If one believes his own claims, he had an extreme pathological hatred for England that in the course of the next twenty years developed into a paranoid obsession: "I had never been to China; I knew nobody in China and I carried no letters of introduction; but I had a plan. My plan was to go to the westernmost province of China, Szechwan, because that province adjoins Thibet [sic] and my purpose was to start trouble in Central Asia."[245] Shanghai is Trebitsch's first destination. From there he at once attempts to advance into the interior of China, "where

Figure 2.8
"Before I practised Buddhism I was the most accomplished liar in the world, but since accepting the doctrines of Buddha, it is absolutely impossible for me to lie" were the words of Ignácz Trebitsch-Lincoln during one of his lectures in Shanghai. The former British MP and "international spy" was regarded by many as one of the twentieth century's most dubious characters.

it would be possible . . . [to have] success as a 're-organizer.'" Via Hankou, he reaches Chongqing—still according to his reports—by boat and then travels downstream again to Yichang. Recently driven out of his stronghold in Chongqing, the military power holder Yang Sen resides there in 1922/23. Trebitsch urges Yang Sen to enter into an alliance with his opponent, Wu Peifu, then one of the most powerful northern warlords.

Trebitsch's renown grows still greater, if we can believe his version of the story, in the course of 1923, because in Luoyang he is appointed a personal advisor by Wu Peifu, to whom he had likewise recommended himself as an advisor. If the story is true, one could best imagine him as a mixture of

PR agent, would-be financial manager, and arms dealer. Unfortunately for him, in 1925 Wu Peifu denies to the press having any ties with Trebitsch-Lincoln.[246] Well documented are, to the contrary, Trebitsch's failed attempts to solicit German loans during trips to Europe with Chinese delegations. The longer he stays in China, the more Trebitsch realizes that "to these Chinese generals money was everything and their country nothing."[247] Did he, who claimed to have become a factor in China's political life, perhaps see himself in this mirror? At any rate, in the following years the Kuomintang's growing strength brings to an end his career as an advisor in China. Once again, the converted Jew, "that arch-rogue and impostor," faces a financial catastrophe.[248] Trebitsch has memories of being a "grey eminence," he was a man firmly convinced he could influence history. His enemies, to the contrary, regard him as a swindler, cheat, and grossly exaggerating braggart.

Trebitsch's retreat from the Chinese political stage does not mean the end of his relations with the Middle Kingdom. He of course tries briefly to make contacts in Europe, but England once more rebuffs him. Resentfully, Trebitsch turns his back on the Old Continent in order to try for a new start in the United States. He sees himself as a victim, as misunderstood. No one listens to him, a man who merely wanted to help China: "It has been my misfortune all through life to have been associated with fools, who spoiled and nullified all my efforts. And so it was in China. I have been successful there far beyond anything ever achieved by a foreigner. But when war broke out Wu Pei Fu would not listen to me."[249] Trebitsch must have suffered great psychic oscillations in those days. His thoughts move between inner retreat and outwardly directed attacks; his mood is depressive and his mind confused. In an effort to endear himself to England, he praises the British Empire as the greatest political institution on earth, and he desires to return to China, which prompts a British civil servant to write: "I think Lincoln is a little mad, and it seems to me that efforts should be made to prevent his return to China."[250] Nevertheless, already in 1925 he manages to return to the Far East, and indeed to Tianjin. There he has his most important mystical epiphany, a spiritual limit experience: "On the 27th of October, 1925, in the Astor House Hotel in Tientsin, where I was staying at the time, I made the great renunciation, I quitted the world . . . I forced the doors of the lunatic asylum open and—walked out."[251]

This proclamation followed his turn to the study of Eastern religion, as manifested in the Theosophical Society of the Russian Helena Blavatsky. He sets off for its headquarters in Southern India, but becomes stranded in Ceylon as "Dr. Leo Tandler" and learns, after acquiring a few words of Pali, the fundamental principles of Buddhism. In Ceylon, Trebitsch learns of his son's tragic fate, condemned to death for murder and awaiting execution in England. He at once sets off to visit him one last time, but it is already too late. Subsequently he enters the United States with a forged passport as "H. Ruh." There he pleads in vain with the British authorities for permission to visit Tibet. His dreams of withdrawing to the high plateau of the Himalayas, secluded from any civilization in a monastery (and if necessary to hatch plots against the British Empire) were not to be fulfilled in his lifetime; nor was his wish to play a role in Lamaist politics. In October 1927, he surfaces in Peking, which moves a member of the British delegation to comment: "He ought to have been hanged years ago, instead of merely being deported as a traitor."[252] At the Hôtel du Nord, he unfolds, this time using the name Anagarika Pukkusati, his Buddhist activities, whereby he more than once snubs the Theosophical Society. He begins to think again of his political abilities: He would like if at all possible to make contact with the Panchen Lama—after the Dalai Lama Tibet's second most important spiritual leader. We do not know whether this is for religious reasons, to gain admission to this holy land, or—as the British suspected—for political reasons. "It appears that LINCOLN has been commissioned by the Soviet Government for the purpose of helping to remove PANSHAN LAMA which is the condition put forward by DALAI LAMA for the signing of the treaty with the Soviet Government for access via TIBET to INDIA."[253]

Trebitsch will in the following years, to be sure, never succeed in meeting this representative of Lamaist spirituality. This apparently does not prevent him from claiming to be the reincarnation of both lamas.[254] In August 1928, he holds a lecture at the Tianjin Rotary Club that makes a good impression on the public (with the exception of the British diplomats present). Despite having apparently turned away from everything political, he is still able to stir up trouble. In his 1932 *Autobiography of an Adventurer,* he writes of England—who would not rub his eyes in disbelief?—as a bulwark of civilization against the Bolshevist threat. Unfortunately, so his conclusion, his personal tragedy consists in having to regard this country as an enemy.[255] It is thus no wonder that he, as incredible as it seems, decides to become a true Buddhist monk: In May, he goes through the required ceremony at a monastery near Nanking, whereby Trebitsch-Lincoln transforms himself into Chao Kung, as he calls himself thereafter. Despite this spiritual elevation, he finds no peace at the age of now fifty-two years. He seeks more, still wants to withdraw into a monastery in Tibet and then return to Europe in order to set up an international Buddhist center.

In Shanghai, Chao Kung finally finds the surroundings that make it possible to act out his inner state of mind in a rhythm of "morbid melancholia and mystic ecstasy."[256] Since his ordination as a monk, he no longer wears Western clothing in public. In a letter to the publisher of the *North China Daily News* he writes, "I have gone further in associating myself with the Chinese

People than any foreigner before; I have a Chinese name, I wear constantly Chinese Clothes; and am the first foreigner to have been admitted into the age-old Order of Buddhist Monks in China."[257]

In late 1933 he and a dozen of his "European disciples" are ordained Buddhist monks and nuns in a monastery near Nanking in the presence of numerous guests, among others Soviet Ambassador Bogomolov. A few weeks later, he and his "pupils" set out to bring Buddhism to the West with the goal of opening a monastery somewhere in Europe. This time his peregrinations end in England, which again denies him entry. The Prophet of the East must start his return trip to China, first to Shanghai, then to a monastery in the coastal province of Zhejiang. His financial means are modest, but often he receives money from Buddhist benefactors, allegedly also from the wife of Silas Hardoon, who died in 1931.[258] In 1935/36 Trebitsch moves to Tianjin, where the British suspect he is engaging in not only pro-Soviet, but also pro-Japanese activities.

But this new turn in his political attitudes likewise brings him no peace. *The New York Times* writes about his alleged ties with Pu Yi, China's last emperor and Japan's puppet in Manchuria.[259] Trebitsch is plagued by homesickness, he wants to return to his homeland, and in late 1937 writes a letter to Miklós Horthy, the Regent of the Empire of Hungary: "Tortured by nostalgia, broken of body and soul, a tired wanderer on this earth returns to his native soil," sums up a Buddhist nun who brings his request to Hungary.[260] But the adventurer's plea to be permitted to return to his origins remains unanswered. In 1938 Trebitsch returns, now for the last time, to Shanghai. Apart from his flirtation with the Nazis and an appeal to President Roosevelt to receive him personally in order to speak about world peace, the former British MP falls silent. A few broadsides against the ignorant and ungrateful Western states testify to a still marked paranoia: "unless governments of European belligerent countries resigned at once so a peace conference could be held, the tibetan Buddhist 'Supreme Masters' would eliminate them from the scene of action."[261]

In July 1943 Anna Ginsbourg, who is working as a correspondent for the Russian newspaper *Nascha Shisn,* meets Trebitsch, now living in the international YMCA, barefoot, wearing only "soft Chinese shoes," who, according to Ginsbourg, has the appearance of a "typical Jewish rabbi with black, lively eyes, a slightly hooked nose and a grey beard." Asked whether he regards himself as a Jew, he replies with a qualified "Yes." The itinerant Hungarian monk expounds on his picture of an unimproved world, blames the Jews for the "Jewish problem" and criticizes the concept of Zionism. Anna Ginsbourg takes leave of Abbot Chao Kung with the feeling of having met a brilliant and engaging personality, a Buddhist monk with all the merits of a great Jew.[262]

Three months after this meeting on October 6, 1943, death claims Ignatius Timotheus Trebitsch-Lincoln, one of the twentieth century's most dubious characters. He had all the talents in the world to do good works. Instead, the confidence man and scoundrel used them for his personal ambitions, especially to satisfy his greed for wealth and power. He was neither Jewish nor Christian nor Buddhist, but rather a sectarian, for he wanted to spread his respective personal worldview with missionary zeal and messianic faith. Despite his nefarious demeanor, he is more a footnote in history (at any rate he manages to get an—even if including errors—entry in the *Encyclopaedia Judaica*).[263]

"If General Two-Gun Cohen had never lived, Bernard Shaw might very easily have invented him" is the first sentence of an article in *The New York Times* with the title "Dr. Sun's No. 1 Boy" about *Morris Abraham Cohen,* born in a Polish-Jewish shtetl on August 3, 1887.[264] Several things link him with Trebitsch-Lincoln, whom he, despite his years-long stay in China, probably never met: These include involvement in petty crimes during his youth, a world-traveler existence, and especially the tendency to flaunt his own personality in a swaggering manner. Cohen's relationships with British civil servants stationed in China also in some ways resemble those of Trebitsch: "He is a pure adventurer with an unsavoury record," notes the British vice-consul in Chongqing.[265] Furthermore, Cohen likewise receives an article in the *Encyclopaedia Judaica,* although the entry is, however, replete with exaggerations and falsehoods.

Morris Abraham Cohen grows up on London's famous-infamous East End, the part of London where the notorious serial killer Jack the Ripper stalked his victims. Here little Abraham (he added the name Morris only later) accompanies his father, Josef, to the synagogue and is proud when he wishes his friends "Shalom" with a powerful-deep voice. In a world of poverty and simultaneously of freedom, "Fat Moisha," his nickname, tries to assimilate to British society. At eighteen, his parents send him to Canada, to inhospitable Saskatchewan, so that he can work off his excessive energy on a farm, but there he again falls afoul of the law. Between prison terms, he earns his living as a peddler, gambler, and speculator. Besides this, he has a lot of time to foster his relationships with the Chinese, who came to Canada in the second half of the nineteenth century when there was an outbreak of gold rush fever, and later when cheap labor was in demand for the expanding Canadian railroad network. Morris is indebted to the owner of a Cantonese restaurant for a patchwork of images of what is happening in the Middle Kingdom: "I didn't quite swallow all he told me, but it stirred my imagination. . . . I'd known poverty myself and what persecution meant . . . And though I'd never seen

China, I could guess that the life of the under-dog would be a whole lot worse there than it was in the white man's world."[266]

In February 1912—the Emperor has just abdicated and made way for Yuan Shikai as provisional president—Morris Cohen is officially sworn in by his Chinese friends as a member of Sun Yat-sen's "Tongmenghui," the Revolutionary Alliance for the establishment of a Chinese Republic. "Anyway I walked down those twisty, shabby stairs and out of that poor little grocery shop . . . pledged to devote my life to the service of Sun Yat-sen, the overthrow of the Manchu dynasty and the liberation of the Chinese people."[267] Before this happens, however, years are to pass. During the First World War, Cohen serves as a petty officer in the Canadian Army in France, where he encounters Chinese fighting for the Allies. As Trebitsch once did before the British Parliament, he criticizes those of his fellow citizens who cannot understand Orientals. The increasing unemployment that set in after the war, as in many countries, was among other things blamed on the Chinese immigration wave. Cohen wants to help his Chinese friends improve their country's image in the West. In 1922 his dream begins to become a reality: He takes a ship to the Far East, previously asked by Sun Yat-sen whether he could arrange contacts with a contractor for Canadian railroad construction. Upon his arrival in Shanghai, Cohen first perceives how different China is: "I knew many Chinese of all sorts and conditions and, arriving in their own country, I expected to feel myself at home right from the start. But I didn't. I felt that I was a stranger in a very, very strange land and I felt lonely."[268] Like many others before and not a few after him, he encounters an exotic world in the Middle Kingdom:

> I heard that awful Chinese music—I've never got to like it even today—and the rattle of the mah jong pieces and I learnt after a bit to jump out of the way when I heard a shout of 'Ohé!' and heavy breathing behind me, because that meant porters on the march and they might be carrying anything from a giant jar of oil to a dead man in a basket. . . . I saw the signboards with that vertical writing on them with characters that just stop short of being an actual picture of something and leave you wondering what on earth they can mean. . . . I'd only been twelve hours in China but already China was beginning to get under my skin.[269]

It is George Sokolsky who introduces the six-years-older Morris Cohen to Sun Yat-sen. However, Madame Sun impresses him more than does the father of the Chinese Republic. He writes that he had expected Madame Sun to be charming, gracious, and dignified, and she did not disappoint him, but he had not thought that she would be so pretty. This meeting at Rue Molière 29 in Shanghai marks the start of Morris' ties with Sun. Until the death of the leader

Figure 2.9
"If General Two-Gun Cohen had never lived, Bernard Shaw might very easily have invented him." Morris Abraham Cohen acquired his nickname because he always carried two pistols. Cover of Charles Drage's book on Morris Cohen, London, 1956.

of the Republican Revolution, he stands at his side as his bodyguard, holding the title of an adjutant—on Morris' calling cards were the initials A.d.C. for "aide-de-camp" (Chinese "fuguan"). He performs his work conscientiously, accompanies Sun on every trip between Shanghai, Hong Kong, and Canton. Because he always carries two pistols, he acquires the nickname "Two-Gun Cohen" in the Western community, an almost legendary designation associated with him to the end of his days. The death of Sun while Cohen is on furlough at home is a severe blow to him. He returns in order to serve the leaders of the revolution and Sun's possible successors as a courier and weapons dealer. These include, for example, Sun Fo, Sun's son and Minister for the Communication System; T. V. Soong; Wu Tiecheng, after 1932 mayor of Shanghai; or also Marshal Li Jishen, a follower (until 1929) of Chiang Kai-shek.

In the years 1929 to 1936, Cohen works as a weapons supplier for Chen Jitang, a general by the grace of Chiang Kai-shek (at least until his arrest). To be sure, he is referred to in the Western press as a "Leader in the Chinese Army," but in truth and deed he commands no troops at all, although the respect shown him doubtlessly increases with his promotion to the rank of major general. After the Japanese aggression against China in 1937, Cohen serves as a mouthpiece for "free China" and works untiringly to win Western support: "If China had as much arms as she has sympathy the war would be over. She does not expect or wish for one foreign soldier to shoulder a rifle for her. China does hope that the nations that are friendly and that have signed treaties guaranteeing her integrity and sovereignty would help her in armaments."[270] When Madame Sun visits Canton, Moishe, whom she awards a sort of pension as a reward for his service to Sun Yat-sen, does not stray from her side. In Shanghai and Chongqing, he meets Emily Hahn, who calls him an "original out of a book." After the Japanese attack Pearl Harbor, Cohen—like Sir Elly Kadoorie, Emily Hahn, and other Westerners—is interned in the Stanley Internment Camp in Hong Kong. In 1943, he is released and returns to Canada, where he becomes active as a spokesman for China: "China will be the economic salvation of the American continent and Europe. The country is just entering the second stage of evolution, the machine age. It will require a great deal of machinery after the war. . . ."[271]

Morris Cohen continues to play off his Chinese contacts to benefit the Middle Kingdom, the Jews, and—his extravagant lifestyle also demands this in a financial regard—himself: He brings Zionist representatives in contact with Wellington Koo, China's ambassador to Great Britain, in order that they can try to secure China's support for the founding of the state of Israel. He supports the departure of Jewish community members from China and finally—the communists have in the meantime taken power in the country—pardons for Canadian nuns sentenced to long prison terms.[272] Mao's victory over Chiang Kai-shek destroys the network of contacts that Cohen has built up over the years. Some of his employers are now living in Taiwan; others switch sides to the new masters. Cohen is literally caught between a rock and a hard place. Even immediately after the end of the Civil War, he believes that communism is an anomaly and could not possibly be accepted by the Chinese people. In 1952 he sets out, again almost penniless, to visit the Generalissimo in Taipei. But the two seem out of synch, and not much is left for Cohen but to return to Europe, where with the aid of his friend Charles Drage he publishes his heavily revised autobiography, *Two-Gun Cohen* (1954).

In late 1955, reports surface in Western newspapers that Cohen is offering himself as an unofficial mediator between the Nationalists and the Communists: "The only way to settle disputes is to go straight to the people and put the guns on the table. I believe the Communists want to enjoy life as much as we do. It just needs somebody to get the top men together and let them know the way to go about it."[273] The peacemaker role, combined with a sort of romantic mysticism, seems to please him, which does not, however, change the fact that such an approach is doomed to fail: A government representative in Taiwan emphasizes that the rumor is too ridiculous to be commented on with an official statement. Whether disappointed by the failure of his wish to mediate or offended by his treatment: Although still officially a member of the Kuomintang, in the following years Cohen increasingly becomes a communist apologist. The communist leadership in Peking invites Cohen to several anniversary celebrations—and he repays his hosts with sympathetic commentaries: "I see that everywhere the standard of living of the ordinary people is much higher than before. I have never seen so many smiling faces. Here I have seen socialism. I am very glad to see in China many democratic parties working together under the leadership of the Communist Party."[274]

In 1966, just at the start of the Cultural Revolution, he travels across his beloved China for the last time. His relationship with the rulers seems marked by a certain sentimentality (which they probably reciprocated for propaganda reasons), so that Cohen does not dare to look behind the facades. "Two Gun Cohen Likes Red Guards," reads the title of an article on his visit in the *London Times* of December 7, 1966, which refers to Morris Cohen as the last great Oriental romantic, a "man of mystery."[275] He spent the first months of his stay in China in the 1920s happily and in peace: "I enjoyed a kind of family life that I'd not known since my boyhood."[276] On September 13, 1970, "Gen. Morris Cohen, Bodyguard of Dr. Sun Yat-sen" dies, "a flamboyant person," in academic terms a poorly educated man who—according to Cohen himself—had nevertheless committed his life to China because he loved the Chinese people.[277]

IV. DIPLOMATS

In a certain sense, a subgroup of the couriers and representatives made up the professional class of state commissioned envoys—the diplomats, whose loyalty definitely had to be to the country whose government sent them to the Far East. Their latitude to act was in general more limited than that of freely acting emissaries. Their activities centered on communications with state offices, and they generally lived outside the surrounding host society or respectively within an area assigned to foreigners, such as the embassy quarter in Peking. Only a few high-ranking diplomats of Jewish origin found their way to China in the first part of the twentieth century. Always mentioned as the best known is the Soviet Russian Ambassador Adolf Ioffe (Yoffe), who concluded the famous 1923 Agreement with Sun Yat-sen to help reorganize the Kuomintang into a tight party structure, but without communist ideology. Two relatively unknown American diplomats offer a revealing view of how this professional group saw things and their experiences in and with China.

"HIROHITO, By the Grace of Heaven, Emperor of Japan, seated on the Throne occupied by the same Dynasty changeless through ages eternal, To all to whom these Presents shall come, Greeting! Having duly examined the Commission issued by Mr. Franklin D. Roosevelt, President of the United States of America, under date of the twenty-ninth day of the fourth month in the year one thousand nine hundred and forty, appointing Mr. Samuel Sokobin to be Consul of the United States of America to reside at Kobe. . . ."[278] In 1940, the coastal city of Kobe represented for *Samuel Sokobin* the beginning of the end of a diplomatic career that up to then had, for almost twenty-five years, led the Jewish-American envoy of Polish-Russian origins to many different consular posts. With the exception of the city of Saltillo in Mexico, they were scattered across the Middle Kingdom: Peking, Tientsin, Shanghai, Nanking, Antung, Chungking, Kalgan, Swatow, Mukden, Harbin, Foochow, and Tsingtao.[279]

Known only to a few insiders, Samuel Sokobin, born in Newark, New Jersey, on April 28, 1893, could be called a pioneer of twentieth-century American diplomacy in China, and yet at the same time an outsider.[280] For political and perhaps personal reasons, he was never to rise above the rank of a Class IV Foreign Service Officer, but thanks to his urge for adventure, he gathered the most varied experiences in a country that in the first third of the last century could not be toured without difficulties, even by official state representatives. Although Western representatives no longer had to fear, as they did in the eighteenth century, being expelled or arrested by the authorities, even a hundred-and-fifty years later there were still enough other dangers lying in wait for people like Sokobin: bandits, unpredictable warlords, Chinese hostile to foreigners, and later the war-hungry Japanese.

Born in the same year as George Sokolsky, Sokobin attended Cornell University for a short time before he applied for a State Department language program that in the frame of the War Reparations (Boxer Rebellion Indemnity Scholarship Program) gave American students a chance to live in China for a certain period. His knowledge of Yuan Shikai's career, the Maritime Customs Administration of China, or the Yangtze as a trade route seems to have been great enough for the twenty-year-old to obtain employment as a translator for the United States Embassy in Peking.

Sam Sokobin appears on a stage that is marked by China's attempt to reorient itself after the fall of the Qing Dynasty. The possibilities for this are of course few, after Japan presents President Yuan Shih-kai the infamous "Twenty-one Demands" in 1915 (had the demands been implemented, Japan would have acquired temporary hegemony over China). England advises giving in, America protests. The West offers little support overall. China is again divided, and the warlords play their own games. After the Treaty of Versailles and the West's betrayal, public anger vents itself in calls to boycott foreign businesses and in the attempt to gain the support of Soviet Russia. Sokobin becomes—the demonstrations on May 4, 1919, by citizens and students in Peking and other places, had taken place only a few days before—the Vice-Consul in Antung (Dandong), a locality in the estuary of the Yalu river on the border of present-day North Korea. Sokobin has now already been in China for five years and longs for a furlough. "The climate of China is not a particularly healthful one, and I quite understand why so many consular officers have asked for permission to return to the United States."[281] He determines that despite the demands of certain Chinese circles, there is no boycott of Japanese goods in Dandong, even though most of the city's residents stem from Shandong Province (where the former German concession areas are located that the Treaty of Versailles assigned to Japan).

The year 1919 is still not past, when Sokobin receives the assignment to sound out, as Vice-Consul in Zhangjiakou, on the border of Inner Mongolia and just south of the Great Wall, the possibilities for American trade with Mongolia. Often he visits Urga (Ulan Bator), the capital of Outer Mongolia, which belongs to his consular district, once via the Gobi desert, once with a detour via Harbin and Manzhouli. Outer Mongolia declares itself independent in December 1911, but does not find peace, because of its position as a buffer zone between Russia and China and as a secondary theater of the Russian civil war between Reds and Whites. In the struggle against the hated Chinese, some Mongols asked for aid from the notorious, virulently anti-semitic White

Guard Lieutenant General Baron von Ungern-Sternberg, whose brutal rule was, however, so unpopular that it was in the end easy for Soviet troops to take the city in the summer of 1921.[282] Sokobin's reports are analytical, precise, and include personal impressions: about the Mongolian dignitaries who leave Zhangjiakou for Shenyang in order to take part in a conference with the warlord Zhang Zuolin, the (good) relations between the Russians and the Chinese, the Soviet influence in Mongolia, and the close-meshed Russian agent network that even includes Korean Bolsheviks.[283] He describes the tragedy of the Russian Jews in Urga, who with their monopoly in the fur and skin trade become the target of terrifying attacks by Cossacks.[284]

With all the means available to him, Sokobin supports the commercial activities of American entrepreneurs—Andersen, Meyer & Co., The China American Trading Co., Brenner Brothers, the Eitington-Schild Company, and others—gives them advice or personally accompanies them to inhospitable areas north of the Great Wall. He supports the documentary filmmaker Gene Lamb no less strongly on his difficult journey from Zhangjiakou via Ningxia, Lanzhou, and Kashgar to India.[285] His engagement is unsurpassed, and Western visitors honor him with thank-you notes. His work is not free of risks. Once there are rumors that the Mongolian authorities plan to arrest him during his next visit to Urga, because he considers Mongolia to be part of China.[286] Several times Sokobin becomes entangled in precarious situations in which American citizens are arrested, and he himself is accused of dishonest machinations. In December 1922, exactly one month after receiving a decoration from the Chinese government, he only barely escapes death on a business trip in Mongolia while accompanying a businessman; soldiers search his car and actually shoot his companion dead.[287] In his next post, in Shenyang, the Manchu's first capital, he receives the assignment to analyze the policy of Marshal Zhang Zuolin, the ruler of Manchuria and High Commissioner for the Mongolian border areas, in the midst of the general chaos at the time. China's Northeast, rich in raw materials, also offers itself to Sokobin as an area to study the spreading, almost spider-web-like railroad network, whereby he turns for help to George Sokolsky, "a mutual friend." In Mukden, he also lends his support to hard-pressed fellow-countrymen, for example, when a native attacks a Western woman with her child:

> I stated that the district in which he [the husband of the American woman—author's note] was now living was at its best a bad place, full of Chinese brothels, low class tea-houses etc. . . . The Consulate General still doubts whether it is a symptom of any infection of Manchuria with the anti-foreign virus prevalent in parts of intramural China.[288]

In the summer of 1927, Sokobin receives a new post in Fuzhou, the treaty port located midway between Shanghai and Hong Kong that above all in the nineteenth century was known for its tea exports. His activity in the coastal region necessarily coincides with the historical events occurring in China in those months of anti-Western outrages and communist revolts during Chiang Kai-shek's Northern Expedition and afterwards: He reports on robberies and incendiary attacks, on the spread of anti-Western caricatures, on complaints by Westerners against Chinese authorities and on the Nationalists' widespread anti-religious movement. Sokobin occasionally presumes to report on topics outside the everyday, for example, on Chinese books about Western civilization. He probably caused his superiors in Washington a certain amount of confusion with his personally colored 1 February 1928 report, "Comparing Conditions in Manchuria and Fukien." He writes, "Irony indeed for the writer, passionately devoted to the cause of international peace, to learn that his dispatches on Manchurian railways caused interest only to a military observer! What those dispatches attempted to bring out was what every writer and every diplomat and every economist had told the Chinese would happen—the country would prosper."[289] Perhaps what bothers the State Department is Sokobin's praise for the successful policy of Zhang Zuolin, who kept the northeastern provinces, in contrast to the rest of China, from degenerating into stagnation and misery.

For health reasons, Sokobin leaves the coastal province and China for four years in all before receiving an assignment to Qingdao in 1934. His reports from the former German concession deal, for example, with the increasingly intense Japanese interference in the fate of the port city, the particular position of Qingdao as more than an administrative unit belonging to Shandong Province, or the struggle for autonomy from the government in Nanking.

With the approach of war clouds from the East, Sokobin's relations with the State Department also worsen. In 1936, he apparently speaks disparagingly to an envoy from the United States in China concerning a drunken U.S. Navy soldier who had disrupted a Japanese parade in Qingdao. A year later his criticism of the American Air Force (he thought U.S. fighter planes had unnecessarily provoked the Japanese fleet) again earns him a reprimand from his superiors. In March 1938, the State Department informs him that he has been "bucking the State Department," especially regarding the evacuation of Americans from Qingdao.[290] However, after more than seventy years we can no longer verify these accusations. Apart from a few trivial offenses, such as for example an unexcused absence or a travel expenses claim that seemed too excessive for the authorities, nothing in the sources points to serious misconduct by Sokobin at any time in his career.

At a reception in honor of diplomats who had been victims of slander after the "loss of China," John Stewart Service, himself a prominent victim of China Lobby criticism and later of McCarthy Red Scare attacks, tries to explain the cold treatment Sokobin received. In his reports he had—instead of praising the heroic Chinese struggle—reported on the Japanese success against the guerrilla resistance and the exploitation of raw materials and thereby undercut the American (and Chinese) propaganda image of the Nationalists' consistent success. "He was cruelly and ridiculously accused of being 'pro-Japanese.' And, with a perverted idea of justice, his transfer was arranged to Kobe, Japan. He was never returned to service in China."[291] On a return trip to Japan from a furlough in the United States, the outbreak of the Pacific War finally overtakes Sokobin. He is interned in Manila and only months later repatriated. His last consular post was to be in Birmingham in 1944. At the age of 93 years, Sam Sokobin passed away, a surely underestimated figure, "a bit out of step" (John Service). With his twenty-five years of practical experience in confronting the adversities and amenities of China, he would have been very well qualified to give the Occident important insights on this country.[292]

Lewis Einstein, born the son of Judah Benjamin in New York in 1877, confided, at least in written form, somewhat more in his capacity as a diplomat of the old school, art collector, and "man of letters," as *The New York Times* reported when he died in 1967.[293] In contrast to Sokobin, he left behind an autobiographical collection of memories first published after his death with the title *A Diplomat Looks Back*.[294] He also differs from him because he resided in the Middle Kingdom for only a relatively short, although for China fateful period. What links him with Sokobin is probably the admission of disgrace hedged by clauses concerning his treatment by the official side: "There could have been more courteous ways of dismissing an old public servant," he writes somewhat peevishly in his memoirs.

Equipped with a master's degree in history and able to speak, besides English, fluent German, French, and Italian, Einstein joins the diplomatic service of his country in 1903. His family belongs to the wealthy entrepreneurial class and maintains good relations with New York Republican political and business circles. Barely thirty years old, he is a member of the American delegation at the famous 1906 Algeciras Conference on the future sovereignty of Morocco. Then he gets an assignment to Constantinople, where the young Turks are starting to undermine the pillars of the Ottoman Empire. Three years later—it seems as though life so-to-speak attracts the American-Jewish diplomat to revolutions—he is assigned to Peking, likewise to a society that has become aware that its political system is disintegrating. In March 1909, with his wife and a small dog he sets out on the Trans-Siberian Railway for China:

> At Peking the little griffin was the first that had been seen of his breed. Orientals love pets and many Chinese would try to fondle him, but for some instinctive reason the dog hated the yellow race and barked at every coolie. . . . Racial prejudice was reciprocated in kind by Mongol horses, many of which will not allow Europeans to ride them.[295]

However, it was not Einstein's assignment to give such reports on the condition of quadrupeds in East and West. Rather, his task was to represent and advance his country's economic interests in the North of China: in particular, the oil and tobacco industries, as well as the railroad construction branch and the related loan transactions by American banking consortia. Einstein believes that he, and he is not the only one, is writing history: "If there had been no Chinese Revolution impending, no Wilson Administration at Washington, and finally no European War, we might perhaps have built the first arch in that long bridge over which we expected China to travel with our guidance."[296] He regrets the advance of the Japanese in southern Manchuria and at the same time deplores the inefficiency and corruption of the Chinese central government. His memoirs deal further with the opium problem or, for example, with the outbreak of a pneumonia epidemic in Northeastern China in 1910.

Einstein does not yet seem to be disturbed, as is Sokobin a few years later, by the unpleasantness of the strange, occasionally even barbaric environment in the border areas of China. His descriptions of life in the capital city have a nostalgic quality, because it was inevitably passing away. The Tartar city's massive walls had protected the Western residents of Peking against a new siege by the Chinese, "but protected us much less effectively from the odour of garlic and of rancid oil which rose every evening above the Chinese city."[297] He looks back on his time in Peking with a sort of inner satisfaction: "With little of the pomp of the large capitals, our life in China could not have been pleasanter. Everything was absurdly easy and abundant, and there was a daily round of gaieties." This included, for example, the praised visits to the Temple of Heaven or the not always successful excursions in search of antiquities in the famous Liulichang Alley (a part of downtown Peking famous for its antique shops). To be sure, Einstein is also a product of his times, viewing the faults of the Chinese rather one-sidedly. In his case, this is partly compensated for, because he honestly tries to look behind the façade in order to understand Chinese customs and practices. He observes eunuchs who plead with "their" princesses to distance themselves from Western decadence, or he attends official banquets where dignitaries "belched and clucked" in between consuming duck tongue and deer tendons. He is sometimes also surprised, e.g., by the unexpected practice of a few

Manchu princes to receive official guests at "the most unseasonable hours" with a glass of ("bad") champagne.

> There were not many points of sympathy between the reigning family and ourselves, and something beside linguistic difficulties stood in the way of any closer intercourse. We could never expect to penetrate those hidden recesses in the Oriental mind where East and West cannot be bridged. If these differences are instinctive or derived by their training I cannot say. I suspect the latter. . . . [298]

Einstein uses meetings with Manchu Dynasty representatives as the occasion for reflecting on the similarities between ancient Rome and the Chinese Empire, two civilizations whose relationships to religion and family were similar. "The Divine Augustus would have sympathised with the Regent if he could have read as I did in the Official Gazette an Imperial decree by which Prince Ch'un had cancelled the divinity of the God of War and reduced that fallen deity to the humbleness of an ordinary mortal."[299] He remembers a remark by another Manchu prince that a fortification like the Great Wall could never have been constructed in a country with a constitutional state system.

Even before the actual Revolution and the fall of the Dynasty, Einstein receives another transfer, this time to the American deputation in Costa Rica. Further stations in his career as a diplomat are Constantinople and Sofia, where entanglement in a legal affair in 1915 prompts his resignation. Only in 1921 (in the meantime the Republican Harding has become President) does he, a man who—according to Theodore Roosevelt—represents the fine tradition of an alliance between American diplomacy and literature, again have a chance to serve his country as an envoy, and in the newly created country of Czechoslovakia. In 1930, he finally turns his back on the State Department to work on creating an extensive journalistic oeuvre. The diplomatically trained "homme de lettres" is thoroughly aware of the limited viewpoint of a governmental representative in foreign countries; not least of all this is probably thanks to his stay in the Peking embassy quarter. "The old career [diplomat] looked at life through the window of a chancery with something of the detached aloofness with which the aged look at people in the street. Its secret wickedness was a romantic myth, its plotting intrigues fantastic tales, and its principal sins were those of Sybarites."[300] Combined in Einstein were cultivation, openness, foresight, modesty, humor, and amiability, with empathy for the other, for foreign *Lebenswelten,* and value conceptions. Handed down to the contemporary reader are realistic, sometimes skeptical, sometimes also ironic pictures and evaluations of times that are past from the historian's viewpoint, but from that of the cultural scholar, in contrast, quite vivid, because their character is indestructible.

V. EXPLORERS AND TRAVEL AUTHORS

For centuries, the Middle Kingdom was not regarded as exactly suitable territory for adventuresome private "globetrotters." At the center of the Occidental discussion of China were rather missionary journeys after the conclusion of the "unequal treaties," the establishment of commercial and political bases in the treaty harbors and outposts in the far reaches of the immense Empire. The slow, unstoppable opening of the country in connection with the violently suppressed Boxer Rebellion and later the fall of the Imperial Dynasty attracted—besides adventurers and would-be advisors—a group of Westerners with an interest in tourism. These were the forerunners of all those who finally in the last third of the twentieth century discovered China as a country to visit and entered the historical annals as "globetrotters."

Even before the first travel authors toured the "original" China, the pioneers of the Western expedition travelers paved the way for a view of the exotic. In the nineteenth century, Russian expeditions in particular had a reputation for setting the pace of such undertakings. Thereby, people were not interested in the Chinese core area, but rather in the remote and inhospitable fringe and border areas with their great variety of ethnic groups, thus territories that, on one side, played a strategic role for East and West, and, on the other side, also promised information on the first contacts between East and West centuries ago. The majority of these expeditions were financially supported by governments, sometimes also by private patrons or institutions, but at the center of such strenuous and adventurous undertakings were individuals who stubbornly and persistently pursued their goals. Regarded as the best known and most successful China explorers of the first third of the twentieth century are Sven Hedin, born in Stockholm in 1865, and the three-years-older *Marc Aurel Stein.*

"The most prodigious combination of scholar, explorer, archaeologist and geographer of his generation" is Owen Lattimore's description of the Hungarian-Jewish "giant" of archaeological research in Central Asia.[301] In contrast, the Director of the Chinese Institute for Archaeology asserts that, "Sir Aurel Stein of Britain is unquestionably regarded as the most villainous of the foreign archaeologists, followed by Professor Pelliot of France."[302] These very different evaluations of Western activities in the Middle Kingdom have cast—similar to the wanton destruction of the Qing Emperor's Summer Palace (Yuanmingyuan) by Lord Elgin in 1860, or the plundering of the Imperial City after the Boxer Rebellion—their long, dark shadows across relationships between China and the West up until today. The most serious accusation on the Chinese side against Stein, Pelliot, Hedin, and the other "discoverers" from the West is their theft of cultural treasures.

Stein was thereby not a conqueror by birth. He was born in Budapest on November 26, 1862. His parents, Nathan and Anna Hirschler Stein (both lifelong Jews), baptized him with the name Márk Aurél, because they regarded their Judaism as a hindrance to his career. Thereby the Steins did nothing more than what many enlightened Jews regarded as expedient—and not just in Hungary, which passed the so-called Emancipation Law for Jews only five years after Marc Aurel's birth. Stein is sent to Dresden at the age of ten years, where he learns Greek, Latin, French, and English. Later he studies Sanskrit and Farsi (Persian) at the Universities of Vienna, Leipzig, and Tübingen, before he dedicates three years to the study of classical and Oriental archaeology and languages at Oxford (but without learning any Chinese). At the age of twenty-five, he journeys to Asia for the first time, specifically to British India, from which he, in the meantime working in the service of the colonial government in Lahore, sets out on his first expeditions in the Kashmir region.

In 1900, Stein, still not yet a British citizen, embarks on his first expedition to Turkestan, with a great longing to uncover cultural, historical, and archaeological secrets. He wants to follow in the steps of Alexander the Great (whom he idealizes), wants to see how far the Hellenistic influence of the West once reached into the East, over what routes the caravans crossed the mountains of Pamir and Karakorum, and where Buddhism (and, with less influence, Manichaeism) originally stretched out their tendrils toward China. In his memoirs, *On Ancient Central Asian Tracks* (1933), Stein names several times as his personal patron saint the Chinese monk Xuan Zang, who in the seventh century traveled from China to India in order to look for "the law that Buddha has passed on to the world." In the region between the Kunlun Mountains on the Tibetan border and the Tangshan Mountains south of contemporary Kyrgyzstan, Stein definitely needed the protection of a patron saint. Here in this ancient cultural region without equal, the paths of Oriental and Occidental traders, pilgrims, and warriors once crossed on the Silk Road opened by the Han Emperor Wudi (141–87 BC). In the meantime, it was almost uninhabited, and once flourishing cities and oases had gone to rack and ruin, buried under the sands of the Taklamakan and Gobi deserts.

Already in the nineteenth century, the region around Kashgar (in Western China) had not the best reputation. Stein's first expedition even had armed escorts, who if necessary were to drive off highwaymen and bandits. From the mid-eighteenth century on, the Manchus try to bring the so-called East Turkestan under their control, whereby there are frequent uprisings by the Muslim Uyghurs against foreign rule. In 1884, the Chinese Empire unceremoniously annexes the "new territories" (Xinjiang). Not much later, the British open a consulate in Kashgar, the Queen's western-most listening post in the Middle Kingdom. The first consul-general, George Macartney, and Lord Curzon, the British Viceroy in India, make every reasonable effort to support Stein's expeditions. The explorer is in good personal condition and feels well, even if his living and working conditions are sometimes exhausting. In Western China, especially in the Taklamakan Desert, his youthful dreams come true. He carries out excavations in Yotkan, Dandong Oilik, Karadong, and Endere, discovers the extended settlement of Niya, and exposes as forgeries some "art objects" offered by Islam Akhun, a crafty dealer who for not a few years kept Orientalists in the West on the run.

Stein is successful, at least in the view of Western observers, but he lacks—according to his biographer, Jeannette Mirsky—"cultural sensitivity."[303] Thus for example he does not want to understand that the "Chinese queue" was since 1644 regarded in deed and truth as a sign of the Han's loyalty to the Manchus. His lack of Chinese language skills probably causes him more than just a little worry, for in his written notes he frequently laments: "But for a serious study of Chinese, the language of its rulers and administrators, I regret I never had had needful leisure."[304] On his second expedition (1906–1908)—once again the role falls to Stein to be *not* the first to uncover ancient ruins, but rather the first to excavate and reconstruct their history. In Miran, an oasis town on the edge of the Taklamakan desert, the British-Hungarian archaeologist discovers over two hundred Tibetan documents written on wood and paper. He makes probably the most spectacular discovery of his second journey to Western China in Dunhuang in the present-day province of Gansu. Through bribery, as well as skillful maneuvers with a monk and warders, he manages to acquire and ship abroad large numbers of ancient Buddhist, Confucian, and Taoist manuscripts from a hidden library in the Mogao Caves, the "Caves of the Thousand Buddhas."[305] This was a "find" comparable to that of the Dead Sea Scrolls discovered in caves near Qumran.

For Stein and others it is obvious that without a large-scale rescue intervention by the West, valuable Chinese cultural goods would be lost forever: due to weathering, above all to art thieves, archaeological dilettantes, souvenir hunters, or prospective antiquity dealers. A Uyghur contemporary of Stein, to the contrary, describes the Englishman as the "thief of the paintings of Miran."

Stein's fourth archaeological mission (a third in 1913–16 went further toward the interior of China, to the western branches of the Great Wall in Inner Mongolia) means for him the end of his contacts with China. He does not understand the increasingly hostile attitude of many Chinese to foreigners after the bloody events in Shanghai of May 1925, and thus in the fall of 1930 there is not much left for him to do but to terminate his expedition, undertaken at the request of the Fogg Museum in Boston. His inflexibility to Chinese demands forces him to withdraw. His days of glory as an historian and archaeologist have finally come to an end.

Despite the failure of his last expedition to China, Stein is acclaimed in the West for revealing to the public the secrets of an area formerly rich in culture and contacts between the Middle Kingdom and the West that were thought to be long since lost. "This great Hungarian is the pride of two nations and the wonder of all," the British Orientalist Sir Denison Ross said of Stein.[306] With the passing of years, less is heard in the Occident about Stein, who set out not to find eternal peace in China, but rather to discover there what the East had absorbed from the West in the course of the centuries. On October 26, 1943, the doyen of Central Asiatic archaeology dies in Kabul, shortly before the start of another expedition to study the many side-branches of the Silk Road in Afghanistan.[307] Stein rests in Kabul's Christian cemetery in the shadow of the Hindu Kush's foothill ridges.

A 1935 black-and-white photograph shows *Carl Schuster* bending forward with a modest, almost affectionate attitude, to examine a traditional piece of embroidery. He is conversing thereby with an elderly peasant woman in a village somewhere in the remote Chinese province of Sichuan.[308] East and West seem to come closer here in the countryside than in the world city of Shanghai. Born into a prominent Jewish family in Milwaukee on November 9, 1904, Schuster, like Stein, is a researcher of past life and expressive forms in remote areas of China. He differs because his research interest has up until today received far less attention than that of Stein, even though seventy years ago the American sought traces of customs that were still practiced in rural China at the start of the twentieth century and in part later. Schuster studies art history and Sinology at Harvard and journeys to the Middle Kingdom because of an interest in the symbolism of traditional folk art. In 1929–1932, he furthers his knowledge in Peking and thereby meets Baron von Stael-Holstein, a Baltic refugee and scholar of the highest rank and reputation. He undertakes adventurous trips by railroad and on foot to Western and Southwestern China, during which he collects samples of the embroidered cotton textiles that were still manufactured using traditional methods by village women at the end of the nineteenth century.

After extended journeys to Shanxi, Sichuan, Yunnan, and Guizhou, and regions bordering on China, Schuster decides in 1934 to submit a dissertation to the University of Vienna with the title *Chinese Peasant Embroideries*.[309] One of the most important insights which he reaches, thanks to his extensive research, is that the embroidery patterns of bed sheets, for example in the rural areas of Southwestern China, display greater similarity to the folk art of Eastern Europe, for example, that of the Western Carpathian Mountains, than to what was generally understood as Chinese art within the core of the Chinese empire. He also sees similarities between the patterns on silk from the Tang Dynasty found by Marc Aurel Stein in Turkestan and the peasant embroidery he studies. He knows the great significance of this rural Chinese art genre, in danger of dying out, because for him it is clear that specifically Chinese art is first of all urban art, "whereas the peasant art belongs to that common fund of primitive or primordial art which is practically ageless and knows no geographical limits."[310] He also regards it as proved that Chinese peasant embroidery still displays meaningful symbolism that only later in the Tang Dynasty yields to more decorative elements.

In 1935–1938 Schuster returns to China, once more to the fringe areas of the Middle Kingdom. Again, his aim is to discover as much as possible about the origins and significance of textile art in the rural regions. For him it was clear that the native tradition of this peasant art had only survived across the generations because the country had not changed politically and socially for a very long time and had remained untouched by outside influences. In those years, he also became aware of the different assessments of originality in the West and in rural textile art:

> [I]n the ateliers of the West individuality is at a premium, and copying has been elevated to the dignity [sic] of a crime: every 'work of art' must be unique. . . . How different this is from the impersonal, anonymous art of the countryside, where every piece is necessarily a copy or, in terms of such conceptions, a 'forgery'![311]

Schuster's return to Europe is merely of brief duration. Shortly before German troops occupy the Netherlands in May 1940, this pioneer of scientific research in the area of folklore and symbolism leaves Europe for America. There he works—night after night in the New York Public Library, as stated in an obituary—on his theories, attempts to decipher the riddles of various peoples of the world that he so loves and values: family trees, body and hand structures, myths and rituals, mosaics, motifs of tattoos, etc. Although scorned by many contemporaries because of his universalistic approach and his theories, Carl Schuster, who with his concepts stands close to the structuralists around Claude Lévi-Strauss, strives up until his unexpected death on July 3, 1969, to solve the mysteries of folk traditions in Patagonia, Siberia, and the Philippines and decipher their symbolic codes.[312]

"More comfortably than tourists, more open-minded than researchers, we want to wander together through the most fascinating—and oldest—cultural circle of the world. Not for the sake of its places of interest, but in order to see; not in order to criticize it, but in order to learn to understand it," notes *Richard Katz,* a journalist and author born in Prague, in the foreword to his 1931 reportage *Funkelnder Ferner Osten!* (Glittering Far East!). This work consists of notes on a trip to China, Korea, and Japan that the editor for the Ullstein publishing house in Berlin and reporter for the *Vossische Zeitung* undertook from July 1929 to July 1930.[313] Katz is an extremely sensitive observer, who with much wit and humor describes the everyday life and character of the Chinese, above all where his intellect, shaped by the Occident, cannot help him to explain the exotic. He knows that he cannot understand the Chinese character within a year, but he can at least try:

> We will as little completely succeed as the experts or those of our countrymen who spend their lives in the Far East. For us as for them the soul of the yellow peoples will remain a mystery. Only the bright reflexes are visible to us that are refracted through that mysterious prism. Yet we want to take pleasure in them, wherever they sparkle to us . . . But better to consider a blue spark to be green, than to not see it flash at all. Better to misunderstand yellow words than yellow humanity.[314]

In contrast to Stein or Schuster, Katz approaches the Middle Kingdom from the South, from Hong Kong, which definitely changes his perspective: "As long as the Europeans' city remains healthy and has space, they [the English—author's note] are not interested in the natives, five thousand whites lay claim to twice as much space as a quarter million yellows. Yellows are quantity, the Englishman calculates, and quantity does not decide. Quality decides."[315] Richard Katz's journey progresses northward along the coast to Shanghai, a Western oasis built on speculation in the midst of the Chinese wilderness. "Showy Shanghai took root with its parasitical system of international treaties on the good-natured giant that is called China and that has nourished itself from the soil of East Asia for millennia." And in prophetic words he, who a few years later will suffer the emigrant's fate, writes: "Yet these reserves are disappearing. Orchids are luxury plants. The gardener is glad about them, but he removes them if they threaten the life of the tree. . . . Our generation will yet see the most colorful, sumptuous city of the East wither."[316] Katz recognizes the signs of the times and anticipates that the "yellows are provoked."

Katz finds his way further north, again following the coast to the former German Tsingtao (Qingdao): "That is indeed Swinemünde, the bright beach with the protective deciduous forest behind it, the casino, the coffee pavilions and here . . . really and truly, 'STRAND HOTEL' is printed black on white below the high-gabled fourth story." Born in the Hapsburg countries, Katz is of the naïve view that the Germans had not only invested labor and money in Qingdao, but also the goodwill for understanding. "Our occupation, like our early settlers, did not play the masters, but rather they sought amicable relationships with the Chinese, and this still proves itself today in the social coexistence of the white population with the yellow."[317] He tries to record the exotic scenes and to explain them socio-historically, using his knowledge of the Chinese philosophy of life:

> The people here are not "xenophobic," they are what Confucius said of himself two-thousand-five-hundred years ago: "I create nothing new; I believe in the old and live it," and Confucius is still their teacher today. Sun Yat-sen's revolutionary teachings may establish themselves in the large cities . . . but what are the few large cities, what do the million Westernized Chinese signify in comparison with the millions of villages, in comparison with the hundreds of millions of peasants who still today live as in Confucius' time?[318]

On a pilgrimage to Taishan, one of the five sacred Taoist mountains of China, in Shandong Province, Katz muses on the rise and fall of the dynasties, on the momentary low point of a curve "that hereafter turns upward with the same regularity. The Chinese people probably bear this insight semi-consciously in its soul, and probably for that reason it toils on so unswervingly and imperturbably, while brigands and generals compete to extort from it the yield of its labor. . . ."[319] In Peking, then called Peiping, Katz strolls along dusty Legation Street (where many foreign representations have their offices), which seems so cavernously empty after the loss of the title *China's capital city.* On his trip to the Great Wall, the Prague journalist runs up against the realization that there must be a connection between the five-thousand-year-old culture and the sterile landscape. The unique, self-contained culture of the Chinese plain would not be imaginable without the forbidding mountain ridges that protect it from the North.

For Katz, it is a proven fact that the old China was significantly more democratic than Western scholars often assumed. In the West, people invented false conceptions about the China of the Imperial period, which the present Chinese government (around 1930) further eroded:

> Now selfish generals rule over China more absolutely than any Emperor ever did, and behind the mask of the Republic stands a military dictatorship that precludes any intervention by the people in the government. . . . It was the tragic error of the Western educated Chinese physician Sun Yat-sen that he thought he could bring his people freedom with this constitution and instead brought civil war. Now Chinese students talking politics are repeating his error in that they want to destroy the old culture of their people without having taken from the new one more than horn-rimmed spectacles and golf trousers.[320]

Attending theater performances stimulates Katz to reflect on the different value conceptions of the Chinese compared to those of Europeans: "The lad who masculinizes as a field commander or acts girlishly satisfies Chinese taste along the same lines as the Pekingese puppy that resembles a [Chinese guardian] lion, or the goldfish with a dragon's head." Under the title "Enjoyable China Notes" he describes phenomena that are very hard for a Western mind to understand, and he sees the three enemies and dangers of the white man in China embodied in the pidgin expressions "chit" (bill), "maski" (all the same), and "squeeze" (squeeze out money).

Thereby Katz again finds himself rather on the level of the majority of the average Old China Hands. Even an entire year of travel in Asia does not bring him personally significantly nearer to China, regardless of how much the man from Prague tries: "A year suffices to recognize the danger. They are too different here in the Far East. My good yellow friends who come to the pier to bid me farewell would become my enemies if I remained with them my life long. . . . It is a matter for us of the differences in thinking and feeling. We could no more overcome this in a decade than in a year. For it has developed over millennia. . . . Therefore, it is better that he departs. To people of his own sort. . . "[321] It is not just among foreign cultures and peoples that one can feel like an outsider, as is shown by Richard Katz's subsequent fate: "People of his own sort" will force him to return to Czechoslovakia in 1933, and seven years later immigrate to South America. Only many years later does he return to Europe, where he passes away in Switzerland in 1968.

A life fate similar to that of Katz characterizes *Arthur Holitscher,* born in Budapest in 1869. He is also described in the *Biographical Handbook of German-Speaking Emigration after 1933* as an author and journalist, he also chooses Switzerland (1934) as the ultimate destination of his flight from the Nazis, and he likewise stays for only a short period—three months in 1926—as a traveling observer of revolutionary conditions in China. In contrast to Richard Katz, Holitscher engages himself politically, which finds enduring expression in his travel chronicle, *Das unruhige Asien* (Restless Asia), published in the same year.[322] After completing secondary school, Holitscher works as a bank employee in Croatian Fiume, which at the time belongs to the Hapsburg monarchy. He follows this with stays in Vienna, Paris, Rome, Berlin, Brussels, and Heidelberg. At the start of the twentieth century, he lives for five years in bohemian circles in Munich. Later he acquires a special reputation through his travel reports from the United States, *Amerika heute und morgen* (America Today and Tomorrow, Berlin 1912) as a new kind of author oriented to politics and culture. Deeply shaken by the horrors of the First World War, he becomes a radical pacifist and socialist. In 1921 he takes part in the Third Congress of the Comintern in Moscow. "Never a member of the KPD, Arthur Holitscher was guided by personal, ethical and pacifist principles to adopt a general emancipatory, socialist outlook," states the 1983 *International Biographical Dictionary of Central European Emigrés*.[323]

A relatively progressive attitude also characterizes his reportage from the Middle Kingdom, which Holitscher—like Richard Katz—entered from the "Achilles heel" of Hong Kong and that immediately fascinates him:

> Uphill meandering funeral procession, downhill meandering marriage procession, round-about the colorful, densely packed turmoil and confusion of the narrow lanes and mountain paths bearing a thousand banners, waving placards, golden, lacquer black, alizarin, in the morning sun, whose rays glide upwards along the labyrinthine paths of the high mountain flanks—this is China, my first morning in Hong Kong, the first, unforgettable day in the legendary Middle Kingdom, empire of the dethroned son of heaven, of earthly reason placed on the throne.[324]

From his not always unbiased perspective, Holitscher gazes across the panorama of "these children, the Chinese, this ancient, inexhaustible, lively, irrepressible people!" He enjoys the extravagant play of light, sound intensity, luminosity, and noise, puzzles over the facial features and respectively the "folk character" behind them. "They are not exactly hostile, their laughing and smiling is not evil or scornful, but one feels among them not untroubled and does not go, as in Agra, as in Benares, dreaming and beatified through the streets." Holitscher's travel destinations are limited to a few cities, to Hong Kong, Macao, Canton, Shanghai, Suzhou, and Peking. In the former Portuguese colony he is a witness of scenes in gambling dens, while in Canton, the city on the Pearl River, he watches the "red parade," not without offering comparisons with similar events in the Soviet capital.

In an effort to improve his understanding of the political situation, he obtains information in discussions with Borodin. He learns from him, for example, that communism was for the Chinese synonymous with "decent, clean government" or that America's attempts to exert influence, in contrast to those of Russia, merely had effects on the fringes of the population. Thoughts of this sort intermingle in his book with a characterization of the Chinese as a "sagacious, inscrutably unsentimental people." He views the "yellow peril" as a bugbear of the European bourgeoisie and a reaction, as a distraction from the fear of China, the "fateful country of the Eastern world, the birthplace of a new world order."[325]

In the "Chicago of the East," as Holitscher calls Shanghai, he fumes at Europeans who do not want to learn the truth about the people in whose midst they live or about the mixed police troops that guard them. They know that it would be a matter of life or death, "as soon as the lurking dragon monster of the Chinese people merely stirs all around and that a blow of its paw could knock down and crush the whole foreign people into a bloody pulp."[326] Peking—Holitscher calls the city the "Jerusalem of the celestial Middle Kingdom"—receives the Hungarian-Jewish loner at the New Year's Celebration that announces itself through the racket of firecrackers, and permits the Chinese, he thinks, to settle accounts—both worldly and celestial. Together with a friend, he visits markets, as well as the Lama and Confucius temples. He concludes that should his friend ever return to Europe, he would die of homesickness: "In many cases he dies physically, even before the spirit has found enough time to properly reflect on the pain caused by the sudden separation from the mythically strange, mysteriously absorptive people of the Far East."[327]

Holitscher dedicates his final glimpse of China to the goal apparently strived for by all Chinese, both the "nervous, decadent Southern Chinese" and the "strong, big-boned Northern Chinese," that "has seized the enormous empire, the four-hundred-and-fifty million and hurled it forward, pressed it upwards along the path of the future." It was merely a few reactionary instincts of the Chinese, according to Holitscher, that impeded, but could not stop this great "epochal idea" of liberation from the yoke of the past. These were "avarice, barbarous disregard for the suffering of the neighbor, corruption and predatory militarism."[327] Three months sufficed for Holitscher to see how thoroughly: "The Chinese have lost their religion and morals today. The veneration of the sages, the fathers of the Chinese concept of morals, is only an empty form, its content long since vanished."[329] Yet such flaws in no way shake Holitscher's conviction that China would continue to exist, to remain China. "[T]he millennia old empire that has gone through all forms of civilization, politics and morals, freedom, slavery, all divine, human, animal and again divine stages of the embryo of humanity without perishing, without having to give up one iota of its inborn power and glory."[330]

"Hard country. Fare-thee-well China," are the concluding comments in the reportage of Arthur Holitscher, a man who lived to see some of his books publicly burned by the Nazis in 1933, and later became himself a political refugee. The exiled and penniless author and journalist for among others the newspapers *Internationale Literatur*, *Neue Deutsche Blätter*, and *Aufbau* dies in a Salvation Army home in Geneva in 1941.

VI. PHYSICIANS

In the Western reportage on the fate of China in times of war and revolution, the physicians' guild plays a significant role. Names like Norman Bethune or George Hatem stand for all those professional colleagues who gave up their Western lives in order to devote themselves to relieving the hardship and misery in the wake of the Chinese tragedy in the years of the Japanese occupation. Many of these medically trained helpers originally came from a Jewish milieu and placed themselves more or less voluntarily in the service of the Chinese cause. Before their arrival in the Middle Kingdom, quite a few had served as doctors caring for the wounded on the side of the Republican government during the Spanish Civil War. Among these so-called Spanish doctors was *Fritz Jensen*, born Friedrich Albert Jerusalem in Prague on December 26, 1903. The family—his father originates from Bohemia, his maternal ancestors from Hungary—is regarded as prosperous and very liberal. Even before little Friedrich starts school, they move to Vienna, where he is soon attracted to politics by the social convulsions of the pre-war and war periods. On the heels of the Hapsburg monarchy's fall, economic distress, and the related domestic political tensions, the population also radicalizes. Under the influence of the journalist Karl Kraus, Friedrich increasingly sympathizes with the causes of leftist movements. Between 1923 and 1929, the young man studies medicine with the famous anatomy professor Julius Tandler, who will later also flee to China. The right-wing terror moves Friedrich Jerusalem to join the Austrian Communist Party late in 1929 and become a member of the Union of Proletarian-Revolutionary Writers of Austria, founded in 1930.

After the failed Nazi Putsch in Vienna on July 25, 1934, the Nazis arrest and imprison Fritz Jensen—he has in the meantime adopted this name. Almost a year passes before his release from the Wöllersdorf concentration camp (KZ). After a brief intermezzo as the head of a private medical practice in Vienna, he leaves his homeland, first for Spain, where he works as the Head Physician of the XIIIth International Brigade. Following Franco's victory, he journeys to China from Liverpool on May 20, 1939, on board an old freighter bound for Hong Kong. He thereby joins the group of wandering Jews who, because of the worldwide socio-political upheavals, fought as voluntary medical helpers against fascism, Nazism, and Japanese militarism.

Jensen's first encounter with the Middle Kingdom, in the areas under Chiang Kai-shek's control, is sobering. In his own words "cold and heartless": "From the warm solidarity and flaming internationalism with which the Spanish people had received us, we came abruptly into the iciness of a Chinese civil servant atmosphere. Thus it came about that I, seduced by my own political and human inadequacy, suspected a Chinese characteristic in the cold that struck us, instead of recognizing in it the easily wounded pride of the 'Hsiau Hschien Hscheng' (the 'small gentlemen'), who were only a thin upper layer of the 'better society.'"[331] Jensen initially works on behalf of the China Defense League for the Chinese Red Cross in the province of Guizhou, then in southern Jiangxi for the Gong Ho movement of the New Zealander Rewy Alley, and at the same time as the family physician of Chiang Ching-kuo (Jiang Jingguo), Chiang Kai-shek's eldest son.[332] At the latest in 1943, higher aims bring him to Chongqing, where he at least gets a chance to talk with Zhou Enlai and the writer Guo Moruo. He also meets his future wife there, the partisan Wang Wu'an.[333] Shortly before the war ends, Jensen, who in the opinion of an American professional colleague, is a man devoted to making the world a better place, works for the British Red Cross in the provinces of Yunnan, Guizhou, and Guangxi. Later he serves with UNRRA in the frame of fighting cholera, and again in Chongqing, although he has long since had his fill of the Kuomintang government's pervasive corruption and inefficiency. Only later does he manage, like many others, to obtain a position in the areas "liberated" by the communists in Jiangsu Province: as an advisor on questions of medical and social care for the China Liberated Areas Relief Association (CLARA). After this, he spends the period before returning to Europe in December 1947—Jensen resided for eight years in the Middle Kingdom—primarily in the communist area:

> Heroism had become a mass phenomenon here. The most convincing was not the shining heroism, visible from afar, of the assault on the enemy position, but rather the incalculable courage in a milieu of scarcity, the gray heroism that lived on two bowls of rice a day, that clad itself day and night in the same coat lined with cotton wadding, that was only protected from the icy cold of Northern China by a small charcoal pan, that with frozen fingers painted the ornamental characters of important state decrees on crude, home-made paper.[334]

In the year the PRC is founded, Jensen's work *China siegt* (China Triumphs, 1949) is brought out by a Viennese publishing house. At the time, Europeans have little interest in the Middle Kingdom, and Jensen writes as a leftist who reveals comparatively little about his own personal impressions and encounters. Nevertheless, his comments offer the reader valuable insights about China that, even more than half a century later, are still worth reading. Once again, this shows how in their contact with the Orient individual Europeans have felt themselves challenged to self-reflection, to thinking about their own position in the world and in this country. Thus, e.g., on a deserted path leading past trackless mountain chains and luxuriant rice fields, Jensen, the Jewish intellectual from Central Europe, encounters a Chinese peasant, bent under a heavy burden, who is afflicted with a serious eye ailment. The usual pity stirs in the relatively well-off Jensen, and then suddenly the old Chinese begins to laugh at the foreigner with his long, funny nose. The latter is confused, but then he starts to understand:

> I saw myself with the eyes of a Chinese. . . . Instead of the pity I wanted to feel, envy crept into my heart. The old peasant with his heavy burden and his emaciated body was at least at home, was not out of the ordinary and knew the paths.

> From the translation of what he said, I recognized the pity that he, despite my good clothing and my seemingly high position, felt for me, and I, who was ready to feel sorry for him, accepted his laughter and his sympathy as deserved. I was a stranger and his natural enemy. My presence in a troop of soldiers seemed to the old peasant to be proof that I had been sucked in by an evil wind from better circumstances into a depth at which I could not find my bearings. I suddenly understood what a difficult step a Chinese has to make before he can disregard the externality of a European and recognize him as his equal.[335]

Jensen does not remain in Vienna, where the winds carried him after his return to Europe. In 1953, he returns to Asia, this time as a correspondent. He reports on the armistice in Korea, the changes in China, and the first war in Indochina. In 1955, he receives an assignment to report from Peking as a commentator for the communist *Volksstimme* (People's Voice) in Vienna and the SED (the Socialist Unity Party was the governing party of the GDR from 1949 until 1990) mouthpiece *Neues Deutschland* (New Germany) on the Afro-Asian countries' conference in Indonesian Bandung. However, his plane, the "Kashmir Princess," does not reach its destination: The flight, in which Premier Zhou Enlai is supposed (mistakenly) to be traveling, crashes over the ocean—very probably due to an act of sabotage, carried out on behalf of the Kuomintang secret service. As a legacy of the deceased, the volume *Opfer and Sieger* (Victims and Victors, 1955) appears posthumously with free adaptations, fiction, and reports by the temperamental author Fritz Jensen, who—as stated in the foreword—did all he could for "his great cause."[336]

Likewise a "Spanish doctor," another Austrian, *Walter Freudmann*, reaches China only a few months later than Jensen (although the two never met). Little is known about his younger years. He also studies medicine and presumably belonged to the Austrian communist party.[337] In his 1947 book *Tschi-Lai!—Erhebet Euch* (Rise up), he reports on his experiences as a doctor in China and Burma in the years 1939–45.[338] His preparation for the "riddle of Asia, the depths of the ancient Chinese culture" is likewise comparatively modest; he explains to the astonished embassy women of the Kuomintang representation in London: "We want to help the Chinese people in the difficult hours of the war in whatever way doctors can."[339] On the luxury liner to China it quickly turns out that Freudmann and his friends hardly fit in with the businessmen, missionaries, and colonial adventurers who are his fellow travelers. Arriving in Hong Kong, one of his visits is to Madame Sun, whose warmth toward the Austrian remains unforgettable: "We experienced that true human greatness is able to get along without any externality. Her own actions, the self-sacrificing activity that animated her whole being, inspired us more to be active for China than all the speeches we had heard till then."[340]

Freudmann works in almost the same places as his compatriot Jensen: In Chongqing, at the Chinese Red Cross headquarters in the province of Guizhou, at the front in Hunan, in Hubei as well as Jiangxi, and finally in the southwestern province of Yunnan. Freudmann's records are significantly more personal than Jensen's, even if they have no less political content. He also has similar experiences with the prevailing economic mismanagement in the areas controlled by the Kuomintang: a constant struggle against bureaucracy; the misappropriation by officers of the food rations of the living, dying and sick; the forced recruitment of peasants as soldiers; the disguise of a brothel as a hospital; and the great indifference to everyday misery. Despite such adversities, Freudmann can achieve something with his work, supervising sanitary measures, training nurses, introducing inoculations, and setting up delousing stations. His criticism of the Chinese public health system culminates in biting irony and sarcasm. For example, in his report on a visit to a division infirmary: "The inhumanity that came to expression in the picture that offered itself would have fit better in a German concentration camp than in an institution that is called an infirmary. . . . Each of them [the patients—author's note] had his free ticket for ascension to heaven in his pocket."[341]

It is first in China's war capital of Chongqing that Freudmann becomes aware of admirable Chinese characteristics:

> It was a beautiful, warm evening and we decided to return to the hotel on foot. Seductively the colorfully illuminated street scene lured us, colored oil lamps, lanterns and electrical light fixtures. Street vendors prepared quick dishes in portable ovens. Everywhere there is a captivating crowd of people and lively, cheery babble of voices. On this evening China first seemed to us—Chinese.[342]

Part of this picture is also the rickshaw coolies running about "like automatons," whereby the exploitation is clearly visible, or the "children covered beyond recognition with scratches and scabs." Like Jensen upon his encounter with the hunchbacked peasant, Freudmann also feels a need for self-criticism: "We felt the glances of hundreds of young girls and boys resting upon us, often distrustful glances. We saw ourselves suddenly in ugly, worn European street clothes that in themselves bore the stigmata of European crimes against Chinese."[343]

Besides the social misery, in an almost poetic tone he also describes his atmospheric encounters with the Chinese landscape, the burial mounds scattered everywhere, the desolate temples, and the simple village life:

> The view of the squalid human habitations depressed us. In the muted stillness of the rural evening, the nearly derelict temples, with their harmoniously sloping gable roofs, their fantastic and varied, even if faded figures and ornaments, radi-

> ated an unforgettable magic. Just as unique and unforgettable was also the impression of the village streets in the evening, where on the edge of the sidewalk in front of almost every hut, smoking chips were stuck in joints in the irregular paving or in cracks in the walls of houses that threw a fantastic flickering light on the edifices.[344]

It is as though Freudmann wants to recover a bit from the horrors of a war he experiences as extraordinarily barbarous, simply through nearness to the Chinese landscape:

> How glorious it was to walk through the Chinese landscape again after the confining and excruciating days. . . . The delicate colors of the silver shimmering rice fields, the dreamy lines of the villages exerted a strange, almost lyrical charm. I inhaled; the entire landscape seemed just to have been wafted there, to be of indescribable lightness. It shimmered like a cloud in white light. It enticed one to quixotic hopes.[345]

Freudmann accompanies the reader to the old Chinese institution of a touring company that has set up a marionette theater in a marketplace:

> A crowd of people, children and many adults bunched together around a little stage, only half a meter wide, and followed the masterfully presented play of the small, delicate dolls and puppets that performed scenes from an ancient Chinese opera. . . . This place, whose atmosphere spoke to us so poetically, in which people lived with an entirely other bearing than in the large cities, showed us that the technology of Western civilization with its revolutionary institutions would still need a long time to penetrate the dusky endlessness of the Chinese space.[346]

Freudmann also makes every effort to get a transfer to the "liberated areas," but in contrast to Jensen, he does not succeed in making his services available to communist military units. In the wake of American efforts to win back Burma, he instead receives an assignment in 1942 to the theater of war there, to help train the Chinese army medical corps. It is clear to him that quite a number of Kuomintang generals have collaborated with the Japanese. Although he knew "that Europe had risen up against fascism, against the oppressors of peoples, that the struggle against Hitler and Mussolini was at the same time a struggle against dictatorship, against inhumane and barbaric forms of government—the Chinese people were not allowed to learn anything about that."[347] The Austrian doctor concludes his historical survey in *Tschi-Lai!* with these prophetic words: "In rising numbers, the Chinese people are laying claim to a humane existence and there can be no doubt that no power will be able to stop the aspiring modern China on its path to full political and economic independence, democratization and social welfare."[348]

Magdalena Robitscher-Hahn, who was born in the Czech city of Karlsbad (Karlovy Vary) in 1899, lives to experience a tragic life fate. The daughter of a bourgeois family, the Sudeten German Jewish girl attends the Gymnasium in Karlsbad and then studies dentistry in Munich after the First World War. After further studies in Freiburg and Leipzig, she completes the program in 1922 and returns to Prague. However, the Czechs do not recognize her German diploma, so that she can only find a position as an assistant in a dental practice. She marries shortly after this but a few years later loses her husband to tuberculosis. Robitscher-Hahn must care for their son alone, and earns a doctorate at Charles University in Prague, in order to be able to open her own dental clinic in Czechoslovakia. At the same time, she is politically active, chiefly in anti-fascist organizations like the Universal Association for Peace, or as a member of the Bertolt Brecht Club. Soon Hitler's Germany threatens her homeland, initially by occupying the Sudetenland in October 1938, then by forcibly creating the Reich Protectorate of Bohemia and Moravia. Three days after the German occupation begins, she flees with her son across Holland, England, France, and Cuba to Bolivia, where she finds work. Then, however, a Nazi informer denounces her, and she is only permitted to give medical treatment to native Indios on a private basis.

After the defeat of the Third Reich, Robitscher-Hahn wants to return to her homeland, but as a German-speaking Jew, she is denied Czechoslovakian citizenship. With luck and personal engagement, the impoverished woman obtains a temporary position with UNRRA, which proposes that she move to Taiwan in order to set up a dental clinic there. After a few weeks, the undertaking fails, and she is transferred to the mainland. With the exception of her friendship with the Prague-born writer Egon Erwin Kisch, who wrote the book *Secret China* (1935), and reading Edgar Snow's works, she has little previous knowledge of China when she arrives in Shanghai in the spring of 1946. The liberated port city is swarming with American soldiers who, as she notes in her posthumously published memoirs, *Im Geist Yanans* (In the Spirit of Yan'an, 1980), seem anything but honorable.[349] As a foreigner in China she is also the "victim of a boundlessly unleashed curiosity . . . that one must escape." Peking seems to the European woman a "magical city": "Its fairytale buildings, roofs, palaces under the usually cloudless shrine of heaven, enlivened by dancing swallows, seem to belong to a sunken world."[350] Initially she works in Taiyuan, the provincial capital of Shanxi, which at the time (July 1946) is still controlled by the Kuomintang-loyal warlord Yan Xishan.[351]

Already on the journey from Peking to Taiyuan through the fruitful loess landscape, Robitscher-Hahn becomes aware that here she is experiencing more than the majority of the foreigners living in large cities. It also soon becomes clear to her that she is working "on the wrong side," because corruption is omnipresent, and the conditions in the hospital are catastrophic. In addition, she discovers to her horror that many of the Japanese working in the hospital may have participated in war crimes and that even disguised Nazis are prowling about there. She would like to reach the "liberated areas" as soon as possible, but civil war is imminent: In June 1946 George Marshall manages for the last time (in Manchuria) to persuade both sides to declare a cease-fire. A month later, this has already been broken. She succeeds in October of the same year in flying from Peking to Yan'an, into the Shaan/Gan/Ning border area, in the northern Shaanxi, Gansu, and Ningxia group of provinces.

The contrast with the Kuomintang area is obvious: No city walls with barbed wire, soldiers, and strict controls, to the contrary—remarkable for the European—numerous bookshops in which a few works of world literature are to be found, as for example Gorky's *The Mother* (1907): "The people here seem well-nourished, wear warm clothing, even if old and faded. I saw neither beggars nor neglected children, as everywhere else in China. On the walls I found hand-drawn posters, almost all opposed to American intervention." Robitscher-Hahn works in a so-called "international peace hospital," a designation for the rather simply equipped mobile medical centers with which between 1938 and 1948 a population of 140 million people was cared for in eleven provinces of Northern China. In addition, the European woman gives instruction on dental care in medical schools, above all in the area of oral hygiene. She herself lives in one of the cave dwellings common in that area: "Everything is incredibly primitive, as is not even common in South America. It is hard to describe how little the people here possess and how hard life is."

In November 1946, the Yan'an infirmary is evacuated, and attacks by Kuomintang troops are imminent. Robitscher-Hahn also goes along into the mountains, to Wayaobu, now called Zichang. The route is difficult, but the European woman feels "infinitely well" among the simple soldiers and peasants after packing takes place with "endless talk, so that you would think that nothing could ever come of it, and that is typical of China." She encounters especially "civilized behavior and human dignity . . . such as I have experienced nowhere else in the world."[352] On the march through valleys and along the mule tracks of the loess landscape, she has time to study the character of her companions. She praises the "deeply-rooted group feeling," the prevailing order that was created not through punishment, but rather through criticism and counter-criticism:

> In a much too long period that was rich in the feudal oppression of the people and in which the teachings of Confucius marked the lives of people . . . the Chinese people went through a process of cultural and civilizational maturation in

> which they, like pebbles in a mountain stream, were ground against one another; this, it seems to me, has pre-shaped them for collective labor and collectively living together.[353]

In the mountains of Shaanxi, she continues her work, makes daily school visits, and instructs students in dental care and in the principles of modern hygiene. The child mortality rate still amounts to 65 percent, which is largely attributable to the unsatisfactory hygiene prevailing in rural areas. Although it is far distant in time and space, she feels very closely linked to her homeland and not infrequently reflects on the Holocaust and all its horrors. It is understandable, therefore, that she feels tied to these strange people who are so grateful for all aid. To her son, studying in the United States, she writes candidly before her return to Yan'an and expresses the life feeling of a person without a homeland:

> My leave-taking from our mountain village and from my fellow workers was unsettling and I have, since I left Prague, never again felt such homesickness . . . Here there is no gossip, and the one is really the other's friend; consideration and benevolence are the slogans of all these people, and that by far offsets all the strange and sometimes also bad qualities (slower and more difficult logical thinking, primitivism of life conceptions, etc.). . . . I really believe that China could be a new homeland for us.[354]

Robitscher-Hahn never realizes her wish, although the Chinese invite her to remain there. UNRRA recalls her to Peking, where she receives another chance to fly back to Yan'an, but then she finally has to depart: Kuomintang troops occupy Yan'an on March 14, 1947. In a letter from Yan'an of March 5, 1947, she complains to her superiors about the great neglect of the liberated areas by the aid organization. She leaves the area controlled by the communists and starts a long journey in the neighboring province of Shanxi, through devastated landscapes, past poppy fields, and through Hebei. This last episode of her stay in China appears almost symptomatic for the subsequent sealing-off of the country against any foreign interference: "The young [soldier] looked at us with a hate-distorted face and glowing eyes. The last thing that I saw of the Red Army was this face."[355]

The return from the Far East to Europe is hard for the Sudeten German Jewess. Once again, she must fight for her citizenship: Three days after her arrival in Prague (in February 1948) the communists come to power in Czechoslovakia. She never obtains permission to leave the country again, does not see her son for more than fifteen years, and suffers a nervous breakdown. After that, she is transferred to the health service far away in the Bohemian-German border region. Only after her retirement in 1961 is she permitted to return to Prague. A year before this she writes in an application to the Czech Foreign Ministry of her "warmest wish to be able to visit China . . . again."[356] She waits for an answer in vain. During the 1968 Prague Spring, she takes advantage of a visit to Bavaria and never returns. She spends her final years in an old age home run by the Jewish community in Frankfurt, "grown lonely and alienated." On October 10, 1977, a life ends which, as she says herself, was "rich in disappointments and lost illusions."

VII. INDEPENDENTS AND FREELANCERS

With the designation "independents and freelancers," I distinguish a group of Western visitors from persons who came to China with a specific assignment. It is obvious that we cannot always clearly demarcate categories—overlaps sometimes reflect reality better than clearly defined boundaries. The Shanghai Municipal Police also had to deal with this phenomenon when it set up a file with the notation "secret" for a certain *Erwin Reifler*. "Dr. Reifler, Austrian, is believed to have arrived in Shanghai from Berlin during the early part of 1932. . . . According to French Police information, Reifler was in close touch with E. Kisch . . . during the latter's stay in Shanghai. . . . Dr. Reifler has the reputation of being a left-wing socialist without any communist leanings."[357] International concession detectives had not done their work ineptly; it had not escaped them that Reifler was a "capable China scholar" who had already in his young years occupied himself with the study of Oriental languages, especially Chinese. To be sure, at the time the officials could still not foresee that the history of modern linguistics would remember Reifler as a pioneer of computer-technology supported translation from Chinese into English.

Erwin Reifler, born in Vienna on June 16, 1903, develops his interest in the Far East in the private library of the legendary Austrian envoy Arthur von Rosthorn, who when China enters the First World War on the Allied side is declared a "persona non grata" by Peking and repatriated. In his native city, the assimilated Jew, for whom the faith of his fathers means considerably less than the language of his ancestors, studies, besides philosophy, classical and modern Chinese. In 1927, he concludes his studies with a dissertation on "State and Administration in Ancient China." On three occasions, he guides Chinese government delegations visiting the Danube city. At the start of the 1930s, he works as a translator for Chinese police officials who are continuing their studies at the Police Academy in Vienna. In 1932, Reifler finally departs for China, according to his wife, initially in order to open up markets there for the Bata shoe company, and after the project fails, to continue his scholarly career.[357] In Shanghai he teaches German at the noted Jiaotong University; he uses the opportunity to deepen his knowledge of Chinese and instructs a small group of interested foreigners in the basics of their host country's language. He uses the pictorial method, according to the conception that the simplest elements of Chinese script are pictograms. In contrast to journalists or doctors, he concentrates on the heart of the Chinese culture, the Chinese language. His interest in this area also includes comparative linguistics. He also seeks to learn more about Judaism from an Englishman, Rabbi Rev. Mendel Brown, the head of the Sephardic community of Shanghai and spiritual leader of the Ohel Rachel Synagogue. Two years later, he visits Hong Kong for further education, returns to Shanghai in 1939, and marries Mendel Brown's daughter, Henrietta.[359] When the Second World War breaks out in Europe, Reifler becomes stateless because he declines to accept a German passport. Because he had arrived in Shanghai before 1937, unlike most European refugees he does not have to live in the Hongkou "ghetto." Reifler and his wife reside at Avenue Roi Albert (now Shaanxi Nan Lu) No. 188, where he enjoys Chinese society and ambitiously continues his studies in comparative linguistics: "The Sinic and the Semitic Languages" is the title of a 1940 contribution for *Israel's Messenger,*[360] in which he compares (classical) Chinese and Hebrew. Right at the start, with a reference to *Genesis*, Chapter 10 (the Table of Nations), he mentions the possibility that not only the Hebrews, but also the Chinese could stem from Noah and introduces the well-known arguments that emphasize the commonalities in the ethical standards of both peoples.[361]

Reifler does not challenge such comparative methods, but rather in his own research seeks sources of scientific knowledge outside the *Bible*. Thereby comparative linguistics seems to him to be quite promising. Above all he is interested in vocabulary comparisons and less in grammar. He determines that Hebrew and Chinese words—stemming from a common source—frequently agree fairly well in pronunciation and meaning. "If the results of my researches into this particular field of comparative philology should prove to be correct, I shall be very glad not only to have been able to contribute my little share in proving the accuracy of the *Bible* report but also to have done a little bit in improving the attitude and understanding of the descendants of the ancient Hebrews towards their Far Eastern brothers to the greater honour of God and to the advantage of mankind and in the interests of peace."[362] Research on the etymology of Chinese characters is another of Reifler's hobbies, whereby he does not shy away from drawing parallels to other languages. As "Professeur de Sinologie à l'Université de l'Aurore," he writes a contribution for the bulletin of this French educational institution in Shanghai in 1944. He tries to convince the reader that certain types of words in classical

Chinese, such as pronouns, interrogatives, or also vocalizations, in contrast to the conception of many linguists, should not be understood according to the over-simplifying "borrowing" theory, but rather as independent words with various meanings.

On November 19, 1940, at the invitation of the American Junior Chamber of Commerce in Shanghai, Erwin Reifler gives a lecture on the topic of "The Much Misrepresented Chinese Language—A Revolutionary Approach." The public receives his report so well that the Chamber of Commerce decides to hire him to teach evening courses on the Chinese language. In the advertising for the eighteen-month course, the stated aim is to teach students Chinese in a manner so interesting that "an educated foreigner can easily go beyond the usual standard coolie Chinese" usually taught by private tutors. The "Reifler Method," which is used in these "High Speed Chinese Language Classes," takes into account the fact that: "Students [are] adults with a logical intellect and not children with excellent memory."[363] Up until his departure from China in 1947 and beyond this, Reifler maintains close contacts with Sinologists from Dehergne to Needham to Wittfogel, to whom he ultimately owes his permission to enter—with a so-called non-quota visa—the United States.

Among specialists, the name Erwin Reifler is closely linked with the so-called Chinese-English Machine Translation Project, on which he worked starting with his debut as a professor in the Far Eastern Department of the University of Washington in Seattle—and after 1956 as the director of this translation project. This project received financing from the Rockefeller Foundation and later the U.S. Air Force. Initially, it worked on computer-supported translations from German into English, then from Russian into English, until finally Chinese also attracted sufficient attention on the side of the relevant political circles. The idea originally consisted in making Chinese scientific-technical publications as easily accessible as possible to the respective specialists in the United States. After composing the final report in September 1962, Reifler increasingly entertains hopes of obtaining a professorship at a university on the East Coast in order to be able to pursue his, in the last few years, increasing interest in the history of metrology, the science and system of weights and measures. But this wish is not to be fulfilled. In 1965, just sixty years old, this man of many outstanding qualities dies in Seattle, where he had worked for so many years.

While for Reifler, the writing system has great significance for the social cohesion of Chinese society, for *Olga Abramovna Lang* the family social system is what, despite the multiplicity of dialects and even languages, plays an integrative role in the great empire. Olga, born in 1898 in Russian Yekaterinoslav, today Ukrainian Dnepropetrovsk, grew up in a socialist Jewish family. She studied Russian and European history and literature during the First

World War in the city that was then still called Petrograd (St. Petersburg) and was also active in the "Socialist-Revolutionary Party."[364] After further studies in Moscow and work for the All-Union Central Council of Trade Unions, Olga Lang journeys to Germany in spring 1927 in order to live with her husband. There she develops a gift for the observation of societal processes that later also distinguishes her in the Middle Kingdom.

Olga Lang works as a reporter for the Soviet labor union newspaper *Trud* and occasionally as a freelancer for other Russian newspapers. She reports on the political-economic situation in Germany, on the workers' fate, about which she writes a book that is published in Moscow in 1932 with the title *Bilder deutscher Arbeiter* (Pictures of German Workers). Her first marriage soon comes to an end, and in a restaurant on Potsdamer Platz in Berlin, she meets the already famous social scientist and communist Karl August Wittfogel, whom she marries in 1929. Together with and through Wittfogel, a combative anti-Nazi, she is increasingly pulled into the maelstrom of political events in Germany. She joins the communist party and works as an assistant at the Soviet Embassy, helping to analyze German newspapers. Following Hitler's takeover of power, Wittfogel, who had hoped to avoid arrest by fleeing abroad, is taken into custody and sent to a concentration camp. Olga calls on friends at home and abroad to help free her husband from the clutches of the Gestapo. After nine months—she apparently found shelter with Brecht and Kokoschka in this period—Wittfogel is released. The two depart as quickly as possible, first to England, then to China (Wittfogel obtains a position at Columbia University in New York and regularly travels from there to the Middle Kingdom to supplement his research work on Chinese society with studies on site).

Little is known of Olga Lang's life in China (1934–1937). She appears to have worked chiefly in Peking and made excursions to Wutai Shan, one of the four most sacred mountains of Buddhism, to Taiyuan, Tianjin, Shanghai, Wuxi, Fujian, and Guangdong. In pictures from those days we see Olga standing in front of ancient temples, on a donkey ride, at a picnic, on the steps of Yanjing University—usually in the company of Western friends, occasionally also together with Chinese faces, for example, with the scholar Hu Shi. She also learns written and spoken Chinese. Because she is interested in the family as the core of Chinese society, Olga Lang adopts the concept of "Oriental society" from her husband and mentor as an aid in doing her field research. Lang concentrates her efforts on the complicated transformation process set in motion within a specific domain (the family) by Western influence on a "civilized Oriental country." The results of her lengthy studies appear under the title *Chinese Family and Society,* published by Yale University Press in 1946.[365] Despite traditions surviving from the past, she concludes that hardly any corners of the immense empire have not been caught up in the new currents. It is clear to her that in the future the Confucian image of the old-style family, which even in the past was never realized in its ideal form, will have to be regarded in a different light.

In the year the Sino-Japanese war breaks out, Lang leaves the Middle Kingdom and settles in the United States. During the Second World War—her marriage to Wittfogel ends in 1939—she works for the Department of Defense translating texts into Russian and helps soldiers prepare for their service in Asia. After the war, she again works as a translator at the Nuremberg Trials and then studies Chinese and Japanese at Columbia University. She writes her doctorate on one of the best-known Chinese authors of the twentieth century: Ba Jin, originally Li Yaotang, who due to his intellectual proximity to Russian anarchism uses as his pseudonym Ba Jin (a combination of *Ba*kunin and Kropot*kin*). That she chose this important author for her work was by no means accidental. It was after all he who exerted great influence on young readers and intellectuals of that time, on just those persons whom she so often encounters during her years of studying the Chinese family, and whose novel *The Family* (1931) had made his literary breakthrough. Olga Lang's book appears in 1967 under the title *Pa Chin and his Writings*.[366]

Even though *The New York Times* calls Lang's book a "brilliant biography,"[367] she never gets a chance to teach a course on the Chinese language and culture at her new academic home, Swarthmore College in Pennsylvania, whose students include many Jewish immigrants. Instead, she teaches Russian language and literature until 1968, after which she returns to New York, where she dies in 1992—reclusive and lonely. Martin Ostwald, professor for Classical Philology and Lang's colleague at Swarthmore, recalled that she could quote Pushkin's poem *Yevgeny Onegin* almost entirely by heart: "Of all the émigrés on the faculty, the most interesting—and most difficult—was Olga. . . . She was a Mensch, . . . a civilized human being."[368]

"I like the Chinese!" is the caption of a caricature that shows a cheery group of young and old Chinese heads that the artist *Friedrich Schiff* lightheartedly drew during his seventeen-year stay in China. Like his somewhat older compatriot Reifler, Schiff was also born in Vienna. Although Schiff was often considered the best known "Chinese Austrian," in contrast to Reifler he came to the Far East by chance. Born in 1908, he probably inherited his artistic sensitivity, openness to the world, and love of adventure: His father, a gifted portrait painter, was also a free thinker who had converted from Judaism to Catholicism; his mother, Regina Eibenschütz, was the daughter of the Budapest Synagogue's Cantor. Frederick, as Schiff was later to call himself, attends the Graphic Academy and Research Institute before gaining admission to the Viennese Academy of Fine Arts at the age of sixteen. Already in his youth, the boy acquires a reputation as a talented portraitist of famous and less famous people.

By traveling to China on the Trans-Siberian Railroad in 1930, Schiff seems to be expressing a desire to escape the narrowness of the now relatively small Alpine republic and to find elsewhere the cosmopolitanism lost by the former Imperial and Royal Hapsburg monarchy. With its large-city atmosphere and its contradictions, in the coming years the cosmopolitan city of Shanghai in every regard offers the somewhat more than twenty-year-old artist sufficient material for a very personal way of dealing with China:

> If one wants to paint the portrait of this city, one must do so with the most contrasting colors, and to every spot of color that one puts on the canvas, immediately add the complementary color. For this city, and the life in it, consists in the sharpest contrasts: Here there are luxury apartment houses furnished with all the achievements of modern technology. . . . Right next to them live coolies in the most primitive of dwellings. Under the straw roofs of the sampans, the hundreds of narrow houseboats that press against the shore, people are born, and they die on the cramped decks without ever having known another home. . . . Here there was ancient wisdom and alongside it an almost bestial degeneration or ruthless grubbing and chasing after material goods.[369]

What other Western residents of the Huangpu metropolis overlook or try to describe in articles and books, the painter and caricaturist Schiff tries to represent visually. By means of deftly produced sketches, watercolors, and—less often—oil paintings, he conveys to the observer a gallery of impressions of Republican China, chiefly of Shanghai, but also of Peking and Hong Kong. Like others, he is also aware that in the 1930s money alone dictates life in the Huangpu metropolis; especially as an artist, he is dependent on customers. The Viennese Schiff shares this insight, and his subsequent engagement as a creator of caricatures and an advertising designer for Western concerns, with Shanghai's most famous cartoonist, the Russian Sapajou (Georgii Avksentievich Sapojnikoff). Schiff opens his own institute, the School of Applied Art, and designs prospectuses, invitations, menus, and other marketing items. He is in demand in almost all societal circles, and thanks to his diligence and restless activity soon begins to attract mention in Shanghai press gossip columns. In the "Maskee" (pidgin English for "never mind"), a club belonging to the Viennese Horst Riehmer, his paintings, such as the notorious "Miss Shanghai," have priority over menus and concert announcements. The Viennese artist belongs to the Shanghai nights, just as does the "Shanghai Girl" he created: sketches of a long-legged, slim, attractive Chinese woman who, according to Schiff himself, stands out with her "graceful figure, the slimness of her stature, her poised carriage and her beautiful aristocratic hands."[370] In

Figures 2.10–2.13
The Viennese Friedrich Schiff belonged to the Shanghai nights, just as does the "Shanghai Girl" he created. He intends his images of China to represent a specific worldview, a very personal relationship, indeed devotion and love for the country.

those years, Schiff's works appear not only in numerous exhibitions or as pictorial material in domestic and foreign newspapers and magazines, but also in travel books and as illustrations, for example, for the visual representation of the character of cities such as Peking or Hong Kong.

Schiff's subjects reflect the spirit of the times, as well as former *Lebeswelten* that, although belonging to the past, display the enduring characteristics of the Chinese spirit and value stances—or perhaps also what the Westerner generally understands by this. He captures everyday activities on paper in a manner that urgently shows the viewer that the literature on China in the West has for decades lived from sometimes quaint, sometimes sentimentalized, but above all, however, always catchy and falsifying subjects. There are the boys who are constantly at the service of the whites, the amahs, the compradors, the speculators, the flower girls. In Schiff's street scenes bicyclists, pushcarts, and funeral processions dominate. It is conspicuous how expertly the Viennese pictorially captures the Chinese knack for creating space by shifting life into the street. The 1930s "Paris of the Orient" exudes the charm of leisure entertainment, but also the dim light of the demimonde and the vices that Schiff also cannot avoid: With elegantly flung off strokes he toys with gracefully dancing beauties, overweight businessmen at casino gaming tables, panderers, and opium smokers. He documents poverty and exploitation with scenes of exhausted coolies, beggars, child labor, and prostitution. Thereby Schiff unmasks the suppressed to the viewer and puts him on a first-name basis with the adversity and misery of the impoverished classes.

Schiff is an amused, but at the same time, an incisive observer. He does not rebel like Arthur Holitscher with words, but he does render contours with brush and pencil. At times, he convincingly portrays arrogance (in whites) and malicious joy (in Chinese) in the faces he sketches with brisk strokes. Thereby he not only documents East-West mental states, but also holds up a mirror to the viewer. In the course of the years, his themes change. The Japanese bombs dropped on Shanghai in autumn 1937 also unsettle him; he records his impressions of the refugee catastrophe in a collection of sketches of Chinese children and mothers that arouses profound sympathy in the viewer.[371] Increasingly he also finds a subject for his creative ability in the Jewish immigrants, their treatment by the Japanese, the crimes of the occupation, and finally the victors. Schiff's pictures of China dispense with the Western stereotypes of the pre-war period that were common after 1945: The postcard subjects of the Viennese Jew—he explicitly considered himself to be one—include no rickshaw coolies. They are replaced by "heroic" soldiers who conquer the hearts of many a pretty Chinese girl.

With a caricature that in a humorous manner represents the end of Western dominance in China, Schiff takes leave of Shanghai in 1947 and moves to Buenos Aires, where he lives until 1953. In a talk on Chinese art, he presents the art of painting as a means of interpreting psychological differences between East and West:

> But it makes all the difference. For it is just this often criticised trait of the Westerner—that of pursuing restlessly and recklessly abstract conceptions of improvement—which gives him an immeasurable advantage over the Chinese in world-affairs. To live or if necessary to die for an idea, the success of which might enable others to benefit, means the height of the ludicrous to the ordinary Chinese mentality.[372]

Julius Tandler, whose portrait Schiff masterfully painted in China, is rightly given considerable space in Stadler's *Vertriebene Vernunft* (Expelled Reason).[373] Not only subsequent generations of Holocaust survivors, but also the Shanghai Municipal Police have understood this. They note in a February 1935 report, "Enquiries show that Julius Tandler, former professor of anatomy at the University of Vienna and former head of the Health Department in that city, arrived in China some time during the earlier part of 1933 on invitation of the Nanking Government as an expert. . . . , while in Shanghai they [Tandler and his assistant Bergmann—author's note] did not come to the notice of the Municipal Police in connection with political or any other undesirable activities."[374]

Tandler was born on February 16, 1869, in Jihlava, the former Moravian Iglau (in the Czech Republic between Bohemia and Moravia). The family moves to Vienna when young Julius is three. He grows up under humble circumstances, and his school performance is mediocre. In contrast, he completes his medical studies successfully and writes a dissertation on a medical topic. Like Schiff's father and many other Austrians, he converts from Judaism to Catholicism even before the turn of the century. During the First World War, he serves as the dean of the medical school in the capital city. Because of his great scientific expertise, the government employs him as an advisor for health questions and social welfare. He works first on the national, then on the municipal level, serving from 1920–34 as the Viennese City Councilman for the Welfare System and Social Administration. His thesis that "the people are the organic capital of the state" refers to the need for political action that he sees equally for the state and the medical profession. He himself becomes, in the meantime a member of the Social Democratic Party, a great "master-builder of 'red Vienna,'" and because of his innovations in the social system, a highly valued expert advisor for the League of Nations. He fights to protect the weak and disadvantaged. To be sure, there are also those who call him, despite his conversion, a Jew, Freemason, Marxist, or a denier of Christian values. As a university teacher, he is regarded as an authority figure, and he governs in an authoritarian manner.

The initial years of the "Austro-fascist dictatorship" probably affect Tandler more than he publicly admits. He, the physician and politician, requests a furlough from the Viennese city administration in order to accept an invitation from the Nationalist government in Nanking to aid China in setting up medical schools and facilities. At the start of his work in Shanghai in 1933, he serves as an anatomy teacher and reorganizes the medical curriculum. When proceedings are undertaken against him in connection with the prohibition of the Social Democratic Party in his homeland in the spring of 1934, Tandler, who is nearing retirement, wants to confront the authorities. To the astonishment of many in China, after his return to Europe he is promptly arrested. After his release, Tandler—in Austria despised, in China celebrated—returns to the Middle Kingdom. He again remains for several months, collects impressions and experiences, returns home, and departs on a third journey to the Far East. Finally at the start of 1936 he accepts an offer from the Soviet government to advise the authorities there on health policy (simultaneously he turns down an invitation from the Nanking authorities to set up a medical-military academy in China's capital). Unfortunately, he does not seem to relish Russian food and, as well, his heart condition worsens. The news agencies report his death in Moscow on August 25, 1936.[375]

Tandler records his legacy of Chinese experiences in a book he publishes in Vienna in 1935 with the simple title *Volk in China* (People in China).[376] In the foreword, the author modestly explains that his book is neither about China, nor about travel adventure, but merely about "experiences and adventures of a predominantly social nature, because a range of favorable opportunities granted me insight into these questions that are of general interest." Like many others, on his first visit to a Chinese city, presumably Shanghai, Tandler may have felt like this as he hurried through the streets in the midday sun:

> In the fog of unfamiliarity and of otherness, they promenade past me. Otherwise I read in people's faces joy, suffering, love and hate. Here I sense feelings in the mask-wearers' souls. They do not bare themselves to me, however. I cannot read the text of this poem of humanity, can scarcely recognize individual letters, but the melody remains completely closed to me. I saw them working, eating, heard them speaking, all the sounds reaching me through the mysterious fog of complete foreignness. I have of course already been in other countries where foreign people used languages that were incomprehensible to me. But I read their sorrow and their joy. I have seen poverty and have understood it, have shared in foreign suffering in the understanding harmony of my own soul. Here it is different. The bodily misery, insofar as it reveals itself to the doctor—that

> I have doubtless recognized. The tone of these patient sufferers' souls has remained incomprehensible to me.[377]

China an eternal riddle? The Chinese as actors who calculatingly deny the crazy foreigner access to their interior life in order to intentionally repel foreign influences? One is almost tempted to believe this. Tandler tries to understand by looking behind the coulisses and does not linger in the narrowness of the foreign concessions. He records with precise statistics the population density of the great empire that so dramatically decreases from East to West. He investigates a fateful aspect of Chinese history, the fact that the people never undertook to tame and breed horses and cattle (for this reason, large tracts of arable land remained uncultivated). He locates, as did Mao Zedong later, the chief problem of the country's economic development in the impoverishment of the peasantry by existing property ownership and tenancy relationships. He comments on illiteracy, acknowledges progress in the government's social experiments, and studies the occupational groups of workers, artisans, and coolies. During a trip on the Grand Canal, which once linked Peking to Hangzhou, he gazes in amazement at this bold structure, constructed thousands of years ago as a means, not an end: "No man speaks of this. There is no kowtowing before technology in this country. . . . Here people live through, and by doing, the work their ancestors did, work, are happy and suffer, just as did their productive ancestors." In the twilight, he sees mute, ghostly sails flit by and the pale landscape with its doleful burial mounds. Upon his arrival in the city of Tai-Chow (Taizhou) he is led through dark, narrow alleyways: "Never will I forget this nocturnal march through the city, the walls of yellow faces with the lively sockets of curious eyes. I thus had a certain delinquent feeling of the intruder in myself."[378] Finally, Tandler dedicates a chapter to the healthcare system, sees in the ancestor cult the reason for the population explosion and finally predicts the future of a country that could lastingly affect the rest of the world. "World history, however, is taking place on the Pacific Ocean and on its coasts and will be decisive for the fate of all mankind. Blinded by the petty quarrels in Europe, those responsible do not see what is preparing to happen among the millions of the peoples of Asia."[379]

NOTES

1. George Sokolsky, 1956 typescript, pp. 1–10, in: George E. Sokolsky Collection, Oral History Collection, Columbia University.
2. Letter from Sok to Eugene Chen, May 4, 1923, in: Hoover Archives, George Sokolsky Collection, Box 35 (Correspondence).

3. William Henry Donald, who lived in China from 1904 on, was one of Chiang Kai-shek's numerous foreign advisors, and apart from Owen Lattimore probably the most famous.

4. Sokolsky, *We Jews* (1935), p. xi, or respectively xiv.

5. Letter from Sok to John B. Powell, September 14, 1921, in: Hoover Archives, George Sokolsky Collection, Box 97.

6. Letter from Sok to T. V. Soong, July 9, 1928, in: Hoover Archives, George Sokolsky Collection, Box 108.

7. Letter from Sok to T. V. Soong, April 9, 1930, in: Hoover Archives, George Sokolsky Collection, Box 108.

8. Letter from Sok to T. V. Soong, January 10, 1930, in: Hoover Archives, George Sokolsky Collection, Box 108.

9. Letter from Sok to T. V. Soong, April 9, 1931, in: Hoover Archives, George Sokolsky Collection, Box 108.

10. Among those who attributed a pro-Japanese attitude to Sokolsky were the two American journalists Thomas F. Millard and John B. Powell, who were both supportive of Kuomintang policies. Sokolsky probably had a few good contacts with Japanese politicians, especially with the moderate Foreign Minister Baron Kijuro Shidehara, but he never justified the Japanese attack on Shanghai in 1932 or Japan's war against China.

11. Cited in: Cohen, *Chinese Connection* (1978), p. 168.

12. Letter from Sok to T. V. Soong of October 7, 1932, Hoover Archives, George Sokolsky Collection, Box 108.

13. Letter from Sok to Hu Shi of September 12, 1930, Hoover Archives, George Sokolsky Collection, Box 64.

14. Letter from Sok to J. B. Powell of April 10, 1933, Hoover Archives, George Sokolsky Collection, Box 97.

15. Letter from Sok to Ludwik Rajchman of July 30, 1931, Hoover Archives, George Sokolsky Collection, Box 98.

16. Sokolsky, *Tinder Box* (1932), p. viii.

17. Letter from T. V. Soong to Sok of August 30, 1932, Hoover Archives, George Sokolsky Collection, Box 108.

18. Sokolsky, *Tinder Box* (1932), pp. 346.

19. Ibid., p. 342.

20. Asia, XXXII, December 1932, pp. 620–26.

21. Cohen, *Chinese Connection* (1978), p. 272.

22. George Sokolsky, Autobiography—Working Copy, (Miscellaneous Articles 1947–51), Columbia University, George E. Sokolsky Collection, Box 6.

23. Klingaman, *McCarthy Era* (1996), p. 344.

24. *The New York Times*, December 14, 1962, p. 16.

25. Cited from a letter by Harold Isaacs to Warren Cohen of October 24, 1972, in: MIT Archives, Harold R. Isaacs Papers, Box 29.

26. Peffer, *Chinese Philosophy of Life* (1927), pp. 431.

27. Ibid., p. 433.

28. Peffer, *What About China?* (1921), p. 591.
29. Peffer, *White Man's Dilemma* (1927), p. 292.
30. Peffer, *Death of Chinese Civilization* (1930), p. 499.
31. Peffer, *Collapse* (1930), p. 8.
32. *The New York Times*, November 7, 1943, *New York Times* Magazine, p. 7.
33. Ibid., p. 7.
34. *The New York Times*, November 14, 1948, p. 12.
35. *The New York Times*, August 10, 1952, p. SM11.
36. Ibid., p. SM43.
37. *The New York Times*, April 14, 1964, p. 37.
38. Folder: Poems, TRAVEL (for his 60th birthday) by Harold R. Isaacs, in: MIT Archives: Harold R. Isaacs Papers, Box 25.
39. Folder: Obituaries, 1986: In memory of Harold R. Isaacs, Poem WORDS read by Robert Isaacs, in: MIT Archives: Harold R. Isaacs Papers, Box 23.
40. Letter from Harold Isaacs to Maurice E. of October 11, 1951, in: MIT Archives: Harold R. Isaacs Papers, Box 27.
41. *The New York Times*, July 31, 1932, p. 7.
42. Memorandum by Isaacs of April 6, 1971, in: MIT Archives: Harold R. Isaacs Papers, Box 28.
43. The Comintern, also known as the Third International, was a communist international organization founded in Moscow in 1919 (and officially dissolved in 1943). Its relationship with the Chinese Communist Party was extremely complicated and—for many Chinese communists—painful or even tragic.
44. On the life of Agnes Smedley see, for example, Kinnon, *Agnes Smedley* (1989); Baruch Hirson wrote a biography of Frank Glass: Hirson, *Cecil Frank Glass* (sine anno). In the Stalin-Trotsky conflict, Glass bet on Trotsky and was consequently expelled from the South African communist party. In Shanghai he worked, among others, as a Tass correspondent, but also composed contributions for Powell's *China Weekly Review*. Until the end of his life (he died in Los Angeles in 1988), Glass remained a committed supporter of Trotsky, the Russian revolutionary who was assassinated in Mexico in 1940. Under the name Li Fu-ren (Li Fu-jen), Glass wrote several contributions to Trotskyite newspapers including *The Militant, New International, New Masses,* and *Fourth International*. The author is grateful to Professor Tom Grunfeld, Empire State College (SUNY), for access to this valuable document.
45. Letter from Hri to VR of June 5, 1931. All these letters (in the following: "Letters from Hri to VR") are courtesy of Peter Rand (Boston University).
46. Letter from Hri and VR of June 13, 1931.
47. Letter from Hri to VR of June 16, 1931.
48. Letter from Hri to VR of June 18, 1931.
49. Letter from Hri to VR of July 1, 1931.
50. Letter from Hri to VR of July 24, 1931.
51. Letter from Hri to VR of July 24, 1931.

52. Letter from Hri to VR of July 24, 1931. The upper case letters correspond to the original.
53. Letter from Hri to VR of September 1, 1931.
54. Letter from Hri to VR of September 1, 1931.
55. Far Eastern Press Correspondence, January 3, 1932 (Archive Peter Rand).
56. Kinnon, *Agnes Smedley* (1989), pp. 83.
57. Letter from Hri to VR of February 14, 1932. The many omitted words, replaced with ellipses (. . .), are typical of Isaacs' writing style.
58. Wang, *Memoirs* (1980), p. 172. Wang Fanxi (originally Fan-hsi), born in 1907, was one of the best-known supporters of the Trotskyite line within the Chinese Communist Party. For his convictions, contradicting the trend of the CCP (he took Trotsky's and not Stalin's standpoint in the China question), he was expelled from the party and spent most of the 1930s in prison. In 1949 Wang fled with his followers from the newly founded PRC to Macao. After 1975, Wang lived in Leeds, England, where he died in December 2002.
59. Letter from Isaacs to the Central Committee of the Chinese Communist Party of May 20, 1934, in: MIT Archives: Harold R. Isaacs Papers, Box 26.
60. In his path-breaking studies, Isaacs not only exposes Stalin as a traitor to the Chinese Revolution, but also uncovers a massacre committed by KMT troops against communist intellectuals (among them the husband of Ding Ling) in February 1931 in Shanghai as part of a conspiracy by the leadership of the CCP to silence bothersome critics within their own ranks. See on this in greater detail Isaacs, *Re-Encounters* (1985), pp. 3, 15, 22, 33 or in Isaacs, *Tragedy* (1968), pp. 334.
61. Letter from Isaacs to "Dear Don" of April 21, 1973, in: MIT Archives: Harold R. Isaacs Papers, Box 28.
62. Letter from Isaacs to "Dear Ronny" of July 22, 1944 (on the flight from Colombo to Bangalore), in: MIT Archives: Harold R. Isaacs Papers, Box 24.
63. Letter from Isaacs to "Dear Ronny" of August 4, 1944, in: MIT Archives: Harold R. Isaacs Papers, Box 24.
64. *Newsweek*, April 23, 1945, p. 60.
65. In a letter to Viola, Isaacs writes about the communists (after a personal conversation with Zhou Enlai in Chongqing in early 1945): "They are efficient. They are ruthless. They will play any card any time. They will play for and with anybody if it will serve their ends. They are much to be counted on. They are much to be feared." Cited in: Rand, *China Hands* (1995), p. 250.
66. Thus Enid Schoettle, in: Obituaries: In memory of Harold R. Isaacs, Remembrance by Enid Schoettle, p. 6, in: MIT Archives: Harold R. Isaacs Papers, Box 23.
67. Original quote of William Jones, from: Retirement Notes by Harold Isaacs, May 19, 1976, p. 1, in: MIT Archives: Harold R. Isaacs Papers, Box 23.
68. Letter from Isaacs to "Dear Ronny" of August 4, 1953, in: MIT Archives: Harold R. Isaacs Papers, Box 24.
69. *Christian Science Monitor*, May 9, 1950, p. 3.

70. Isaacs, *Scratches* (1958). The book appeared four years later under the title *Images of Asia,* published by Capricorn Books.

71. Isaacs, *Images* (1972), p. 35.

72. Letter from Isaacs to Yu Xinhui of April 22, 1982, in: MIT Archives: Harold R. Isaacs Papers, Box 26. Lu Xun is considered to be the founder of modern Chinese literature.

73. Besides a selection of short stories by sixteen authors, *Straw Sandals* also contains biographical data on all these writers, a foreword by Lu Xun, as well as information on the social and cultural-historical background of how this unique collection came about. Lin Biao was an important Communist military leader who greatly contributed to the victory in the Civil War, but was later condemned as a traitor. He died in a mysterious airplane accident in 1971.

74. Copy of a memorandum on a slip of paper by Isaacs of March 4, 1976, in: MIT Archives: Harold R. Isaacs Papers, Box 25. The slip stems from Madame Sun, but we still have not identified the person who so vehemently opposes his visit to China. "Traitor" refers to Isaacs.

75. Isaacs, *Re-Encounters* (1985).

76. The author Ding Ling was only 23 when she became famous with the story "Miss Sophie's Diary" (1927). She had a very difficult lot not only under the Kuomintang, but also under the communists. In 1958, for instance, she was expelled to Manchuria, spent several years in prison, and was only rehabilitated in 1979. Her colleague Mao Dun (the author of *Midnight* and *Spring Silkworms*) adapted much better to the respective party line, which made it possible for him to survive the Cultural Revolution unmolested. Chen Hansheng, one of the most famous economists of China at the time (his book *Landlord and Peasant in China* (1936) is still regarded as a major source for research on the peasant rebellion in China), was denounced during the Cultural Revolution as a member of Chiang Kai-shek's extreme right CC Clique (even though he was once a Comintern member). *See also* note 146 below.

77. Isaacs, *Re-Encounters* (1985), p. 155.

78. Letter from Isaacs to "Dear Alexandra" of December 23, 1982, in: MIT Archives: Harold R. Isaacs Papers, Box 26.

79. *The New York Times*, 10 July 1986, p. B8.

80. Isaacs, *Re-Encounters* (1985), p. 124.

81. White, *In Search of History* (1979), pp. 119.

82. Ibid., p. 19.

83. Ibid., pp. 22, 24.

84. Letter written by White to "Mom and Gladys and Bobby" of June 1, 1940, cited in: Theodore H. White Papers, Harvard University Archives, Box 2, Folder 10.

85. White, *In Search of History* (1979), pp. 45.

86. Ibid., p. 50.

87. Ibid., p. 55.

88. Ibid., pp. 4, 61, 64.

89. Ibid., p. 67.

90. Letter written by White to Dean Hanford of July 1939 (with a copy for John Fairbank), in: Theodore H. White Papers, Harvard University Archives, Box 2, Folder 6.

91. White, *In Search of History* (1979), p. 69.

92. Ibid., p. 89.

93. Ibid., p. 92.

94. Letter from White to John K. Fairbank (1940), in: Theodore H. White Papers, Harvard University Archives, Box 2, Folder 23.

95. Letter written by White to an unknown person of July 11, 1943, in: Theodore H. White Papers, Harvard University Archives, Box 4, Folder 12.

96. White, *In Search of History* (1979), p. 104.

97. Ibid., p. 72.

98. Letter from White to Mr. Walsh of 1943, in: Theodore H. White Papers, Harvard University Archives, Box 4, Folder 10.

99. Report (no recipient, no title) by White of March 25, 1940, p. 7, in: Theodore H. White Papers, Harvard University Archives, Box 2, Folder 8.

100. Letter written by White to Dr. Wang Shih-chieh, Minister of Public Information, of 15 September 1943, in: Theodore H. White Papers, Harvard University Archives, Box 4, Folder 3.

101. White and Jacoby, *Thunder* (1946), p. 169.

102. Letter written by White to "Till and Peg" of June 1, 1943, in: Theodore H. White Papers, Harvard University Archives, Box 4, Folder 11.

103. Cited in: Epstein, *Jew* (2000), p. 95.

104. Letter written by White to an unknown person of July 11, 1943, in: Theodore H. White Papers, Harvard University Archives, Box 4, Folder 12.

105. White, *In Search of History* (1979), pp. 183.

106. Cited in: Davies, *Dragon* (1972), p. 366.

107. White, *In Search of History* (1979), p. 201.

108. Remark by an American Brigadier General in a conversation with Theodore White in Chongqing, in: White, *In Search of History* (1979), p. 240.

109. Ash, *History of the Present* (1999), p. xviii.

110. Letter from White to "My Dear Premier Chou En-lai" of March 30, 1960, in: Theodore H. White Papers, Harvard University Archives, Box 15, Folder 13.

111. Letter from Livingston T. Merchant, Under Secretary of State for Political Affairs, to Theodore White of March 5, 1960, in: Theodore H. White Papers, Harvard University Archives, Box 15, Folder 12.

112. Letter from White to A. Doak Barnett, Ford Foundation of April 21, 1960, in: Theodore H. White Papers, Harvard University Archives, Box 15, Folder 12.

113. Letter from White to "Dear Mr. Chairman" of February 8, 1963, in: Theodore H. White Papers, Harvard University Archives, Box 15, Folder 12.

114. Quoted in: Thompson, *Theodore H. White* (1992), p. 134.

115. White, *In Search of History* (1979), p. 125.

116. Letter from White to "My Dear Mr. Prime Minister" of August 19, 1975, in: Theodore H. White Papers, Harvard University Archives, Box 15, Folder 13.

117. Letter from White to Zbigniew Brzezinski of January 15, 1979, in: Theodore H. White Papers, Harvard University Archives, Box 42, Folder 3.

118. Quoted in: Thompson, *Theodore H. White* (1992), p. 139.

119. Thompson, *Theodore H. White* (1992), p. 153.

120. Ibid., p. 156.

121. *The New York Times*, February 10, 1985, p. 2.

122. *The New York Times*, May 16, 1986, p. A1.

123. Letter from White to "Mama, Gitty and Bobby" of January 23, 1940, in: Theodore H. White Papers, Harvard University Archives, Box 2, Folder 7.

124. Acton, *Memoirs* (1985), p. 288.

125. Cuthbertson, *Nobody Said Not to Go* (1998), p. 19.

126. Hahn, *China to Me* (1988), p. 2.

127. This information is provided by Cuthbertson in his Hahn biography: Cuthbertson, *Nobody Said Not to Go* (1998), p. 141.

128. Hahn, *No Hurry to Get Home* (2000), pp. 220.

129. Hahn, *Mr. Pan* (1942).

130. Cited in: Cuthbertson, *Nobody Said Not to Go* (1998), p. 161.

131. *The New York Times*, December 10, 1944, p. BR5.

132. Hahn, *China to Me* (1988), p. 130.

133. Ibid., p. 156.

134. Hahn, *China A to Z* (1946).

135. Hahn, *Chiang Kai-shek* (1955).

136. Hahn, *Cooking* (1968).

137. Letter written by Emily Hahn to "Dearest Victor" of July 23, 1945, in: Emily Hahn Collection, The Lilly Library, Indiana University, Hahn mss.

138. Letter written by Edgar Snow to "Dear Mickey" of April 18, 1956, in: Emily Hahn Collection, The Lilly Library, Indiana University, Hahn mss. II.

139. Roger Angell, "Ms. Ulysses," in: *The New Yorker*, March 10, 1997, pp. 52–55, here 52.

140. In a letter by Emily Hahn to Randall Gould of May 7, 1945, Mickey refers to Stein as "well known as an opportunist who has changed around often, and he thought the profitable time had come to be Red," in: Emily Hahn Collection, The Lilly Library, Indiana University, Hahn mss.

141. Strauss, *Biographisches Handbuch der deutschsprachigen Emigration nach 1933* (1983), p. 1112.

142. Stein, *Far East* (1936), p. 177.

143. Cf., for example: *Christian Science Monitor*, May 8, 1943, pp. 2 or respectively March 31, 1945, p. 3.

144. Stein, *Red China* (1945).

145. *The China Weekly Review*, December 15, 1945, pp. 51.

146. *Miss Sophie's Diary* is a story by Chinese author Ding Ling in which a young woman describes her sexual feelings and unhappy life. Ding Ling was a Chinese social activist who shocked many conservatives with progressive feminist ideas. Her

husband, Hu Yepin, was a poet, worker and communist who died in a Kuomintang prison. *See also* note 76 above.

147. Stein, "The Other China," in: *Foreign Affairs* (October 1945) Vol. 24, 1, p. 62.

148. Stein, "An Interpretation of China's Conflict," in: *Yale Review* (1946) Vol. 35, 4, p. 635.

149. *The New York Times*, December 16, 1948, p. 22.

150. *The New York Times*, February 11, 1949, p. 1.

151. Willoughby, *Shanghai Conspiracy* (1952).

152. Ibid., p. 77.

153. McCarthy, *McCarthyism* (1952), pp. 5–7.

154. Canham, *Commitment to Freedom* (1958), pp. 342.

155. A few biographical details about Israel Cohen are found in: *Encyclopaedia Judaica* (1972), Vol. 5, p. 677.

156. Cohen, *Journal* (1925), p. 127.

157. Ibid., p. 130.

158. Ibid., p. 168.

159. Ibid., p. 194.

160. During the McCarthy Red Scare, the FBI and other interested authorities tried in vain for years to learn Asiaticus' identity. See on this, e.g.: Newman, *Lattimore* (1992), pp. 45.

161. Asiaticus, *Kanton bis Schanghai* (1928).

162. Shippe's meeting with Wittfogel had repercussions after the former's death: Following the conclusion of the German-Soviet Non-aggression Pact of 1939, Wittfogel breaks with communism and develops into one of its severest critics. During the McCarthy era and the hearings before the American Congress, Wittfogel uses his acquaintanceship with Shippe as an occasion to testify against the China expert and "top spy" Owen Lattimore.

163. Asiaticus, *Criticizes* (1938), pp. 237–244 and 248–252.

164. CWR, April 10, 1937, p. 217.

165. The New Fourth Army was put together from the survivors of the communist fighting forces left behind for guerrilla actions in Central China during the Long March.

166. *Amerasia* was at the time edited by Philip Jaffe, the intellectual and great admirer of the communist revolution in China. He was under observation by the FBI immediately after the end of the Second World War (he was suspected of being a Soviet spy), a fact that was unknown to John Stewart Service, employed at the time in the U.S. Embassy in Chongqing and a co-worker of General Stilwell, and was to be fateful. Jaffe had in 1945 been given political reports written by Service (criticizing the Kuomintang) so that these could be published in the journal *Amerasia.* Service was arrested and accused of espionage (which could not be proved). The China Lobby campaign lasted for several years, and finally in 1951, Secretary of State Dean Acheson saw himself forced under public pressure to suspend Service from diplomatic work as an apparent security risk. Only in 1957, when the paranoia of the McCarthy

Red Scare had subsided, did the U.S. Supreme Court hand down a judgment against this "inappropriate" dismissal.

167. In China Shippe is still venerated today. His book *Von Kanton bis Schanghai 1926–1927* was also published under the title *Xibo wenji* (Collected Works of Shippe) in Jinan, Shandong Province.

168. Autobiographical typescript Max Granich (1974), Tape 6, page 2, in: Grace Maul Granich and Max Granich Papers 1929–1993 (New York University, Tamiment).

169. Autobiographical manuscript by Grace Granich (sine anno), n. pag., in: Grace Maul Granich and Max Granich Papers 1929–1993 (New York University, Tamiment).

170. Letter of July 12, 1937 (Department of State, Division of Far Eastern Affairs, unsigned), in: Grace Maul Granich and Max Granich Papers 1929–1993 (New York University, Tamiment).

171. Autobiographical Typescript, Max Granich (1981–82), p. 104, in: Grace Maul Granich and Max Granich Papers 1929–1993 (New York University, Tamiment).

172. The 1936 Xi'an Incident occurred when Chiang Kai-shek was kidnapped by Marshal Zhang Xueliang, son of Zhang Zuolin and a former warlord from Manchuria. As a result, the warring Communists and Nationalists agreed to stop fighting and combine their forces against the Japanese threat. In this incident, Madame Sun's house was surrounded by members of the Kuomintang, because they wanted to use her as a bargaining chip to press for the release of Chiang Kai-shek, who was then imprisoned in Xi'an.

173. Granich, *Humiliation* (1938), p. 6.

174. Werner, *Sonjas Rapport* (1977).

175. Ibid., p. 32.

176. Ibid., p. 39.

177. Ibid., p. 39.

178. Ibid., pp. 105.

179. Ibid., p. 115.

180. Ruth Werner in a letter to her parents, cited in: Werner, *Sonjas Rapport* (1977), p. 176.

181. Werner, *Sonjas Rapport* (1977), p. 191.

182. Ibid., p. 291.

183. *The New York Times*, July 23, 2000, p. 27.

184. Balinska, *Humanity* (1998). The author of this book is Ludwik Rajchman's granddaughter.

185. Cited in: Balinska, *Humanity* (1998), p. 88.

186. Ibid., p. 91.

187. Monnet, *Mémoires* (1976), p. 135.

188. Cited in: Balinska, *Humanity* (1998), p. 100.

189. Ibid., p. 131.

190. Letter to Foreign Minister August Zaleski of February 22, 1944, in: Balinska, *Humanity* (1998), p. 168. General Joseph Stilwell, sent to China to keep the country

in the war, offended Chiang and many Chinese with his heavy-handed intervention in military policies.

191. *The New York Times*, November 28, 1950, p. 10. At the March Session of the UNICEF Executive Board, the representatives of the USSR, as well as of Poland (Rajchman) and Czechoslovakia, left the meeting in protest, and afterward a majority decided to keep the seat for the representatives of the Nationalist government on Taiwan.

192. *The New York Times*, July 25, 1965, p. 69.

193. Cited in: Leutner/Titarenko, *National-revolutionäre Bewegung in China* (National Revolutionary Movement in China, 1996), p. 396.

194. Ibid., pp. 469.

195. From the notes and information reports of M. M. Borodin (not before February 16,1924), cited in: Leutner/Titarenko, *National-revolutionäre Bewegung in China* (1996), p. 468.

196. The authorship of this testament (including the possibility of Borodin's authorship) has been disputed in the historical guild ever since Sun's death. See on this: Jacobs, *Borodin* (1981), pp. 169.

197. Bennett, *On Her Own* (1993), pp. 220.

198. From a journalist's interview with Borodin shortly before his departure from China, cited in: Jacobs, *Borodin* (1981), 279.

199. Borodin flew the stretch from Ulan Bator (now Outer Mongolia) to Ulan Ude (now Russian Federation). Fanny Borodin was later released and likewise returned, disguised as a nun, to the USSR (*The New York Times*, August 23, 1927, p. 10).

200. Leutner/Titarenko, *National-revolutionäre Bewegung in China* (National Revolutionary Movement in China, 1998), p. 1179.

201. Jacobs, *Borodin* (1981), pp. 309.

202. Mehnert, *Peking und Moskau* (1964), p. 252.

203. Strong returned to her beloved China in the 1950s and was, for example, there in 1959 when the People's Liberation Army suppressed anti-Chinese demonstrations in Tibet. She lived in Beijing until her death at the age of 84 in 1970. Lubyanka is the popular term for the headquarters of the Soviet secret police (Cheka, KGB) and the connected prison, located on Lubyanka Square in Moscow, less than a mile from the Kremlin.

204. *The New York Times*, September 3, 1953, p. 21.

205. Letter from Rayna Prohme to Helen Freeland of March 19, 1927, in: Knodel and Hirson, *Reporting the Chinese Revolution* (2007), p. 72.

206. The following biographical details about Prohme are taken chiefly from Knodel and Hirson, *Reporting the Chinese Revolution* (2007), as well as Grunfeld, *Chinese Communist Party* (unpublished manuscript, 1999).

207. Cited in: Knodel and Hirson, *Reporting the Chinese Revolution* (2007), p. 19.

208. Letter from Rayna to her sister Grace (later married to the South African Trotskyist Frank Glass), undated, cited in: Knodel and Hirson, *Reporting the Chinese Revolution* (2007), p. 25.

209. Cited from the article "We Met at Sea," in: *American Review*, No. 2, May–June 1924, in: Knodel and Hirson, *Reporting the Chinese Revolution* (2007), p. 25.

210. Bennett, *On Her Own* (1993), p. 74.

211. Letter from Rayna Prohme to Helen Freeland of September 8, 1926, in: Knodel and Hirson, *Reporting the Chinese Revolution* (2007), p. 33.

212. Ibid., pp. 36.

213. Letter from Rayna Prohme to Helen Freeland of October 22, 1926, in: Knodel and Hirson, *Reporting the Chinese Revolution* (2007), p. 40.

214. Ibid., p. 40.

215. Letter from Rayna Prohme to Helen Freeland of December 12, 1926, in: Knodel and Hirson, *Reporting the Chinese Revolution* (2007), p. 46.

216. Letter from Rayna Prohme to Helen Freeland of October 29, 1926, in: Knodel and Hirson, *Reporting the Chinese Revolution* (2007), p. 43.

217. Letter from Rayna Prohme to Helen Freeland of January 4, 1927, in: Knodel and Hirson, *Reporting the Chinese Revolution* (2007), p. 52.

218. Letter from Rayna Prohme to Helen Freeland of February 19, 1927, in: Knodel and Hirson, *Reporting the Chinese Revolution* (2007), pp. 66.

219. Sheean, *Personal History* (1937), p. 216. Sheean fell in love with Rayna Prohme and stayed at her side until her death in Moscow in November 1927.

220. Gould, *China in the Sun* (1945), p. 69.

221. *People's Tribune*, April 19, 1927, p. 2.

222. Madame Sun's "Statement" is among others also printed in: *Hankow Herald*, July 19, 1927, p. 1.

223. It is unclear whether Rayna actually accompanied Madame Sun on this trip, as is mentioned in: Bennett, *On Her Own* (1993), pp. 285. More likely is that Rayna departed from Hankou somewhat later, because she spent a few days with Borodin in Kuling (Lushan), a renowned "British" health spa.

224. Letter from Rayna Prohme to Samson Raphaelson of August 1927, in: Grunfeld, *Chinese Communist Party* (1999), p. 30.

225. Letter from Rayna Prohme to Bill Prohme of September 22, 1927, in: Knodel and Hirson, *Reporting the Chinese Revolution* (2007), p. 114.

226. Sheean, *Personal History* (1937), p. 278.

227. Bennett, *On Her Own* (1993), p. 226.

228. *The New York Times*, November 22, 1927, p. 4.

229. At the time of the First World War, many immigrants from Europe to the New World chose to Anglicize their German-sounding names. Milly Bennett's editor at the *San Francisco Daily* changed her name because her first byline coincided with the United States entering WWI, and he was afraid of having a byline with a German sounding name.

230. The biographical data on Bennett, alias Bremler, alias Mitchell—thus the name of her first husband, also used in reference to her, for instance, in Jacobs, *Borodin* (1981)—stem from her own autobiographical legacy, which Prof. Tom Grunfeld has edited and provided with numerous valuable comments: Bennett, *On Her Own* (1993).

231. Bennett, *On Her Own* (1993), p. 13.

232. Ibid., p. 68.
233. Ibid., pp. 70.
234. Ibid., p. 167.
235. Ibid., p. 288.
236. Conversation of Milly Bennett with Liu Shaoqi cited in: Bennett, *On Her Own* (1993), p. 274.
237. Letter from Milly Bennett to "Dear Alfreda and Lester" (sine anno), in: Hoover Archives, Milly Bennett (Mitchell) Collection, Box 1.
238. *The New York Times*, November 7, 1960, p. 35.
239. Memorandum on Trebitsch-Lincoln, sine anno, in: NARA, RG 263, SMP: File 5607.
240. Trebitsch-Lincoln, *Revelations* (1916); Trebitsch-Lincoln, *Autobiography* (1932). This book appeared in German already in Vienna in 1931 under the title *Der grösste Abenteurer des XX. Jahrhunderts!?* (The Greatest Adventurer of the XXth Century).
241. From a lecture given by Trebitsch-Lincoln in Shanghai on April 29, 1932, "The Message of the Buddha to a Shipwrecked World," recorded in a report of the SMP of 2 May 1932 (p. 3), in: NARA, RG 263, SMP: File 5607.
242. Cited in: Wasserstein, *Trebitsch Lincoln* (1988), p. 72.
243. Ibid., p. 126.
244. Trebitsch-Lincoln, *Autobiography* (1932), p. 226.
245. Cited in: Wasserstein, *Trebitsch Lincoln* (1988), p. 199.
246. Cited in: *North-China Daily News* (NCDN), September 14, 1925, n. pag. (in: NARA, RG 263, SMP: File 5607).
247. Trebitsch-Lincoln, *Autobiography* (1932), p. 272.
248. The characterization of November 1923 in quotation marks stems from the British Consul General in Munich, cited in: Wasserstein, *Trebitsch Lincoln* (1988), p. 206.
249. Cited in: Wasserstein, *Trebitsch Lincoln* (1988), p. 220.
250. Ibid., pp. 220.
251. Trebitsch-Lincoln (Chao Kong), *Can War Be Abolished?* (1932), pp. 64.
252. Cited in: Wasserstein, *Trebitsch Lincoln* (1988), p. 229.
253. From a British police report (Paraphrase Secret) from Tianjin to Shanghai of November 2, 1927, in: NARA, RG 263, SMP: File 5607. The names are written in capital letters in the original.
254. See on the incarnation hypothesis the report by the British Consul General in Chongqing of September 1938, cited in: Wasserstein, *Trebitsch Lincoln* (1988), p. 271.
255. Trebitsch-Lincoln, *Autobiography* (1932), p. 291.
256. Wasserstein, *Trebitsch Lincoln* (1988), p. 243.
257. Cited in: NCDN, February 9, 1932, n. pag. (in: NARA, RG 263, SMP: File 5607).
258. Shanghai Municipal Police Report of 23 January 1935 on the "Activities of Abbot Chao Kung (Trebitsch-Lincoln)," in: NARA, RG 263, SMP: File 5607.
259. *The New York Times*, October 18, 1937, p. 16.

260. Cited in: *The New York Times*, July 18, 1938, p. 15.

261. According to excerpts quoted in: *The New York Times*, December 20, 1939, p. 5.

262. "Our Life" (supplement by Nascha Shisn in English), July 7, 1943, p. 2.

263. *Encyclopaedia Judaica* (1972), p. 1364.

264. *The New York Times,* June 27, 1954, p. BR 10.

265. Cited in: Levy, *Two-Gun Cohen* (1997), p. 144.

266. Drage, *Two-Gun Cohen* (1954), p. 36. Cohen's emotional moods, as rendered in this book, probably come closer to the truth than the details about Cohen's influence in China, which were written to create audience appeal.

267. Drage, *Two-Gun Cohen* (1954), p. 37.

268. Ibid., p. 83.

269. Ibid., p. 85.

270. Cited in: Levy, *Two-Gun Cohen* (1997), p. 196.

271. Ibid., p. 237.

272. Even before the end of the Chinese Civil War, the Jewish community of Tianjin turned to Cohen with the request that he work with the Chinese government and Western consulates to arrange their emigration. In 1956 the chairman of the Jewish community of Shanghai asked Cohen, who was in the country at the time, to do something to help them (see: Letter from R. D. Abraham to Charles Jordan, of July 3, 1956, in: AJDC Archive, Catalogue/Record Group: 1933–1944, File: 474).

273. Cited in: Levy, *Two-Gun Cohen* (1997), p. 266.

274. Cohen in an interview with the *People's Daily* (*Renmin ribao*) of 19 November 1956, cited in: Levy, *Two-Gun Cohen* (1997), p. 278.

275. *The London Times*, December 7, 1966, n. pag.

276. Drage, *Two-Gun Cohen* (1954), p. 138.

277. *The New York Times*, September 14, 1970, p. 39.

278. Translation of the official reception of the American General Consul Samuel Sokobin by the Japanese Emperor Hirohito on April 29, 1940, in: American Jewish Archives, Samuel Sokobin Collection.

279. In the pinyin phonetic transcription, the place names are written as follows: Beijing, Tianjin, Shanghai, Nanjing, Dandong, Chongqing, Zhangjiakou, Shantou, Shenyang, Harbin, Fuzhou, and Qingdao.

280. Finding biographical data on Samuel Sokobin was extremely difficult. I obtained a few references from Michael Pollak (Dallas, Texas), who also knew Sokobin personally. Probably Sokobin's only surviving descendant is his nephew, Rabbi Alan Mayor Sokobin (Sylvania, OH), who cordially made it possible for me to examine archival material from the National Library of Australia.

281. Letter from Sokobin to: The Honorable Secretary of State, July 8, 1919, p. 2, in: NARA, RG 59, Decimal File 1910–1929/123, thus 3/22. Sokobin's request is not approved. Instead a few months later he is transferred for a short time to Chongqing in Sichuan Province.

282. See on the "Mad Baron": Palmer, *The Bloody White Baron* (2011).

283. See on this various reports by Sokobin to the State Department: NARA, RG 59, Decimal File 1910–1929/893.00/3958 and 4136; 893.00 B/12; 893.00 B/19; 033.6193 J59.

284. See, for example, Sokobin's report "Conditions in Urga" (now Ulan Bator in Mongolia), of May 17, 1921, in: NARA, RG 59, Decimal File 1910–1929/123 So 3/75.

285. See, for example, the report "Safe Arrival of American Moving . . ." by Sokobin of April 17, 1924, in: NARA, RG 59, Decimal File 1910–1929/033.11 T68.

286. See on this Sokobin's report of August 16, 1922 (in which he denies this allegation) to the American envoy Jacob Schurman in Peking, in: NARA, RG 59, Decimal File 1910–1929/123 So 3/92.

287. The case of Charles Coltman received much attention at the time, whereby Sokobin's description of Coltman's death differed considerably from that of the Chinese authorities (see on this: *New York Times*, December 24, 1922, p. 3; February 15, 1923, p. 24, 29 April 1923, p. 16).

288. See on this the report by Sokobin, "American Woman and Child Ill-treated . . ." of February 7, 1927, in: NARA, RG 59, Decimal File 1910–1929/393.11/528.

289. Report of February 1, 1928, pp. 19, in: NARA, RG 59, Decimal File 1910–1929/693.001/279. Its recipient marked exactly this section with the note "Erase!" A further section with the title "Comparison of Political Conditions" was likewise marked "Erase" and is classified as "strictly confidential."

290. Sokobin admits in an explanatory report to the State Department that he did not foresee the immediate occupation of Qingdao by the Japanese, but vehemently objects to the expression "bucking the State Department" (see: NARA, RG 59, Decimal File 1930–1939/123 So 3/522).

291. Cited from: *Foreign Service Journal*, March 1973, p. 24 (in: National Library of Australia, Papers of Harold Williams/Samuel Sokobin).

292. John Service recalls Samuel Sokobin during an interview in the frame of an Oral History Project of the University of California at Berkeley, 1977/78. Besides his characterization of Sokobin as "a bit out of step," he writes of him: "He did not have any great reputation as a Chinese scholar or linguist, but I think he kept up his Chinese better than most other people. He still reads fairly well" (in: Service, *Duty in China* (1981), p. 492).

293. *The New York Times*, December 5, 1967, p. 50.

294. Einstein, *Diplomat* (1968), pp. xi, 207.

295. Ibid., p. 87.

296. Ibid., p. 89.

297. Ibid., p. 88.

298. Ibid., pp. 91, 96, 99.

299. Ibid., pp. 104.

300. Einstein, *Diplomat* (1968), p. xxxiii.

301. Cited from: Mirsky, *Sir Aurel Stein* (1977), p. 1.

302. Cited from a conversation with the Director of the Chinese Institute for Archaeology at the start of the 1980s, in: Hopkirk, *Foreign Devils* (1984), p. 6.

303. Mirsky, *Sir Aurel Stein* (1977), p. 462.
304. Stein, *Central Asian Tracks* (1998), p. 36.
305. See on this: Hopkirk, *Foreign Devils* (1984), pp. 156.
306. Cited in: Hopkirk, *Foreign Devils* (1984), p. 238.
307. *The New York Times*, October 29, 1943, p. 19.
308. This picture of Carl Schuster and a woman from Sichuan is the frontispiece of: Schuster/Carpenter, *Patterns* (1996).
309. Schuster's dissertation is found together with hundreds of documents, biographical data, letters, as well as photographic negatives, in the *Museum der Kulturen* in Basel (Archive Schuster).
310. Schuster, *Peasant Embroideries* (1935), p. 93.
311. Schuster, *Embroideries* (1937), pp. 30.
312. Structuralism is a theory developed by French sociologist Claude Lévi-Strauss about the relationships between the structure of a language and the culture of a society that assumes that cultural phenomena in another order of reality are phenomena of the same type as the linguistic.
313. A brief biographical reference to Katz is found in: Strauss, *International Biographical Dictionary of Central European Emigrés* (1983), p. 602.
314. Katz, *Funkelnder Ferner Osten!* (1931), pp. 5.
315. Ibid., p. 15.
316. Ibid., p. 21.
317. Ibid., p. 37.
318. Ibid., p. 41.
319. Ibid., p. 52.
320. Ibid., p. 105 and 108.
321. Ibid., p. 298.
322. Holitscher, *Das unruhige Asien* (Restless Asia, 1926).
323. Strauss, *International Biographical Dictionary of Central European Emigrés* (1983), p. 533.
324. Holitscher, *Das unruhige Asien* (1926), p. 196.
325. Ibid., pp. 221 and 225.
326. Ibid., p. 249.
327. Ibid., p. 258.
328. Ibid., p. 284.
329. Ibid., p. 287.
330. Ibid., p. 288.
331. Jensen, *China siegt* (China Triumphs, 1949), p. 10.
332. The China Defense League was founded by Madame Sun in 1938 in Hong Kong for the purpose of providing medical and other aid to the Chinese troops, especially in the "liberated areas." The idea of the Chinese industrial cooperatives (Chinese: gonghe; English: working together) originally stemmed from Helen Foster Snow and was taken up by her husband, and in particular also by the New Zealander Rewy Alley, who founded the first committee in April 1938. The Gong Ho (gonghe) movement tried to find employment in small cooperative businesses for workers and

refugees who had lost their work due to the Japanese bombardment of large cities like Shanghai.

333. The author had the opportunity to interview Jensen's widow in Beijing on September 7, 2001. In later years, Wang Wu'an also held a high position in the Ministry of Public Health of the PR China.

334. Jensen, *China siegt* (1949), p. 137.

335. Ibid., p. 88.

336. Jensen, *Opfer and Sieger* (1955), p. 6. This (political, propagandistic) volume is a collection of selected poems and essays.

337. Walter Freudmann is mentioned, e.g., in: Strauss, *International Biographical Dictionary of Central European Emigrés* (1983), p. 192. Nothing is known about Freudmann's place and date of birth and many other details. After his return from the Far East in 1945, Freudmann worked as a doctor in Vienna. The year of his death is likewise unknown.

338. Freudmann, *Tschi-Lai!—Erhebet Euch* (1947). The dictum "Tschi-Lai" (Rise up!) is part of the first stanza of the so-called "March of the Manchurian Volunteers" (1933) dating to the time of the Japanese invasion and later chosen as the Chinese national anthem.

339. Freudmann, *Tschi-Lai!—Erhebet Euch* (1947), p. 6.

340. Ibid., p. 25.

341. Ibid., p. 81.

342. Ibid., p. 35.

343. Ibid., p. 44.

344. Ibid., p. 63.

345. Ibid., p. 96.

346. Ibid., p. 69.

347. Ibid., p. 198.

348. Ibid., p. 220.

349. This book appears three years after Robitscher-Hahn's death: Erling, *Im Geist Yanans* (1980).

350. Ibid., p. 9.

351. Yan Xishan (1883–1960), one of the most enigmatic warlords, played a prominent role in the years of the Republic, because he joined neither the Nationalists nor the Communists (although he officially bore the title of Commander of a Kuomintang Army).

352. Letter of November 21, 1946, reproduced in: Erling, *Robitscher-Hahn*, 1977, p. 5.

353. Interview with Robitscher-Hahn, in: Erling, *Robitscher-Hahn*, 1977, p. 8.

354. Letter of February 17, 1947 to her son, in: Leo Baeck Institute, Magdalena Robitscher-Hahn Collection, AR 25012, Box 4.

355. Erling, *Im Geist Yanans* (1980), p. 126.

356. Cited in Erling, *Im Geist Yanans* (1980), p. 138.

357. Memorandum about Dr. Reifler of 15/2/1933, in: NARA, RG 263, SMP, File D 3854.

358. Another source (*Who's Who in American Jewry*, sine anno) states that Reifler worked as an assistant to the Austrian envoy to the League of Nations in Shanghai.

359. This event is reported in *Israel's Messenger* on October 13, 1939, p. 10.

360. *Israel's Messenger*, December 20, 1940, pp. 24.

361. In this chapter, he refers to the Sinites, whom non-academic fundamentalists consider to be Chinese.

362. *Israel's Messenger*, December 20, 1940, p. 2.

363. See the documents on the "Reifler Method" published by the American Chamber of Commerce in Shanghai in: University of Washington/Seattle: Erwin Reifler Collection, Box 1, Folder 1, 644–2-78–9).

364. The biographical information on Olga Lang was graciously provided by Ted Wahl, who was married to one of Lang's long-time friends. This woman, born in 1917, was Tatjana Manooiloff Cosman, a Russian orphan. A Russian family first adopted Tatjana in Manchuria and then sold her to an opium dealer. Having arrived in Peking, she worked as a cabaret girl and taxi dancer before she was taken in by the well-known social worker Ida Pruitt, the daughter of an American missionary family. Cosman later—like Olga Lang—worked at Swarthmore College in Pennsylvania, and indeed as a Russian teacher. The author is grateful to Ted Wahl (Media, PA) for various documents, including copies of pictures taken in China in the 1930s.

365. Lang, *Chinese Family* (1946).

366. Lang, *Pa Chin* (1967).

367. *The New York Times*, January 28, 1968, BR 3.

368. Giardinelli, *Emigre* (2002), pp. 39.

369. From one of Schiff's manuscripts (sine anno), cited in: Kaminski, *China gemalt* (1983), p. 12.

370. Schiff in a letter of March 21, 1946 to "Dear Maureen," cited in: Kaminski, *Künstler* (1998), p. 60.

371. Sketches of this are found, for example, in: *The China Weekly Review*, December 4, 1937 or February 5, 1938.

372. Schiff in a lecture in Buenos Aires to the Association of British Artists on July 28, 1949, cited in: Kaminski, *Künstler* (1998), p. 62.

373. Stadler, *Vernunft* (1988), pp. 815–818.

374. Shanghai Municipal Police Report, February 19, 1935, in: NARA, RG 263, SMP, File D 5741.

375. In China the report is spread with a delay of a few days, thus by the *Shanghai Times* on September 17, 1936, under the title "Dr. Julius Tandler Dies in Moscow."

376. Tandler, *Volk in China* (1935).

377. Ibid., p. 8.

378. Ibid., p. 33.

379. Ibid., p. 47.

Chapter 3

Refugees Driven from Europe to the Far East

Shanghai was probably at no time regarded by European Jews fleeing from Hitler as a dream destination, but rather it was the only and final gleam of hope to escape the terror of the Nazi regime. Despite the explicitly formulated warning against flight to this city in the *Handbook for the Jewish Emigration* (*Handbuch für die jüdische Auswanderung*), published in 1938, up until 1941 about 18,000 European Jews found temporary exile in Shanghai, literally the city "above the sea," which—its only trump—required no entry visa. However, with regard to housing, hygiene, and not least of all odors, it was in last place among the preferred exile destinations.[1] The political situation in Europe determined in no small measure the backgrounds of the Shanghai exiles. It was mostly a matter of members of older generations who had decided only at the very last moment to flee from their once beloved fatherland, as well as of a majority of rather bourgeois white-collar workers. The discussions on the labor and resistance movements of their younger coreligionists, who had moved abroad earlier, meant little to them—and they had not been known for political activities in Germany either.

Until Italy entered the war in June 1940, most of the refugees from Europe reached Shanghai by way of a four-to-ten week sea voyage, as a rule—that was also an irony of fate—on luxury steamers of the Lloyd-Triestino Line. They usually sailed through the Suez Canal or around the Cape of Good Hope, and crossed the Indian Ocean, with stops along the way in Bombay, Colombo, Singapore, and Hong Kong. After the blockade of the Mediterranean Sea and until the entry of German troops into the Soviet Union in June 1941, the last remaining possibility to escape was to take the land route via the Trans-Siberian Railroad from Berlin to Moscow and continue on to Chita. There refugees disembarked and boarded the East Chinese Railroad, traveling on toward Harbin in northern Manchuria and from there either via Mukden (Shenyang) or Dairen (Dalian) or—even more time-consuming—via Vladivostok and Japan (Kobe, Shimonoseki, Tsuruga or Yokohama) by ship to Shanghai.

David Ludwig Bloch

David Ludwig Bloch once referred to his almost ten-year stay in Shanghai as a "school of life." In fact, for most refugees, exile in Shanghai was merely a waiting room on the road to a brighter future. A few artists laid the foundations for their further careers in the port city on the Yellow Sea. "Exile, whatever it is like, is the hatchery for creative deeds, for the new," the Czech-Jewish philosopher Vilém Flusser once concluded. Bloch, born in the Upper Palatinate in Germany on 25 March 1910, seems to have committed himself to this credo. Deaf and an orphan from his first year, after completing a training program to become a porcelain painter's apprentice, the young man attends the Academy for Applied Art in Munich, but for financial reasons cannot complete this program. Bloch subsequently works as an advertising graphic artist and poster painter for the Sallinger Department Store in Straubing, a city in Bavaria, until his dismissal in October 1938 as part of the company's "Aryanization." After "Kristallnacht" on November 9–10 with its anti-Jewish pogroms in Nazi Germany and Austria, Bloch is taken into custody and imprisoned in the Dachau KZ. Four weeks later, he is released. After this traumatic experience, he immediately applies for an exit visa, which he receives at the last moment: In April 1940, Bloch departs for the Far East from the harbor of Venice on board the M.S. *Conte Rosso*.

"The heat plagued us, and also the cold, and worry about good old cash; the prickly heat, it burnt; because of it one ran to the outpatient clinic. Red beans and a hard egg, an extra pot for the millet gruel; hold your lip, cried the VIENNESE; stow it, thereupon screamed the BERLINER," reads the text of a drinking song by former Shanghai resident Ruth Gerechter.[2] Bloch is also one of those who have to restructure their lives in Shanghai in order to overcome culture shock. Living in the Concession Française, later in the Shanghai "ghetto," he does this in his own way, as a quiet, unobtrusive observer, initially by painting impressionistic, naturalistically tinted watercolors, later with pencil sketches that he uses to design woodcuts. Over the course of the years, Bloch produces a great number of such woodcuts (actually one would have to speak of wood engravings), which he arranges in cycles with their own names: Yin-Yang, Chinese Children, Rickshaws, and Beggars.[3]

Bloch's works reflect no longing for the Far East; they neither capture the exotically transfigured atmosphere of his surroundings, nor are they oriented to the well-formed, delicate female figures that so impressed Friedrich Schiff.

Nor does he have a nostalgic gaze, he who in all his production concentrates on the known in the unknown, apart perhaps from the motif of the magnificent Western colonial buildings on the Bund as background. In his cycles, he holds firmly to the Chinese themes that would first attract the attention of an unbiased Western visitor to Shanghai. The woodcut technique entails not the subtleties of an individual occupying the foreground, but rather the impression of the whole.

Bloch looks at things that others avoid seeing. In portraits of beggars, he spotlights people living on the margins of society, in response to whose suffering, sometimes intensified by bodily deformities, the viewer experiences equally pity and revulsion. The poor figures have been stamped by fate and voice a silent scream of total hopelessness. With short, hard strokes, Bloch strives to capture on paper phenomena that were widespread then, to represent social interactions pictorially. In the rickshaw coolie cycle, the conventional gestures or movement patterns of this guild occupy the foreground, for example in transporting excessively large loads, in disputes with the police, in struggling against bad weather, or while trying to recruit customers. The viewer almost feels the hardship and difficulty of this work with his own body.

Finally, in his Yin-Yang cycle Bloch flirts with subjects that represent a balance for him: between work and leisure, life and death, dream and reality, man and machine. His strokes are heavier than Schiff's, but at the same time they seem to express his own life situation: not belonging to the mainly wealthy Western society of Shanghai, the loss of his native land, and not least of all the handicap of being deaf. Bloch's woodcuts lack the free, at times mocking character of Schiff's drawings, yet the strokes are unaffected and appear free from ulterior motives. Like other refugees, he belongs to the *Association of Jewish Artists and Lovers of Fine Art* of Shanghai. He is able to display his works at exhibitions, and critics evaluate them positively:

> The most talented and therefore probably the most restless among them is D.L. Bloch. He among them has the least of what one could call style; he is still capable of becoming very different things, he knows that, it tortures him and again pleases him. [His] [e]ye and hand have very much direct power of comprehension, which is devoted to the hidden, although the technique has a premature and sometimes even dilettantish quality, it sometimes creates a true life that makes one take notice. The capable man sometimes looks astonishingly clairvoyantly into what is Chinese, without even making the effort to attempt this.[4]

Even the Japanese propaganda newspaper *Asiana* praises the German artist, without referring to his religious background, let alone reporting in a brief biography the reasons for his exile.[5] In March 1949, now married to a Chinese woman, David Ludwig Bloch leaves Shanghai for America. In the Middle

Figures 3.1–3.4
David Ludwig Bloch once referred to his ten-year stay in Shanghai as a "school of life." China has given him "much stimulation but little bread." His woodcuts focus consistently on the Chinese themes that would first attract the attention of an unbiased Western visitor to Shanghai at that time.

Kingdom, he concludes that he has personally "become acquainted with the great antitheses"; the country has "given him much stimulation but little bread."[6] For him it no doubt holds, as for other emigrant artists as well, that because he had been torn out of his everyday German life he had a sharper perception of himself and of the foreign, whereby he gives contemporary viewers vivid images of Chinese realities.

Lothar Brieger

For a very few intellectuals, the years of their China emigration represent a challenging experience of being foreign. Despite their daily struggle to survive, in one way or another they summon up the willpower and interest to deal with the Chinese environment. The art historian Lothar Brieger, born in Zwickau in 1879, was a critic for the *Berliner Zeitung am Mittag* (Berlin Midday Newspaper). In 1933, the Nazis impose a writing ban on him. Five years later, he flees to Shanghai, where he resides until 1947 and keeps his head above water by selling antiquities and books. As an employee of both the *Shanghai Morgenpost* (Morning Post) and *Neue Zeit* (New Time), he takes an interest in Chinese art and life wisdom, although without being able to forget the daily misery of emigration, above all the intellectual isolation. In one of his first contributions to the fortnightly magazine *Gelbe Post* about Shanghai as a gambling metropolis, Brieger writes:

> Gambling is the lifeblood of the Chinese. From the millionaire to the lowly coolie it runs in each one's blood. . . . The Chinese is by nature a loquacious and boisterous person, especially in restaurants and in the public places of entertainment where he spends his leisure hours. In an odd way, however, the Chinese takes gambling deadly seriously and celebrates it in solemn silence. One can in fact say that only two occasions give the residents of the Kingdom of Flowers the possibility to keep completely mum: prayer and gambling. . . . The Chinese gambler is a philosopher and knows neither remorse nor regret. He believes that luck must be waiting for him around the corner and will somehow find its way to him.[7]

Right at the beginning of his stay, the then already sixty-year-old bohemian and zealous bibliophile attempts to gaze into the Chinese soul. In gambling casinos, he is a restrained observer of Chinese behavior: "The Chinese set no great store by being watched while they let themselves be ruled by their greatest weakness." The so often mentioned Chinese "poker face" also attracts his attention; it is the "best in the world," he judges. As others probably do as well, Brieger searches for his own image of China, which everyone, and he is convinced of this, needs as a starting point for his thinking. "If one holds from the start that China is at the same time sweet and bitter like the mango fruit, then one is from the first moment on a mango Sinologist, and one remains one. The porcelain Sinologist has discovered that China is multi-colored and hard."[8]

Very little information is available about Brieger's years in Shanghai, but they were probably difficult: "His by nature amiable character was surrounded by dark shadows in the last period, a consequence of suffering the humiliations and brutalities of the Hitler regime," states an obituary in the famous German weekly magazine *Weltbühne* (The World Stage) of 15 March 1949. In an edition of the *Shanghai Herald* he is presented as a professor of literature at St. John's University (along with others, such as the architect Paulick or the music scholar Kuttner), but nothing is known about his academic activities there, nor about how closely he came in contact with his Chinese colleagues and students.[9] Only after the war does one read about him again, in a contribution on Chinese music:

> I do not understand much about music and much less about Chinese music. But this much I have already noticed: There are two kinds of Chinese music. The one is the loud music of the percussion instruments, which is supposed to drive out demons. We need not speak of that; we hear enough of it. The Chinese share the other kind, however, with all other people, the soft, wistful, charming music that wants to summon up and chain precisely the demons, the forces of nature. . . . But there is still that instrument that was dear to the Chinese from time immemorial, through which, using the mouth the human soul directly evokes mysterious nature: the flute, . . . and there the two greatest ancient civilized peoples, the Chinese and the Greeks, come together and become human.[10]

As well, Brieger comments on the relationship between emigration and artistic productivity. Emigrants who "were emigrated," that is, forced into exile, are neither needed nor desired, without rear cover, given only the right "to hold their tongue about everything." The art historian is wise enough to see that art does not represent the primary need of people in Shanghai: "First, the necessities of life, then culture" is his motto.

Unfortunately, Brieger never gets a chance to communicate his nine years of experience in China to a larger circle of Occidental readers. In 1947, he returns—at the request of professors from the Berlin Academy of Fine Arts—to Germany. The journey becomes a martyrdom for him, the contact with his lost homeland a catastrophe. The above-cited obituary in *Weltbühne* states:

> Severe spiritual depression resulted from the fact that having in the past year returned from emigration (Shanghai), he did not find his spouse alive. In all practical questions of life, he was as helpless as a child. In Berlin, destroyed by Hitler's megalomania, in the fully changed life circumstances he could not find his bearings. . . . With Lothar Brieger the literary world loses an author of high intellectual niveau and Jewry a valuable and unselfish person.[11]

Willy Tonn

"This W.Y. Tonn is a unique person . . . a Sinologist and Sanskrit scholar, a man of the book against the background of the Bund and the Szechuan Road, but his greatest characteristic feature is his persistence, his ability to ignore the difficulties and to swim against the current. . . . Grown richer through the hour-and-a-half of furlough from my own insufferability and through sorrow over the brevity of the just experienced, I came back to the district with the annoying awareness that we have too few Tonns, but still less public for what the one Tonn has achieved."[12] The extraordinary Willy Tonn was according to a few eyewitnesses the most important personality among the Shanghai immigrants. He was born in Berlin on January 28, 1902, a German of Jewish faith, as he himself emphasizes.[13] His father, Georg, founded a company, Dr. Franz Steiner & Co., which specialized in chemical, pharmaceutical, and cosmetic products, and Willy took over the business after his father's death in 1924. As his biography concisely states, the Nazis transport his mother, Dora, to Riga in January 1942—"end unknown."

After completing secondary school, Willy Tonn studies at Friedrich Wilhelm University in Berlin, first philosophy and medicine, later Oriental languages: Chinese, Manchurian, Sanskrit, Vedic, Pali, Prakrit, and Tibetan, as stated in his curriculum vitae. We do not know the source of his interest in Asia, but perhaps it arose in connection with Oriental medicine, which his father endeavored to introduce into the West. He also possesses extensive knowledge of sociology, psychology, art history, and Hebrew. Automobile trips to neighboring countries, as well as to Greece, Syria, Egypt, and North Africa expand his intellectual horizon and increase his curiosity about the strange, the *other*. In the late 1920s, Tonn publishes contributions in journals like the *Ostasiatische Rundschau* (East-Asian Panorama), *Durch alle Welt* (Through All the World) or *Indian Economic Affairs*.

As his final residence before emigrating in February 1939, Tonn lists Parisերstrasse 38 in Berlin-Wilmersdorf. He tries in vain to obtain a position in the Secretariat at the renowned School of Oriental and African Studies in London and finally feels forced to leave Europe for Shanghai, "from longing for the East, not out of fear of the Nazis," as he later states in a newspaper article.[14]

Shanghai is for him exactly the right place for his China studies, although the everyday struggle to survive has priority. Between 1939 and 1943, he writes regular articles for German, English, and Chinese language newspapers and magazines. In all, he publishes three hundred essays and literary treatises on Asia, chiefly on Chinese philosophy and culture. In July 1939—after only two months in Shanghai—the *Gelbe Post* publishes an article by him under the title "East and West—a Contradiction?" in which he reflects on the subjectivity of Europeans in assessing Chinese customs and practices. For the one, China is the "essence of the most uncivilized and calcified people, stuck at the level of the Middle Ages;" for the other, it is "in its morals the most advanced and developed civilized people." For the Berlin Sinologist himself, both views represent exaggerations:

> A so ancient civilized people as the Chinese bears in its peak achievements the highest virtues and lowest vices; the remainder, i.e., the masses, are the same everywhere; if differences in character are still there, they are determined by

> specific factors; the differences become nuances, although precisely these nuances constitute the core of the essential difference. In any case, one can say that the dictum, "East is East and West is West and never the train [sic! this should be 'twain'—author's note] will meet" is incorrect for the expert on the East, even if not false, while for him the words of Goethe, "The Orient and the Occident can no longer be separated," have enduring validity.[15]

For Tonn it is clear that the Confucian ethics represents the core of Chinese culture. In addition, he adds the five relationships (*wulun*), as well as the five cardinal virtues (*wude*) that characterize the ideal of a "perfect man" or "gentleman," the "*junzi*."[16] In contrast to this, Europe and the greatest share of the world owe their moral laws and thereby the foundations of their culture to the Jews, that is to the ethics of the great teacher Moses. This conception indicates what topic occupied Tonn above all in the ten years of his exile in China: the question of what unites or respectively separates Occident and Orient:

> The ethical teachings of both scarcely differ, their ideal is the correct behavior of the noble man, of the gentleman in the original sense of the word, the gentilhomme; the noble person is, thus spiritually, everyone according to his correct gentle behavior and is not 'noble' by birth. As both teachings are thus rooted in charity and justice, not only that of K'ung-tse [Confucius], but also that of Moses, whose ideal of the kiün-tse [the junzi—author's note] or respectively the zaddick [Hebrew for 'righteous one,' who is regarded as a mediator between God and man—author's note] is the nobly and justly thinking man; thus East and West also have their moral codex in the 2000 commandments and prohibitions of the *Li Chi* [*The Book of Rites*—author's note] or respectively the 613 of the Talmud, from which the West has borrowed many rules.[17]

In a list of his own manuscripts which Willy Tonn compiled, there are contributions on Chinese music, Chinese boxing, Chinese mysticism, Chinese medicine, Chinese proverbs, Chinese cosmology, and Chinese psychology. Besides this, there are also short stories, Chinese jokes, and fairytales, in short, everything that constitutes for the Westerner what is generally "Chinese" in this country.[18] His texts show his understanding of how to make the Westerner aware of phenomena and distinctive features that still play an important role in dealing with China and the Chinese population even today. These include coming to terms with the complexity of Chinese values and behavioral rules, as well as the understanding and functioning of these "Chinese rules of the game." He succeeds in extracting general knowledge about the Chinese manner of thinking from specific topics. In an article on Chinese poetry, he discusses the charm of Chinese characters and concludes that "the

Chinese have ever been far more people of feeling than they are commonly thought to be." Tonn concludes that due to the cosmology of Chinese thought, the Chinese view the universe as a "great chessboard and a grand contest."[19] With the conception of a seventeenth-century erotic novel, *Jinpingmei*, he identifies the, in his opinion typical, "Chinese confession of sin" in contrast to "European servility":

> In Europe external appearances are anxiously preserved; the public, however, does not care about private mischief. Thus, one can be a crooked scoundrel, a base lecher; if he hypocritically manages to outwardly preserve his virtue as a respectable citizen he will likewise be regarded as a gentleman, even if everyone knows how threadbare his cloak of virtues is. On the contrary, the Chinese describes things as they are, and despite his ancient culture is still naive in the best sense, and natural enough not to spread a ridiculous veil over highly self-evident and natural processes. In contrast, he portrays deplorable states of affairs as much more severe than in reality, in order to energetically bring about a remedy.[20]

Another contrast between East and West is the concept of culture as a counterpart of nature, culture as a development of the spiritual life and the most important principle in the lives of individuals and peoples:

> So the Asiatics form the world in their mind "from within" and endeavour to bring it into harmony, to perfect it, whereas the Western peoples see the world, being outside of their sphere, "from without" and try to command it, to master it. Asiatic insight principally depends on intuition, inspiration and innermost manifestation, whereas Western knowledge since Aristotle is mostly derived from measurable, logical and objective investigation.[21]

When the Hongkou "ghetto" is established in 1943, for Willy Tonn, who has adopted the Chinese name Tang Weili, a new stage begins in his personal engagement against "intellectual passivity" and the "cultural low point" of his Occidental countrymen. In order to overcome the "refugees' spiritual paralysis" and to spread "Asiatic knowledge and modern science," he founds—without having obtained permission from the Japanese authorities—a type of adult education center, the so-called Asia Seminar, with the subtitle "International Institute of Culture and Science." A newspaper report on the founding of this "People's University" states that Tonn, "one of the wandering Jews," who refers to himself as the "Fighting Scholar of Shanghai," wants to shake the Westerners in Shanghai out of their lethargy. He knows that the foreigners living in this city possess a unique opportunity, but do not use it: "They could have known how to create a synthesis between East and West." The problem, according to Tonn, is that the foreigners' activities merely concentrate on profiteering, the material side of life, above all on superficial pleasures.[22] That he could not gain anything from such externalities is clear from the report of an auditor and teacher at the Asia Seminar:

> That Tonn was a cultivated man was not apparent at first glance. . . . He made an unkempt impression, unshaven, the shirt collar dirty, the suit wrinkled and full of stains. He spoke in short bursts, incoherently, more to his manuscript than to the listeners. But Chinese flowers gleamed among the weeds and undergrowth of his explanations. His voice had an inner warmth and tenderness that helped to get beyond the lecture's inadequacies. . . . The man revealed how lonely he was and how he sought in his love for China to find a substitute for humanity.[23]

In fact, Tonn's material livelihood worsens from year to year. "I was a rich man in Germany . . . when I left Berlin in 1939. I lost everything: my mother, my relatives, my business, my income, my property, my fortune." In Shanghai, he gradually has to sell the tiny share of his books that he had brought with him

Figure 3.5
Willy Tonn, the "fighting scholar of Shanghai," had a tragic personal destiny: "I was a rich man in Germany when I left Berlin in 1939. I lost everything: my mother, my relatives, my business, my income, my property, my fortune." Unfortunately, his contemporaries never paid him the respect he deserved for his unswerving efforts to bring China closer to the West.

to Asia in order to "make a living at least after the Chinese fashion."[24] Using self-composed job references, he attempts in his need (but in vain) to find suitable work, for example at the University of Kunming, which was not occupied by the Japanese. In 1947, his luck seems to change: the Shanghai press reports that he has accepted a professorship of Linguistics and Comparative Philology at the National Chinan University, as the "first European who [would] instruct Chinese students in the Chinese language . . ." The outbreak of the Civil War prevents him from taking this position, and he feels it necessary to plan a future outside the Middle Kingdom. Once again, he invests all his energy in various projects to further intercultural exchanges, in particular with the founding of two branches of his Asia Seminar, the American Seminar and the Israeli Seminar (in order to prepare Shanghai refugees for life in the USA or respectively in Israel). His greatest plan, the founding of a Chinese-American Cultural Institute in San Francisco, does not arouse any interest—given the threatening clash of ideologies, the world does not seem prepared to pin its hopes on cultural accommodation among peoples.

Shortly before the fall of Shanghai to the communists in the spring of 1949, he leaves his beloved China for Israel, suffering from heart disease and not knowing where his life will lead him. Already a few months after his arrival in the Holy Land, he decides that Israel is not the right place for his life interests and professional activities:

> In the meantime, I have spoken during my previous stay of six months here to leading people, among them the Minister of Education, the presidents of the Sochnuth (Jewish Agency), the American Ambassador here, Prof. Martin Buber, Hebrew University, etc. Here everything is province, and Hongkou to the contrary big-hearted and the cosmopolitan city. . . . I have also spoken to a few nice leading people from the Foreign Ministry, really exceptions; the end effect is, however, the same. The country is very charming, the people less charming.[25]

Aside from two smaller projects on Far Eastern art at Israeli museums, the fifty-year-old Berlin Sinologist can do little to make his mark as a scholar. Nowhere does he find a suitable field of activity for a universal scholar like himself. His talents are not recognized or—which from today's viewpoint seems no more reasonable, but is at least more understandable—not needed. Willy Tonn simply has the great misfortune to live in the wrong epoch. During a stay in a Swiss sanitarium he dies in 1957, one of the tragic figures of the Shanghai emigration. He never received financial compensation from Germany, and with the exception of Hongkou, his contemporaries never paid him the respect he deserved for his unswerving efforts to bring China closer to the West. "Anyone who knew Prof. Tonn mourns his premature return home and the irreplaceable loss of so many unused possibilities in the areas of science, art, relationships to Asia."[26]

Adolf Josef Storfer

In a discussion of Eduard Horst von Tscharner's 1939 book *China in der deutschen Dichtung bis zur Klassik* (China in German Literature until Classicism), a reviewer notes that inadequate and often murky sources often make it possible for Occidental literature "to falsely attribute a wishful image to China or to develop a distorted image of China for some sort of argument."[27] The reviewer is an old-established Austrian who fled to Shanghai barely half a year before this contribution appeared, Adolf Josef Storfer, a man of "deep knowledge, an author, linguist and Sigmund Freud's most loyal evangelist."[28] Born in Transylvanian Botoşani, now in Romania, on the 11th (according to other sources the 6th) of January 1888, Storfer, like Willy Tonn, is not a religious Jew. Storfer referred to himself as non-confessional, and yet in his nature there is, as in the Berliner, a characteristic that especially distinguishes Judaism, the tendency to take cognizance to a considerable extent of the "others." Storfer grows up without a mother; his father, a lumber dealer, regularly takes the boy to a nearby coffee house in order to breakfast together. At the secondary school in Klausenburg or Kolozsvár (now the Romanian city of Cluj), the "robber captain," as he is later called by friends, publishes a socialist weekly newspaper that turns against petit bourgeois society. After an (unjustly imposed) jail sentence, Storfer studies law, philosophy, psychology, and comparative linguistics in Klausenburg. As time passes, Storfer, yearning for the greater world, finds the Transylvanian atmosphere too narrow: He enrolls at the University of Zürich and gets a start in newspaper journalism. As a correspondent for the *Frankfurter Allgemeine Zeitung* he reports to the world on the "White Terror" (the 1919–21 period of counter-revolutionary terror intended to crush communist revolutionaries in Hungary). After an intermezzo in the Imperial and Royal Army during the First World War, he reaches Vienna and is more or less safe there from enemies in the despised Horthy regime. He becomes familiar with psychoanalysis and about 1910 meets its founder, Sigmund Freud. In 1921, he becomes the Director of the International Psychoanalytic Publishing House, which he is to head until 1932, and thereby publishes its journals together with Freud.

Like Brieger, Storfer is considered a bohemian, an original and highly educated man with a limitless interest in everything. An Austrian publicist refers to him as "one of the last polyhistorians of Vienna." In his character, "which was distinguished and honest, there were no cracks. He took

GELBE POST

ERSCHEINT AM 1. UND 16. JEDES MONATS

SHANGHAI, 1. NOVEMBER 1939

AUS DEM INHALT DIESES HEFTES:

Run in Shanghai

Sun Yat-sens Testament

Chinesische Zeitung

Die Fünftonleiter

Mietmädchen in Hongkong

Chinesische Ironie

Schmutz in China

Mandschurische Banditen

Freud und der Mensch

Preis des Heftes in Shanghai 30 Cents

Figures 3.6–3.7
Adolf Josef Storfer, a man of "deep knowledge, an author, linguist and Sigmund Freud's most loyal evangelist." His name will always be connected to his Shanghai "child," the Gelbe Post, *a Journal that tried to bring the East closer to those fleeing the West.*

everything seriously and derived the most naïve pleasure from every sort of mental acrobatics. His modesty, which was genuine, overshadowed his pride, which was likewise genuine. Storfer was the source of the insulting-conciliatory expression: 'You are right, but you do not know why.'" In the 1930s, Storfer occupies himself, aside from psychoanalysis, with etymology, which finds expression in the publication of two books, *Wörter und ihre Schicksale* (Words and Their Fates, 1935) and *Im Dickicht der Sprache* (In the Thicket of Language, 1937). At the age of fifty, Storfer has to leave Vienna; the fate of emigration also drives him to the Far East, because with time running out, both the USA and Switzerland give him a cold shoulder.

On 31 December 1938, Storfer arrives in Shanghai, where aid committee representatives at once accompany him to Hongkou. In a first report, he writes of the inexpensive life, the expensive accommodations, the bad sanitary conditions, and above all, of his dread of the terribly hot summer climate. He hopes to earn his daily bread by giving German lessons:

> I am also prepared to teach without pay at a middle school or college, above all, in order to enter into relationships with Chinese intellectual circles. I have the impression that here there is *a really intellectual life only with the Chinese.* Europeans and Americans here are usually nothing but moneymakers, rather unscrupulous, as one can well imagine given this masterless and rootless city, and are otherwise only interested in sports, local societal gossip and mundane life. A hairdresser has at any rate more status and better life chances than, for example, a professor from the Sorbonne.[29]

On May 1, 1939, five months after Storfer's arrival in the city on the Huangpu River, happy "to be out of Germany," he publishes the first edition of a journal that he founded, *the Gelbe Post*, bearing the subtitle *Ostasiatische Illustrierte Halbmonatsschrift* (Yellow Post: East Asiatic Illustrated Fortnightly Journal). In the first issue, he states that he intends the journal to be as unbiased as possible and will not deal primarily with political affairs. Storfer makes this explicit, placing his emphasis on China-related topics, and right at the beginning trying to correct an image of China that has changed little for centuries in the West:

> Anyone who with his own eyes has seen the burdened coolies, has listened to their sing-song with his own ears . . . should not forget that it is not a nodding Mandarin, such as we once smiled at among the chinoiseries on our grandmothers' Ottoman mantel piece, that is the symbol of this country and not an amply robed wizard whose staff whirls endless scrolls through the air, not a treacherous Chinese knife-wielder of the sort that creepy, mediocre detective stories once believed they could not do without, not a newly rich opium dealer who in contented leisure folds his hands over a fattened paunch, . . . but rather that the real representative of the Chinese urban populace is no one more than the coolie working hard like a robot and yet living only a deprived existence. . . . Hats off to them. Hats off to the coolie; hats off to the hard working Chinese people![30]

Storfer's lines express sympathy for those little blessed by fortune, a sort of humanity that only someone can know who has first-hand experience of being denied it. A similar mentality—to be sure with a note of irony, one of his most masterful stylistic means—is expressed by a contribution entitled "1 Kick = 10 Cents," in which Storfer warns the Western residents of Shanghai against regarding the Chinese as uncivilized and acting accordingly, as otherwise negative repercussions would come to pass for the West:

> The Chinese are neither primitive savages who have yet acquired nothing, nor semi-savages who have only adopted some superficial features of European civilization. If the white man does not understand the savage, this is because he cannot place himself in the perspective of the primitivism of his thinking. As to

> what concerns the Chinese, however, it would be better to say that we are just not equal to the wealth, the complexity of their thinking. . . . A kick may be given at first to pay 10 cents, and whoever imposes this forced rate of exchange may temporarily feel obscenely well about it. But who can ensure that on a later account page horrendous differences in rates might not then result that must be settled.[31]

In his contributions, Storfer tries to enlighten his Western readers about their nearer and wider surroundings, to direct their attention beyond their own fate to the social, cultural, and political conditions in China. The *Gelbe Post* has the reputation of being a mouthpiece for the arts, cultures, and societies of East Asia, with a renown extending far beyond the Shanghai emigrant world. The cover of the *Current and Topical East Asian Album*, a collection of the *Gelbe Post's* first seven issues, states that it contains "100 essays and 150 illustrations about institutions, proceedings, customs, traditions, individual personalities, and general types (statesmen and generals, revolutionaries and gamblers, boys, coolies and beggars, poets, and women of easy virtue) in Shanghai, China, Japan, Korea, Manchuria, etc." Storfer, who stemmed from a European landscape of many peoples *par excellence*, bursts the Shanghai emigrant world's narrow fetters with his longing to capture Chinese life, to go a step farther from a personally suffered fate in search of his foreign neighbors' mentality. Numerous contributions in the *Gelbe Post* deal with the possible assimilation of the Jews in the interior of China.

With his *Gelbe Post,* Storfer ultimately expresses the conviction that only a good understanding of Chinese *Lebenswelten* could guarantee emigrants a relatively secure existence in the Far East. To this belongs the sharpening of critical self-evaluation by the Western community of fate itself. Storfer wants to give readers a chance to relativize their own situation, true to the Chinese saying, "Who has seen little wonders a lot." In this sense the *Gelbe Post* fulfills a sort of mirror function insofar as it shows Westerners that critique need not point in only one direction and that negative stereotypes are always a matter of insufficient understanding, as, for example, in the contribution "Chinese Scorn Over Handshaking" (an excerpt from Lin Yutang's book *The Importance of Living*).

Unfortunately, the *Gelbe Post* is not destined for a long life. After just half a year, Storfer changes the magazine into a twice-weekly newspaper, later into a daily. For readers, the *Gelbe Post* seems too demanding, especially since the emigrants often have more interest in information about the war in Europe than in the events of their immediate surroundings. Storfer increasingly has to struggle with financial and health problems, and thus he complains in a final letter to a friend about an alleged intrigue of his competitors against him.[32] On 28 August 1940, Storfer sells the *Gelbe Post* to an emigrant newspaper tycoon, Ossi Lewin, the owner and publisher of the *Shanghai Jewish Chronicle*. After that not much is heard of him. The Transylvanian Jew at least earns a modest income as an editor for the British Information Service. To this activity he owes finally—just in time before Pearl Harbor—the possibility to flee from Shanghai on board a ship and indeed to Australia, where he gets a job as a turner in a sawmill (he dies in 1944). "Perhaps he did so out of need. Not ruled out at any rate with Storfer would be that the idea had attracted him that turning knobs was a more sensible activity than writing books," writes Alfred Polgar in an obituary of Storfer.[33]

Fritz Alex Kuttner

The dictum "The nature of the cosmos is the number" has been attributed to the Greek mathematician, astronomer and philosopher Pythagoras. We owe another philosophical insight, "Music is a hidden arithmetic exercise of the soul that does not know that it is dealing with numbers," to the German philosopher Leibniz. The productivity and work of Fritz Alex Kuttner, born in Poznan (a city that belonged to Germany before WWII, now part of Poland) on 18 January, 1903, can probably best be placed in this border region between science and mysticism, whereby he doubtlessly paid greater attention in his studies to the idea of rationality than to mysticism. According to Chinese mythology, around ca. 2700 BC, the legendary Emperor Huangdi dispatched one of his ministers to the empire's western border with the assignment to "invent" music. The official cut a flute pipe in a bamboo grove with the length of the imperial foot, which provided the key note of the Chinese tonal system and the foundation of all the empire's measures of length and volume. Then, based on the singing of a heavenly pair of phoenix birds, he fashioned twelve panpipes, each a third shorter than the previous one, from which the principle of the two-thirds spacing of the pure *quinte* (interval of a perfect fifth) or respectively the Chinese tonal system of the traditional twelve *Lüs* is supposed to have resulted. This charming story from the early period of Chinese mythical illustrations points to the topic that Fritz Kuttner chiefly dealt with during his ten-year stay in China, and beyond this to the end of his life: the present and past of Chinese music.

Little is known about Kuttner's early years. According to the written records, his father married four times. In Berlin, the young Fritz, born to his father's first wife, studies—according to the 1966/67 *Who's Who in the East*—economics, and he receives a doctorate in 1932.[34] It appears that there is always more than enough money available for the young man; he does not need regular employment and can accordingly fully enjoy the easy-going, sometimes dissipated society of 1930s Berlin. He regards himself as more a German than a Jew (in later years photos often show him in front of a Christmas tree)—and above all as a scholar. Thus, it must deeply disturb him, he who detests the category "Jew," that it is Hitler, the uneducated corporal, who puts an end to his scholarly career. According to his passport, stamped with the letter "J" for "*Jude* (Jew), Dr. Alex Fritz Israel Kuttner boards a ship bound for the Far East with ten German Reich marks in his pocket on 10 April 1939.

Initially his tracks are lost in Shanghai, until in 1942 the *Shanghai Jewish Chronicle* reports on a music exhibition made possible by the "owner of the music store Philharmonia, Dr. F. A. Kuttner."[35] The music store is located on Avenue Joffre, the main shopping street of the Concession Française, and sources indicate that it was financially possible for Kuttner, at least until the official date when the "Restricted Sector" was established (in February 1943), to rent a dwelling outside the Hongkou "ghetto." After the war ends on 23 May 1945, the President of St. John's University sends a letter to Fritz Kuttner inviting him to teach as a guest lecturer on Western music theory and history for the music department of this renowned university. Therewith a musical studies journey begins for the trained economist, in whose course the Chinese tonal world will enthrall him for the remainder of his life.

"Today's music in China is of almost transcendental ugliness and vulgarity. Why? It is not learned and studied anymore, but solely played by proletarians and bunglers." This is from an undated note by Kuttner (in English) that is included among his personal papers. He must have been deeply affected by the circumstance that ancient Chinese music is not even understood by the Chinese themselves, let alone played by them. "For several years, I tried to find out where one could hear Chinese music well played, but without success. All I was able to hear was very amateurish or even primitive playing, with a poor effort to master the melodic contents of the piece."[36] At the start of his teaching activities, Kuttner feels somewhat hesitant about instructing Chinese students, but he soon concludes that they have at least as much talent for playing Western music as Western students. Yet even the Chinese students do not know much more about their country's music than that it arose more than four thousand years ago. He must himself seek the path to the Middle Kingdom's earliest musical history, whereby the first thing he realizes is that it is a great error to regard, based on the *Analects of Confucius*, the master as "*the* authority for the *whole* Chinese music history."[37] He does not dispute the view advocated by Confucius that the one who knows and hears music becomes a harmonious person—to the contrary. But he is convinced that this philosophical, sometimes mythical, at times esoteric or even trivial viewpoint distorts the true content of scientific knowledge about ancient Chinese music.

Before Fritz Kuttner starts his search to scientifically explain the scales used by Chinese musical instruments, he spends many years in Shanghai doing detailed research on Chinese ideas about music. He thereby discovers that the researcher must first reflect fundamentally about himself and about what is strange for him.—He holds that the study of nationally specific sounds—for example in Poland, Russia, or France—leads, like that of a language, to knowledge that guides far beyond the domain of music and conveys insights into a comprehensive spiritual and *Lebenswelt*. With Chinese music, he discovers a unique nuance that also expresses itself in the overall societal environment:

> And the lack of perspective in the paintings, the lack of harmony and counterpoint in music, which we might call the equivalents of perspective in Western music, these two things: visual and acoustical perspective, were found to be substituted by intensity and refinement of nuances, substituted in China, but maybe—for European taste—not fully compensated. . . . Meanwhile it seems to me that the same principle rules all the other utterances of civilized life in China. I seem to detect the same refined nuanciation in the customs of social and family life, in matters of tradition and etiquette, of tact and behaviour, in short everywhere, when people get into contact or relation to each other.[38]

"The less one knows about a civilization and its music, the more it seems to be unchanged, conservative, homogenous," states another handwritten comment by Kuttner. In understanding music, in recognizing the variety, and above all in understanding the differences among members of foreign peoples he sees the chief pillar for building bridges between East and West.

During his Shanghai years, probably chiefly after the war, Kuttner is very active; besides his teaching, he is also a lecturer at B'nai B'rith, the Jewish fraternal order. Furthermore, in the years 1948–49, using the pseudonym "Marpurg," he writes as a zealous music critic for the newspaper *China Press*, at a time when the headlines of this paper are full of appeals from politicians who warn of an attack by the Kuomintang if peace talks fail. In an introduction to a recital by a Chinese professor, Kuttner criticizes—decades before Edward Said launches the Orientalism debate—a perspective that was overly narrow, because it was under the influence of Occidental ways of perception. "Consequently, the Westerner is unable to find a direct, a naïve and absolute approach to Chinese music—his approach is, by necessity, hampered by the habitual relation to Western music, by the permanent urge to compare Oriental music with his dearly beloved and accustomed Western experience."[39]

In 1949, Kuttner leaves China to build a new life in the USA. The path to doing research on ancient Chinese music is rocky, and with his theoretical interest in the study of Chinese tones and their mathematical basis, he is an outsider. Kuttner zealously promotes an interdisciplinary manner of working for Sinologists and music scholars,[40] but his research, for example on a bronze, seven-stringed instrument stemming from the Zhou Dynasty, or on the so-called *bi* disks, round flat disks with a hole in the center, made of jade and used ritually, attract only limited interest.

China no doubt represented the high point of Fritz A. Kuttner's life—he died in New York in 1991. The Shanghai years gave him the greatest satisfaction, because they decisively informed his later work. Although denied a workplace in the USA commensurate with his needs and talents, he never lacked self-confidence. From the Sinologist's viewpoint, it appears noteworthy that in a footnote on the topic of "Chinese ideas on acoustics as a science" in Volume IV of his monumental standard work, *Science and Civilisation in China* (1962), the great China expert Joseph Needham refers to Kuttner's unpublished work: "And perhaps the work of Kuttner . . . will reopen the question."[41] The latter tried to fill that gap in the research with his 1990 *The Archaeology of Music in Ancient China*.[42] Considered in the discipline to be one of the most significant findings of his decades-long research is that what we call the Pythagorean tone system was known in China 500 to 600 years before the rise of the Pythagorean School.

Karl Blitz

Karl Blitz was born on 5 September 1897 in the Galician city of Czernowitz (Chernivtsi, now part of the Ukraine), the capital city of the Carpathian Bukovina region. Like Kuttner, he discovered an unconventional favorite activity during his years of imposed exile in Shanghai. An entry in the *Biographical Handbook of the German-Speaking Emigration after 1933* describes him briefly as an "author, inventor of Blissymbolics."[43] Like Kuttner, the native Austrian is also intrigued by the culture of China, and his later life work is influenced by a formative element of the Chinese intellectual world. In Vienna, Blitz studies music, mathematics, and chemistry, and graduates from the Technical Institute in 1922. After that, he works in the patent division of a large electronics company before his arrest following the "Anschluss" (annexation) of Austria by Nazi Germany in March 1938 and spends the next thirteen months in the Dachau and Buchenwald concentration camps. Fortunately, just before time runs out, he receives permission to leave for England; later he travels via Canada and the Pacific to Shanghai. There he is reunited in December 1940 with his wife Claire, who in the meantime has arrived via the Trans-Siberian Railroad.

Chinese characters must have strongly impressed Blitz: "I went Oriental," he writes in a chapter called "How Semantography Came into Being."

Perhaps he recalls the poetry of Rose Ausländer, like him a native of Czernowitz: "Four languages, four-language songs, people who get along." Already in his youth he, who always refused to learn any language other than German, regarded Esperanto as a solution to the Babylonian language confusion. In Shanghai, as in his native city, likewise a cosmopolitan multicultural city, Karl Blitz henceforth calls himself Charles Bliss, probably not by accident. Shanghai means for him—despite the adverse circumstances—a feeling of well-being. Unlike many other refugees, he feels well here, even if the climate is hot and humid in the summer. He senses in Shanghai an "atmosphere of world citizenship" that "made people think in broader terms." In every nook and cranny, in the police organization, the administration, even the army, above all in the International Settlement public health department, he discovers harmonious relationships between members of different nationalities. "Consequently most people in the world believe that Shanghai must be the worst place on earth. After six years of study at close quarters I maintain that *Shanghai is the only place in the world which can give us hope and proof that a world government and international co-operation and understanding is possible*."[44]

In Shanghai, Bliss quite clearly sees the power of one's own native tongue; he sees how instead of the foreign residents it is the Chinese who try to absorb fragments of Western languages. He realizes that in the Far East the only possibility to continue to use the language that is familiar from childhood on and nevertheless be able to overcome the linguistic barrier was to invent a script based on ideograms, that is, symbols that represent ideas rather than words—"such as the Chinese use, but it had to be a better one, a writing simple and clear and one which people should be able to type on a typewriter of ordinary size."[45] Thereby he has made the decision to create his so-called meaning script (Semantography). Similar to Chinese script, which since the first and second centuries AD has been divided into six classes of characters, Bliss employs a combination of various symbols (e.g., flower, tree), ideographic symbols (e.g., the word *on*), but also abstract symbols (e.g., idea). The lateral thinker from Czernowitz is convinced that a simple system of a hundred pictorial symbols would suffice "in order to vanquish Babylon in reading, writing, and thinking."

In various lectures, he successfully introduces his invention: First, at the Shanghai Jewish Club in 1943, and later in front of an audience including American officers at a Rotary Club event after WWII. With almost prophetic zeal, he advocates the view that his world script could contribute to preventing wars, or at least to eliminating narrow-minded nationalism, similar to the Chinese language, which successfully united 450 million people of different nationalities. Besides developing his meaning script, Bliss also works as a filmmaker (C.K. Bliss Film Service) and lives from productions commissioned by prosperous Western private individuals or companies. His films capture the typical Shanghai street scenes of that time: toiling rickshaw coolies, beggars vegetating in the streets, foreigners amusing themselves on horse-drawn trams, or the typical street libraries: "It was for me a constant source of wonder, seeing these children consume ravenously those queer and cumbersome Chinese characters . . ."[46]

Six years after his arrival, Bliss and his wife leave the Huangpu metropolis for Australia, where he henceforth dedicates himself to the development of his "language of the non-speakers," a pictorial and value-free language. At first no publisher is interested in the publication of his three-volume, several hundred page manuscript on his universal symbol script, not even when Bertrand Russell promotes the second, expanded edition with the following words: "Supporting Bliss' work means performing an important service to mankind."[47] Only in the early 1970s is Bliss' life work rediscovered in the course of a literature study by the Canadian Ontario Crippled Children's Centre. A group of therapists was searching for a method of communication for physically handicapped children. After extensive study, they concluded that BLISS, as the language was later officially named, could lead to positive changes in users—from the cerebrally paralyzed to the mentally handicapped. The most recent projects (likewise in Canada) deal with BLISS texts and the possibility of using them on the Internet.

With Karl Bliss' very personal Shanghai experience and reworking, he passed on to a technical posterity at least one element of the East-West exchange that is worth more than a brief mention. In another publication, *The Invention and Discovery that Will Change Our Lives* (1970), Bliss, who died in Sidney in 1985, called himself a "scientist in rebellion." Here the already seventy-year-old Bliss discusses in an elementary but urgent manner the question of the meaning of logic, of the word and its potentially explosive force, in the end closing the circle of his life story with his origins: "But thirty-four of our relatives died in deportation and the gas chambers. I dedicate this book to them, and to all the millions who died with them. May my book help to avoid future tragedies caused by words."[48]

General Jakob Rosenfeld

"From KZ inmate to People's Liberation Army brigade physician" is the heading of a contribution about a third Austrian-Jewish physician who found his way to China.[49] Referred to here is Jakob Rosenfeld, born in Galician Lemberg (today's Lviv in the Ukraine) on January 11, 1903. In contrast to his professional colleagues Drs. Jensen and Freudmann, he has no experience in

Spain, but still he travels straight across Kuomintang-controlled territory to the "liberated areas" and offers his services on the Chinese battlefield there. His superiors are later to express their gratitude: "Comrade Rosenfeld, you have come as an anti-fascist fellow soldier far across the ocean to China in order to participate in the anti-Japanese war and now serve in the hostile hinterland in the work of the New Fourth Army."[50]

However, Jakob Rosenfeld does not seem to have been born for revolution: His father, Michael, is a loyal Imperial and Royal (Austro-Hungarian) military officer; his mother Regina, née Wohlmann, stems from an orthodox Jewish home. When he is seven years old, his family moves from the eastern corner of the Hapsburg lands to the rather staid Wöllersdorf in Lower Austria. Until the First World War, his mother prepares kosher cuisine; later, because of food rationing, she sometimes cooks pork goulash. The parents speak German, Polish, and sufficient Hebrew to be able to pray, although the synagogue (in Wiener Neustadt, a town located south of Vienna) is too far away to go there every Saturday. At any rate, Jakob receives Jewish religious instruction, although he does not distinguish himself with his zeal. Instead, the secondary school student is brilliant in the German classics, in Latin and Greek. Then the talented young man studies medicine in Vienna. During his years of study he can pursue his interests without restrictions: music, theater, and fine arts. After earning a medical degree in 1928 and completing an internship, he and his sister open a private practice in Wiener Neustadt. He loves everything "beautiful and pure" and earns enough money to undertake cultural visits to nearby countries. But these golden years do not last very long: The civil-war-like situation in Austria in 1934 following the failed Nazi putsch against Chancellor Dollfuss gives Rosenfeld a premonition that behind the gray clouds a threatening storm is brewing.

In 1934, anti-Jewish laws take effect in Vienna, where Rosenfeld has in the meantime moved. About ten percent of the Austrian capital's population is Jewish, and life becomes a torment for them, especially after the annexation by Germany in March 1938. The persecution also hurts Jakob Rosenfeld, the humanist and philanthropist, who due to the events in his homeland increasingly develops sympathy for the Social Democratic Party. In May of the same year, the Nazis first send him to Dachau, a KZ near Munich, where he suffers as a defenseless victim of Nazi brutality. Transferred to Buchenwald, a notorious KZ near Weimar, he suffers severe bodily injuries as a result of vicious beatings. After a year in "protective custody," the Nazis free him, and he learns that his father—in the meantime deceased—has made emigration plans for him. Jakob has relatively good luck and is able to leave Vienna for the Far East in June 1939 (only years later does he learn of his beloved mother's death in a KZ near Minsk). As an outcast, completely uprooted, yet at least

Figure 3.8
"From KZ inmate to brigade physician of the People's Liberation Army" was the newspaper heading of a contribution about the life and work of Jakob Rosenfeld. He once compared Mao Zedong's Long March to Moses' difficult wandering through the desert. On the left is Liu Shaoqi, President of the PRC from 1959 to 1968, and on the right Chen Yi, a communist marshal and Foreign Minister from 1958–1972.

a survivor, he arrives a few weeks later in Shanghai on the *Lloyd Triestino*. In the international city, he can practice medicine free from harassment: At Avenue Joffre 1252B (now Huaihai Lu), he opens a medical practice as a "Specialist for Diseases of the Liver, Bladder, and Prostate." He spends his free time with friends, Jewish-Austrian emigrants, in the Restaurant Fiaker or the Chocolate Shop, and discusses political and general events. In such an "island of luxury," he also meets his Galician compatriot Hans Shippe. The latter enlightens him on the war situation in China and introduces him, in his apartment on Bubbling Well Road (now Nanjing Xi Lu) to Dr. Shen Qizhen, a Chinese physician secretly working for the CCP. The latter, who speaks perfect German, describes to him the Revolution in China, the fragile, unstable alliance between the Kuomintang and the communists in response to Japanese militarism and the invaders' atrocities.

Thereby the spell is broken for Jakob Rosenfeld, who vows to take revenge on fascism: The attack by troops of Chiang Kai-shek on the communist New Fourth Army under the command of General Ye Ting in Jiangxi in January 1941 is merely another reason for him to volunteer as a doctor to serve the troops in the "liberated areas." For the next eight years, he accompanies the communist troops of the New Fourth Army, as well as of the Eighth Route Army, on their advances and retreats, and thereby operates on soldiers and commanders almost to the point of exhaustion. His area of service extends thereby from Jiangsu to Shandong, from Liaoning into the province of Heilongjiang, and finally from Jilin to Peking. Everyone who meets him finds words of praise for "Luo daifu," the Herr Doctor from Vienna. They treat him like a Chinese. With great enthusiasm, Rosenfeld reads Mao's text on the "new democracy" and discusses literary questions for nights on end with Chen Yi, the New Fourth Army commander. As well the existing relationship between the ordinary soldier and the army leadership impresses him greatly. In 1942–43, Rosenfeld gains honorary membership in the communist party. He feels as though he were now part of a family, but perhaps also experiences a certain substitute for what the Nazis have taken away from him. Images of the concentration camps continually haunt him; abhorrence of violence, terror, suffering, and injustice pursue him until the end of his life.

Occasionally he writes articles that appear in local newspapers (in translation, because Rosenfeld speaks little Chinese, with a few exceptions to meet his everyday needs). He criticizes the superficial pictures of China in the West, because they either take the commercial life of entrepreneurs in the foreign concessions as their topics or concentrate on the "superficial and shallow" Chinoiserie descriptions of a Lin Yutang or Pearl Buck. "If, however, foreigners move their feet a few Li from the large cities of China, then they can recognize the real situation. Four hundred million people live in China. . . . Almost all of them lead a life that is so miserable that one can scarcely describe it."[51] In 1943, he changes his area of service and is transferred to the Eighth Route Army in Shandong. He himself would like to go to Yan'an in order to meet the great revolutionary leaders face to face, which to his regret never becomes possible. Still he believes that as well in Shandong there are signs that, "In the Twentieth Century, China [will] be a country that will run up against no limits to its developmental possibilities."[52] He is overjoyed when he learns that the war in Europe is over, but does not know exactly what to do with his future. Austria is an occupied country, his parents are dead, his brothers and sisters are missing, and he himself has no homeland. Thus, it happens that he also spends the Civil War years in China: first in Shenyang, the former Mukden, the location of the offices of Party Secretary Peng Zheng and the Commander of the Autonomous People's Army of the Northeast, Lin Biao. After this, there is a short stay in Harbin, later in Tumen on the Korean border, and again in Harbin. There he, the Galician Jew, chooses to attend Emmerich Kalman's operetta *Gräfin Maritza* (Countess Maritza) at the Russian Theater. Finally, with the 1948 fall and winter offensive leading to the Kuomintang's total defeat in Manchuria, he accompanies the Red Army troops on their march toward Peking, which surrenders without a struggle at the end of January 1949:

> Over all the houses, on the old ramparts and the countless gables of the "Forbidden City," the Imperial Palace, the red flags waved with the five golden stars, the banner of the Liberation Army. Red, the color of joy and happiness in China, red the color of the Revolution, held sway over the cityscape. Peking had become red. Peking was in a frenzy of joy. The city of schools, the city of students, the cultural center of China sang and danced in the streets, squares and public gardens.[53]

Rosenfeld feels out of place in the midst of this frenzied Communist enthusiasm for the Civil War's end (during the victory celebration he finds himself far from the official VIP stand), and perhaps the new leadership wants to quite deliberately prevent any possible interference by Western foreigners. At any rate, due to his poor health, a vacation in Austria is recommended for Rosenfeld. He follows this advice and departs from Shanghai by ship in October 1949 (after Shanghai's Mayor Chen Yi praises him as a "living Dr. Bethune"). Back in Austria, he finds it hard to acclimatize himself to his old, cherished Vienna. The city lies in ruins; his grief about the death of his mother knows no bounds. He feels frustrated because of his failure to help her. He would like to write a book and report on his experiences in China, but world politics closes the door on this. The People's Liberation Army leaders, whom he personally knows and whose biographies he has made use of in his book, are fighting on the North Korean side against Western troops—a conservative publishing house is now out of the question. The left-leaning publishing houses, on the other hand, which brought out the reportages of Jensen and Freudmann, are more oriented to the Soviets, and this probably discourages Rosenfeld. He vainly strives to return to China: The rejection of his visa application by the PRC representatives in East Berlin severely disappoints him, the man without a country: Rosenfeld feels he does not belong anywhere. In the summer of 1951, he leaves Europe abruptly in order to settle in Israel. To his sister, who is living in London, he writes, "My sudden decision . . . will surprise you, but you know my balmy temperament, briefly I have already been in the 'Holy Land' for four days, received very cordially. . ."[54] On 22 April 1952, he dies in Tel Aviv of a heart ailment that has plagued him ever since his confinement in the concentration camps. Only decades after this commendable helper and philanthropist passes away is his diary discovered.[55] He had dedicated it to Mao Zedong, the "genius of the new China."

NOTES

1. The most comprehensive work on the European refugees in wartime Shanghai was written by David Kranzler: *Japanese, Nazis & Jews* (1976).

2. To mark the 25th Anniversary of the "old Shanghailander," from: Program of the Commemorative Celebration of 21 October 1973 in New York, in: Leo Baeck Institute, David Ludwig Bloch Collection, AR 7199, Box 3, Folder 3.

3. A book with a selection of works completed by Bloch during his stay in China is also oriented to this classification of Bloch's woodcuts: Bloch, *Holzschnitte* (Woodcuts, 1997).

4. *Shanghaier Morgenpost*, 14 November 1941, p. 5.

5. *Asiana*, January 1943, Vol. III, No. 20, pp. 46.

6. Statement made in an interview with the artist on 18 July 2000 in Munich. Bloch died in the USA on 16 September 2002 at the age of 92.

7. *Gelbe Post*, Vol. 1, No. 5, 1 July 1939, p. 107.

8. Ibid., p. 109.

9. *Shanghai Herald*, undated (Kranzler Archive).

10. Cited from: *Die Neue Zeit*, No. 27, 2 February 1946, p. 4.

11. From the obituary in *Weltbühne*, No. 11, 15 March 1949, n. pag.

12. Cited from an article by a certain O. Rapoport in: *Nascha Shisn*, 27 October 1944, p. 3.

13. The autobiography of Willy Tonn is available—together with a large, unsorted accumulation of documents and other material—in the Archive of the Leo Baeck Institute under: Willy Tonn Collection, AR 7259 (Folder 1).

14. *The China Press*, 31 August 1946, p. 1.

15. *Gelbe Post*, Vol. 1, No. 5, 1 July 1939, p. 98.

16. The five relationships are—according to the philosopher Mencius—the right relationship between father and son, ruler and minister (subject), man and woman, old and young, as well as between comrade and friend. The five cardinal virtues include humanity, justice, politeness, wisdom, and reliability.

17. *Gelbe Post*, Vol. 1, No. 5, 1 July 1939, p. 98. "Li," or ritual is important in Confucian philosophy. Rituals serve a moral purpose by regulating people's desires and reinforcing good and appropriate behavior. They contrast with the law, which has a more coercive character, for example, by punishing wrong behavior after it has occurred.

18. This list is found in Leo Baeck Institute, Willy Tonn Collection, AR 7259, Box 2, Folder 2/11.

19. Tonn, *Chinese Chess* (1941), p. 21.

20. *Gelbe Post*, Vol. 1, No. 4, 16 June 1939, p. 81.

21. "The Unifying Spirit of Asiatic Culture" by W.Y. Tonn, p. III (Manuscript), in: Leo Baeck Institute, Willy Tonn Collection, AR 7259, Box 2, Folder 2/10.

22. The article "Sinologist Says Foreign Life in City Below Par" appeared in the *Shanghai Herald*, 22 October 1945, p. 2 (copy in: Leo Baeck Institute, Willy Tonn Collection, AR 7259, Box 3, Folder 3/6 Add. 6).

23. Kneucker, *Shanghai* (1984), p. 156.

24. Cited from letters written in 1946 to a professor in Colorado, in: Meng, *Willi Tonn* (1995), p. 115.

25. Letter from Willy Tonn to a certain E.A. Alexander of 5 September 1949, in: Leo Baeck Institute, Willy Tonn Collection, AR 7259, Box 1, Folder 1/10).

26. Obituary by a certain Dr. Uri Baer with the subtitle "Homeland did not take him up with open arms," in the Israeli newspaper *Jedioth Chadashoth*, 31 December 1957, p. 3.

27. *Gelbe Post*, Vol. 1, No. 4, 16 June 1939, p. 94.

28. Obituary by Afred Polgar, cited in: Stadler, *Vernunft* (1987), p. 171.

29. Report by Storfer of 18 January 1939 of his first impressions in Shanghai, in: Library of Congress, Manuscript Division: Paul Federn Papers, Cont. 17. The italicized phrase is underlined in the original.

30. *Gelbe Post*, Vol. 1, No. 1, 1 May 1939, p. 2.

31. Ibid., p. 2.

32. Letter from Storfer to Fritz Wittels of July 1941, in: Library of Congress, Manuscript Division: Paul Federn Papers, Cont. 17.

33. Cited in: Stadler, *Vernunft* (1987), p. 171.

34. The author is thankful to Mrs. Carol Goodfriend from New York, a long-time neighbor of Fritz Kuttner, for providing many documents about Kuttner's life and work.

35. *Shanghai Jewish Chronicle*, 20 December 1942, n. pag.

36. "Remarks on the Sociology of Chinese Music" by Fritz Kuttner, p. 2 (sine anno), in: Goodfriend Archive.

37. Note from Kuttner, sine anno, in: Goodfriend Archive.

38. Kuttner in an April 1965 lecture on the topic of "The Rise of Music in Ancient China" given in Bloomington and Ann Arbor, p. 2, in: Goodfriend Archive, p. 8.

39. Introduction to Professor Wei Chung Loh's Recital of Classical Chinese Music, at the USIS on Friday, April 18, 1947, by Dr. F.A. Kuttner, Professor at St. John's University, p. 1, in: Goodfriend Archive.

40. Thus, for instance in: "The Archaeology of Chinese Music, Lecture No. 2" for Ann Arbor, April 14, 1965, pp. 7, in: Goodfriend Archive.

41. Needham, *Science and Civilisation* (1962), pp. 126, 176.

42. Kuttner, *Archaeology* (1990).

43. Strauss, *International Biographical Dictionary of Central European Emigrés* (1983), p. 117. More information on Charles Bliss has recently been made available on the Internet, see: http://www.blissymbolics.us/biography/

44. Bliss, *Semantography* (1965), p. 219. In the (English language) original Bliss underlines the sentence that is italicized here.

45. Ibid., p. 218.

46. Ibid., p. 101.

47. Bliss, *Semantography* (1965), dust jacket.

48. Bliss, *Invention and Discovery* (1970), p. 394.

49. Kaminski/Unterrieder, *Von Österreichern and Chinesen* (Of Austrians and Chinese 1980), pp. 828. Only thanks to the Viennese Professor Gerd Kaminski has the name of Jakob Rosenfeld become better known in the West. Kaminski has published two books on the adventurous life of the Viennese physician: Kaminski, *General Luo* (1993), as well as Kaminski, *Ich kannte sie alle* (I knew them all, 2002).

50. From a letter from Marshal Chen Yi, the Commander of the New Fourth Army and later Foreign Minister of the P.R. China, to Rosenfeld, cited from: *China Reconstructs*, September 1977, p. 29.

51. Cited in: Kaminski, *General Luo* (1993), p. 103.

52. Ibid., p. 112.
53. Cited in: Kaminski, *Ich kannte sie alle* (2002), pp. 181.
54. Cited in: Kaminski, *General Luo* (1993), p. 187.
55. The diary is published in Kaminski's book *Ich kannte sie alle* (2002).

Chapter 4

"Foreign Experts" and Supporters of Mao's Revolution

After the communist seizure of power in 1949, Western missionaries, entrepreneurs, adventurers, researchers, and adherents of Chinese exoticism were no longer active in the Middle Kingdom. In the 1950s Soviet advisors made up the majority of the "Foreign Experts" stationed in China,[1] but there were also revolutionaries from the Third World, along with progressive-thinking Westerners—political refugees, enemies of the expelled Kuomintang government, and also adherents of the ideas of Mao Zedong. They all shared the will and the determination to leave their original homeland for a good cause in order to serve China and its people. Called by some the regime's "propagandists" and "useful fools," and by others "idealists" and "brilliant thinkers," they enjoyed a view of the newly founded communist state's politics and society such as was otherwise not permitted to foreigners since the Kuomintang government's withdrawal from the mainland.[2] That assessments of Foreign Experts, especially over the past few years, have undergone significant changes is also due to the end of the Cold War. Issues that were formerly bracketed as political because discussing them was inopportune are today judged more critically and objectively. Finally, it is fair enough to mention the fact that once these Foreign Experts decided to stay in China after 1949, they lost all opportunities to be "free agents." Every aspect of their lives was strictly regimented and controlled by the state.

Israel Epstein

Israel Epstein would have fulfilled all the requirements for a successful journalistic career in the West: intelligence, acumen, a gift for observation, an agreeable writing style—and years of experience as a war correspondent. In short, Eppy, as his friends always called him, was a witty, imaginative, historically thinking, and internationally experienced reporter. He could just as easily have found a place in the annals of Western China reportage as Edgar Snow or Theodore White. But precisely his stubborn way of thinking, formed by the events and spirits of his times, was fatal for his career, at least in the West. Instead, Epstein, born in Poland in 1915, is regarded in the history of Westerners in China as a "model" Westerner, a legendary propagandist in the service of the "new China," pejoratively speaking the Chinese equivalent of a Russian "court Jew."

In his own words, Epstein was as a youth especially taken by the Jewish philosophers Baruch Spinoza and Uriel da Costa.[3] Both decisively influenced his way of thinking and unconventional path through life: the former with his ideas on ethics, the latter with his rejection of rabbinical authorities. Eppy's parents come from Lithuania; both belong to the General Jewish Labour Bund. Like most Russian Jews, they choose the Siberian route to leave the Czarist Empire for the Far East. The family first lives in Harbin, and when Eppy is five, they move to Tianjin. At home they speak Russian and proclaim themselves secular ("I never observed the Sabbath, entered a synagogue perhaps three times in my whole life"). The majority of the Tianjin Jews then could eat ham sandwiches—according to Epstein—without batting an eye. Father Lazar, a book dealer, refers to himself as a social-democratically oriented Marxist ("a portrait of Marx hung on the wall at home"). He rejects Zionism for geopolitical reasons and impresses upon his son never to refer to their Chinese hosts with the insulting terms common in the international concessions, for example, "Chinks." Like most Western foreigners in Tianjin at that time, Epstein attends the English school and has almost no contact with Chinese of his age, although his father continually urges acculturation and interprets the colonial situation in China as the beginning of the end of Western superiority.

After finishing high school, Epstein earns his first journalistic spurs as a reporter with the *Peking & Tientsin Times*. At the age of eighteen, he discusses Edgar Snow's book *Far Eastern Front* and makes contact with Americans in Peking. World affairs fascinate him, especially the confused situation in China, which regards itself as threatened from all sides. He manages to get in touch with United Press International (UPI), and after the Japanese attack in July 1937—he himself was an eyewitness of the Marco Polo Bridge Incident (with the Mukden Incident the start of the Sino-Japanese War)—he leaves the city near the Bohai Sea. (This is the innermost gulf of the Yellow Sea, a busy sea lane because of its proximity to Peking.) In the following years, he reports for the American press directly from the various battlefronts (among others as a freelance journalist for *The New York Times*). At the age of only twenty-four, his first book appears, *The People's War* (1939), published by

Figure 4.1
"I felt that the communists were my sort of people, and perhaps they felt that I was their type," gave the Polish-born Israel Epstein once as reasons for his involvement with China. Cover of the book Aipositan xinwen zuopin xuan *[Selected Reportage on China by Israel Epstein], Beijing 1995.*

the well-known Londoner Viktor Gollancz, a founder of the Left Book Club.[4] Epstein's work is a historically situated study of China's war against Japan and its prehistory, without any personal-atmospheric note, but instead with some half-truths and personal wishful thinking (although the book cannot, unlike many others of the period, be characterized as particularly opposed to the Kuomintang). The idea, for instance, that the city of Hankou fell to the Japanese because the Japanese Empire thought it was empowered to attack by the Munich Agreement sounds plausible, but in the opinion of the reviewers in the *China Weekly Review,* untenable.[5] Epstein also seems to take every word from the mouth of a communist at face value, resulting in an overestimation of the Chinese people's powers of resistance. Of interest from the historian's viewpoint is his opinion that the growing strength of the communist movement in China was due to the swelling impetus of peasant nationalism—a thesis that various historians later seized on in order to explain the communist victory in 1949 as resulting from the events of the war years.[6]

In the war years Epstein, a tireless champion of the United Front, works for a Kuomintang radio station in Chongqing, but chiefly, however, for Madame Sun's China Defense League in Hong Kong. Together with Gunther Stein, he travels to Yan'an in 1944 and a year later returns to the USA to write his second book, *The Unfinished Revolution* (1947).[7] A review of this book by the prominent intellectual Owen Lattimore subsequently appears in *The New York Times.* While the China expert concedes Epstein's partisanship for the communists, he nevertheless praises the book as providing a basis for the reader to form his own opinion. "He convinces me that the trend of the civil war in China is not toward the triumph of an ideology or the winning of dictatorial power by individual generals or politicians. It looks as though what is going to win out is people—millions and millions of people."[8] Similar to the expectations of many other contemporary commentators, Lattimore's optimism is to prove unfounded. The anti-Communist hysteria in the USA subsequently makes it easier for Epstein to accept an invitation from Madame Sun to return to China (1951), and it is good that he quickly left the country, because soon after that newspapers begin mentioning his name in connection with the debate on the "loss of China."[9]

With his return to China, he ceases to display any reticence about expressing pro-communist attitudes: "I felt that the communists were my sort of people, and perhaps they felt that I was their type."[10] In the following years, Epstein writes numerous books and articles that are all full of praise for the "new China" and aim at promoting the social acceptability of a government despised in the West. Personal statements and individual encounters or moods are lacking; he places them, if at all, in the respective political context or in the service of the ruling ideology. *From Opium War to Liberation* (1956) reflects the classical historical understanding of the communist government, while in *Tibet Transformed* (1983) he recapitulates and justifies the official Chinese Tibet policy. Just like the Peking leadership, to make the discontinuity appear as striking as possible, Epstein endeavors to demarcate sharply the achievements of the "new China" and the "semi-feudal" conditions of the country under the Kuomintang. No exploitation, no corruption, no filth anymore—they have been replaced by equality, honesty, and cleanliness in the "new China."[11] Epstein often vehemently objects to the supposedly false picture that the West promulgates of Mao's China. He does not even shy away from criticizing his former colleagues. Under the title "Fooling the People," he attacks the China experts John K. Fairbank, Owen Lattimore and Edgar Snow, who he claims falsified history and spread "counter-revolutionary thoughts."[12]

In China, Epstein is celebrated and flattered and receives Chinese citizenship in 1957. He is one of the co-founders of the foreign language journal *China Reconstructs* (later called *China Today*), joins the Chinese Communist Party, and in 1983 becomes a member of the Chinese People's Political Consultative Conference (CPPCC), an advisory organ in which at one time five of ten non-Chinese members were of Jewish origin.[13] Epstein is the mascot of the group of "Foreign Experts" in Peking, who are expected to bring the power-holders good fortune in the form of foreign recognition. He has contacts with the highest state dignitaries: until her death in 1981 with Madame Sun, about whom Epstein writes the biography *Woman in World History: Soong Ching Ling* (1995), with Zhou Enlai, whose wife supposedly once made possible Epstein's flight from Japanese troops, and with China's patriarchs Deng Xiaoping, Li Peng, and Jiang Zemin. Forgotten are the years of solitary confinement during the Cultural Revolution, which affected almost all the foreigners living in China at the time. "I share your feelings, because I've also spent six years in prison on grounds of false accusations," Deng Xiaoping proclaims on Epstein's seventieth birthday.[14] Even today, supporters of the Chinese state regularly cite him, and even Premier Wen Jiabao insisted on attending the celebration of his eighty-eighth birthday in his Peking apartment.[15] Epstein passes away in Peking on May 26, 2005, and is laid to rest in the Babaoshan Heroes Cemetery.

The Polish Jew spent almost ninety years in China and thereby experienced China's many twentieth century upheavals. Similar to his comrades in fate, there is a close connection between his personal career and later life tasks. To condemn him for his propaganda work from a contemporary perspective would be wrong. Rather, we must again ask about the reasons for each individual's decisions, given the spreading influence of inhumane ideologies during the twentieth century. For Epstein it seemed clear that given the fascist and Nazi threats of those times, he would devote his life to the struggle against these totalitarian worldviews. He compares people to corks floating on water; the individual can always choose the wave on which he wants to swim. Living in an age of extremes, he simply happened to find himself on one that was no less ideological and totalitarian in nature than the others.

Sidney Shapiro

Sidney Shapiro, a hale and hearty gentleman with a typical Brooklyn accent and alert eyes, lives for several decades in a rectangular Peking residential court still spared from the demolition craze dominant everywhere in China's cities, the "Siheyuan," at Nanguangfang 24, not far from the shores of Houhai Lake and the former residence of Guo Moruo. The beautiful garden is resplendent with roses and cactus plants. The living room is simply furnished and contains books by Shapiro himself and some by his intellectual mentors, Mao Zedong and Deng Xiaoping.[16] Like the older Sokolsky and Granich, Shapiro also hails from the Lower East Side of New York; he is born in 1915 of parents from respectively the Ukraine and Lithuania. During his stay in the Middle Kingdom in the last half of the twentieth century, he sought an alternative field of activity: as a translator of Chinese literature, for which he has also become known to Western Sinologists, and, less well known, as the editor of a book on the Jews in ancient China.[17]

In contrast to Epstein, a Pole born in the same year, Shapiro initially does not really know what he is seeking in China. After law school, he joins the US Army in 1941 and is assigned to a language unit with an emphasis on Chinese, but it is on an ocean voyage that he finally reaches the Middle Kingdom in April 1947. Like Epstein, a secularly oriented Jew ("I left God"), in his childhood he at any rate attends synagogue on holidays. Unlike Epstein, he has no knowledge of Marxism, but after arriving in Shanghai, he falls head over heels in love with a beautiful actress who has ties to the communists. In his autobiography, *I Chose China* (2000), he, who until then simply based his picture of China on the American media, recalls his first impression of the Chinese. "When I got to China I found that here were people—I'm not talking just about the Communists or the political people—who were very kindly and considerate, very family-oriented people who, if you were their friend, there was absolutely nothing they wouldn't do for you, to an embarrassing extent."[18]

Shapiro and his wife move to Peking shortly before Mao's troops take power and witness their entry into the city. In a roundabout way, he finds work in the state publishing house, Foreign Languages Press, which specializes in the publication of pro-government pamphlets and books. Shapiro now serves the "new China." He writes about the end of prostitution, the reduction of criminality, the land reform, the overall cleanup. In the *China Monthly Review,* he defends the entry of Chinese "volunteer" units into the Korean War.[19] Shapiro becomes, as he himself says, a man who loves the discussion and study groups of his "unit" above everything. Over time he learns more and more about Marxism and the ideas of Mao Zedong; in contrast to Epstein, however, he never becomes a member of the Chinese Communist Party, although he receives Chinese citizenship in 1963.

In his autobiography, he attempts to convince Western readers that China should be judged by its own standards. His autobiography has an authentic feeling and contains a very personal note; occasionally the presentation seems all too self-centered. Many of his ideas appear naïve from a contemporary perspective, yet one can believe that he then had great confidence in the new socialist morals. As befits a "Foreign Expert," he unreservedly adopts the official line, for example, against religion or respectively popular superstitions. Shapiro believes in communism, in the "new society" to be created, and even criticizes Mao only where the party line permits this (for instance in connection with the Great Leap Forward). "Yet swept along by the Chinese revolution, I was coming closer to socialism, at least in mental outlook. By the early 1960s I knew that in China I had the kind of life I wanted most. . . . I liked the political atmosphere, the cultural and social life."[20] Without scruple, Shapiro adopts the current propagandistic expressions of that time like "barking dogs" (referring to Western critics) or the "unleashed" Chiang Kai-shek. His views on Tibet also conform, as with Epstein, to official government positions. Finally, he even compromises himself as an actor by playing foreign villains.

Of some interest is Shapiro's report on an inspection trip in December 1980 to the province of Sichuan, where at the time the now ostracized Zhao Ziyang ruled as party chief. His reportage reveals—with citations of Chinese academics and factory managers—a hardly concealed critique of state policy that would have been impossible years later.[21] He rather frankly criticizes the party leadership's excessive reaction to the incidents surrounding the demonstrations on Tiananmen Square in 1989. Like most of the remaining old "Foreign Experts," Shapiro regrets the degeneration of the moral order that existed under Mao. And like some of the "Foreign Experts" of Jewish origin, toward the end of his life he reflects on his Jewish roots: "But here [during his 1989 visit to Israel—author's note] was where it started, the primary essence of me as a Jew began here. I found an origin."[22] Shapiro consequently never regretted his decision to adopt China as his second homeland: "China opened up to me the extraordinary opportunity to experience how with human efforts one could lead a country out of the depths of the greatest humiliation up to a decent sort of society."[23]

Sidney Rittenberg

For the one a liar, for the other a loner of remarkable charm: Sidney Rittenberg, born into the family of a prosperous attorney in Charleston, South Carolina in 1921, is in any case one of the most mysterious figures in the group of "Foreign Experts"[24] and without doubt the most powerful. According to rumors, he even tried to topple Premier Zhou Enlai.[25] Of all those in the group, he saw China's prison walls from inside for the longest time: Of his 35 years in the Middle Kingdom, he spent a total of sixteen in solitary confinement, a truly unusual fate.

Rittenberg's maternal grandfather came from Russia; in his childhood, he attends the synagogue and Jewish elementary school, although he later claimed to be non-religious. Sid, as his friends call him, is a good pupil and masters foreign languages effortlessly, a gift that is of advantage to him again in 1942, when he, like Shapiro, is selected by the army for an intensive course in Chinese at Stanford University. Already during his studies, he gets involved as a member of the American Communist Party in fighting for the rights of coal miners and textile workers. He is also active in the civil rights movement against racial segregation, then common in the USA. His involvement earns him a jail sentence.

In the fall of 1945, the U.S. Army sends him as a language specialist to Yunnan's capital of Kunming. "True, I was a reformer, a revolutionary, almost a zealot for the social causes of the day. But China wasn't one of them. I never dreamed, as so many Americans did, of saving China."[26] Then he has experiences that dramatically change his life perspective. The despicable behavior of an American truck driver toward a Chinese girl, as well as the everywhere visible Kuomintang corruption, drives him, as he himself says, into the communists' arms. Whenever possible, he meets with their liaison people. This includes meetings in Shanghai, and as an observer for the UNRRA in Hunan, where he is an eyewitness of a terrible famine. He works in the territory of the New Fourth Army itself, in the Dabie Mountains, and in the border areas of the provinces of Hubei and Anhui, where the troops of Li Xiannian, the later State President, are no longer moving in the wake of the cease-fire negotiated by General Marshall. There it seems that Sid, who by now has assumed the Chinese name of Li Dunbai and works as a translator, for the first time feels the inner urge to intervene in China's internal affairs. He warns Li that the Americans might be lulling the communists into a false sense of security while covertly supporting the Kuomintang. After that, he works as a representative of the United China Relief Organization in Kalgan (now Zhangjiakou), which is then under the rule of the later Marshal, Nie Rongzhen.

In October 1946, Rittenberg's greatest wish comes true: After a journey of several weeks on foot and riding on the backs of horses and mules, the twenty-five-year-old reaches Yan'an, where he personally meets Mao for the first time: "I could scarcely believe my good fortune. This was the Mao Zedong I had been reading about in the daily press, the Mao whose words I had studied in Stanford. I respected his vision for China and admired his philosophical brilliance."[27] From this moment on, he is a captive of a living icon, of an ideology that in the truest sense of the word fetters him, reduces his ability to make decisions to a minimum, and makes him an unresisting tool without his being aware of this. Rittenberg, who works as an advisor for the English language radio station, assumes the position of an intermediary between the communists and the American government. Modesty is not one of his virtues: Proud of his role in the revolution, he enthusiastically participates in "struggle meetings" against the large landowners. He finds them necessary in order to "bring about peace on earth and goodwill to all the multitudes of downtrodden people in the world." He wants to strive ever higher, to place himself fully in the service of this revolution. But the higher one ascends, the farther one can fall. When the news reaches Yan'an of Anna Louise Strong's arrest by Stalin in early 1949, Rittenberg is taken into custody on charges of espionage.[28] He, who personally knows everyone in the communist top cadre and who has become a Chinese Communist Party member, is held in solitary confinement for six years. His release comes only in April 1955, after the Chinese have informed him that they had imprisoned him on false charges.

Like others imprisoned by the communist system, Rittenberg is subjected to brainwashing and, like a number of Westerners, after his release from prison he displays a certain sympathy for those who let him stew in his own juices over the course of many years of confinement.[29] His 1993 autobiography, *The Man Who Stayed Behind,* is a sort of "mea culpa," which the skeptical reader only accepts to a limited extent. He judges too simplistically, at least from a contemporary viewpoint, the conditions in Mao's China, and above all he is the sort of person who loves basking in the spotlight. After his release, he finds work at Radio Beijing and has access, as he writes, to "top-secret meetings." Rittenberg is a good analyst, but a poor observer. With the exception of a single everyday observation, namely the various tones of the street peddlers in the pre-war period, the former U.S. soldier merely hears the mostly shrill sounds of communist politics—and then only those that he wants to hear. Some describe him as a weather vane. With but little guilt, he concedes he believed everything people told him. Yet his seemingly almost pathological drive for legitimization continually emerges, which predestines him to go along with almost all the campaigns of those times. He even enthusiastically participates in the correction campaign beginning in the late 1950s with the Hundred Flowers movement. During the Great Leap Forward, in which millions of people starve, he and his Chinese wife emulate those who brought the greatest amount of cooking pots, old tools and sundry scrap iron to local backyard blast furnaces to produce (inferior) steel.

Rittenberg is especially proud, and rightly so, of his work on the official translation of Mao's writings, a project that includes Chinese scholars and a few Western "Foreign Experts."[30] "My star was rising. . . . Everywhere I was in great demand," he comments. He sees himself as advocating the Chinese position toward other countries. Given his access to the innermost power circles, it seems odd to read that he first hears of the Cultural Revolution on the Voice of America. Again, that does not prevent him from playing an active role in this mass event lasting ten years. He, the "internationalist Communist fighter," journeys all around the country, praises the slogans of Chen Boda, a leading ideologue, holds lectures that newspapers print, and feels like a kingmaker. Smashing the old appears to excite him and further boosts his power instinct. At the start of 1967, he receives the position of Director of Radio Beijing: The foreigner Rittenberg has thereby reached the summit of his power. From then on things can only go downhill. His memories of this period sound like the morbid phrases of someone who no longer knows what he is saying.[31] At Christmas in 1967, it is suddenly all over with the star allure of the whip, agitator and brain behind the operations. The revolution begins to devour its own children, which for Rittenberg, again accused of committing espionage for America, means another period of solitary confinement, this time for all of nine years.

In March 1980, three years after his release from prison, Rittenberg and his wife depart from China for America without having accepted the Chinese government's offer of a seat on the Chinese People's Political Consultative Conference (CPPCC). However, he still serves for a short time before his departure as an advisor to the Academy of Social Sciences. The rejection of the offer by Rittenberg, the fellow traveler, sounds like a hollow phrase in view of the ideals he held high for decades: "I had come to China to serve humanity, to serve people, to change China, to change the world. I had no intention of spending the rest of my life serving those whom power had corrupted, bought by their perquisites, rendered unable to speak or act freely for what I believed in."[32] Rittenberg's chronicle, a no doubt valuable historical document, leaves more questions unanswered than it answers. In many ways, his book seems to be the work of a person who likes to attract attention and thereby comes under fire. His relationship with Jiang Qing, Mao's widow and a member of the Gang of Four, is unclear. Nor can he put to rest the accusation that he had denounced foreigners and Chinese. He tries to whitewash himself by reporting his alleged intervention on behalf of the dissident Wei Jingsheng at his condemnation in 1979, but in the same breath blames Deng Xiaoping for the increasing corruption of the power structures. Mao is for him a "brilliant, talented tyrant" whom he claims he never liked. In many cases, the respective motivations of his actions, and what is invention, what truth in his utterances about his life remain a mystery. One thing we do know is that in his later years he operated a very successful consulting business in the USA that facilitated the access of Western companies to the Chinese market. Perhaps that was the best idea of his entire life.

Sam Ginsbourg

Sam Ginsbourg, born in 1914 in Chita, a city on the Trans-Siberian Railway, spends several decades in the Middle Kingdom and never regretted this decision for the rest of his life. Ginsbourg's father came from Byelorussia, and the family fled from Czarist troops to Chita, where the father amassed a small fortune as a lumber dealer. A few years after Sam's birth, the family moves to Harbin in Northeastern China, where his father works for the millionaire coal magnet Skidelsky.[33] In his autobiography, *My First Sixty Years in China* (1982), Ginsbourg himself describes his family as above all Russian, although they attended the synagogue on important holidays and on Passover they ate *matzah* instead of bread. At the start of the 1920s, Ginsbourg's father attempts to establish a business in Vladivostok, but in vain: In 1926, the family sails to Shanghai, where Sam Ginsbourg will live for more than twenty years. He studies at the French Aurora University and later finds a position with a British engineering company.

In spring 1947, his parents having moved to the USA, he decides to strike out for the "liberated areas" of Shandong. In Weifang, the seat of the East China University, he initially teaches English, then also Russian. After the university moves to Jinan, the capital of Shandong Province, he works, besides teaching, as a translator. In 1953, now married to a Chinese woman, Ginsbourg becomes a Chinese citizen: "From that day on, I was bound not only in thoughts and feelings, but in my status, with the people of China. I was no longer 'a friend.' I was one with the 450 million Chinese. I shared their griefs and joys, their defeats and victories, their pride in a great Party, a great Motherland, a great people, a great Republic. And I have never for a moment regretted, nor lost my pride in being a citizen of MY Republic."[34] The only drop of bitterness is that Ginsbourg never attains Communist Party membership; he must content himself with belonging to the China Democratic League, a sort of bloc party.

In Russian Harbin, Sam Ginsbourg does not yet even take note of China, but at any rate, upon arriving in Shanghai as a fourteen-year-old he develops a feeling for Chinese history on forays through the city. He learns the names of the various warlords, takes an interest in the Northern Expedition and hates Japanese militarism. "But, although not considering myself a Russian any longer, I did not feel any closer to the Chinese people. There was an ever greater admiration, ever deeper sympathy—yes, but it was addressed toward an indeterminate, impersonal mass of people."[35] It is first the outbreak of Sino-Japanese hostilities in 1937 that sharpens his view of China's fate: "I sympathized with the Chinese, admired them, pitied them, wanted to know them better and to do something for them." After the founding of the

PRC, he participates in political discussions, in celebrations of the national holiday and in the constantly recurring campaigns, which he does not always approve of.[36] After the famine years following Mao's Great Leap Forward, Ginsbourg becomes acquainted with the ability of the Chinese "to take it, to pick themselves up and to go into battle again, always to look ahead and to be optimistic about the future."

During the Cultural Revolution, Ginsbourg is first called a "monster," then a "bourgeois academic authority" and finally branded a Soviet spy. Despite his suffering in those years, he remains confident and defends the ruling party and ideology until the end of his life. The Middle Kingdom has become his homeland:

> China has accepted me for what I am, in which everything pulls at me and the pull is getting stronger as the years pass. It's not because there's no anti-Semitism in this country—this is more than most great countries in the world can say today. Here I feel myself not a Jew, but a citizen because here it's not things that own me, as they used to in the old society, but I own everything I have. It is because this country has given me a sense of belonging, a sense of oneness with its people, a craft, a realization of usefulness.[37]

Eva Siao

"Despite all my criticism, I love this country just as one loves a person even if he is not perfect. I react to the many bad events that occur in the world with horror and locate them in world history. But when something bad happens in China, I suffer."[38] With these words, Eva Siao (Sandberg), the best known "Foreign Expert" in the German-speaking world, expresses her feeling for the Middle Kingdom in her autobiography, *China—Mein Traum, mein Leben* (China—My Dream, My Life, 1997). Born in German Breslau (now Wroclaw in Poland) on November 8, 1911, Eva Siao is the daughter of a German-Jewish physician. Already in her childhood, that strange Asian country appears in her dreams, but her real encounter with China must wait until 1940. Before this happens there will be years of searching and going astray which lead the "German Jewess" (she refers to herself as such throughout her life) across the European continent to the Soviet Union.[39] Eva Siao leaves school a year before obtaining her secondary leaving certificate (Abitur), because one of her teachers, a Nazi supporter, learns one day that she is Jewish (against her mother's wishes she attends synagogue with her uncle and secretly learns Hebrew). Her brother is a conductor in Sweden, and after she graduates from the State Institute for Film and Photography in Munich, Eva follows him to Stockholm in 1930. There she works in the photographic laboratory of a Russian Jew and meets Zionists, socialists and anarchists. At a friend's urging, she travels to Moscow in 1934, where she meets among others Isaak Babel and—on an excursion to the Black Sea—gets to know the Chinese poet Siao San (Emi Siao), who is later to become her husband. After a further six years of inner searching, she travels from Stockholm via Moscow, Urumqi (Wulumuqi) and Lanzhou to Yan'an, where by then Siao San has already lived for a year. Although she can finally be together with her lover after a long separation (she also marries him there), she feels lonely and three years later returns to the Soviet Union.

Between 1944 and 1949, Eva Siao lives in Kazakhstan, Moscow and Czernowitz, whereby she earns her living chiefly as a photographer. In Moscow, she is reunited in spring 1949 with her husband, whom she at once follows to China, even before the PRC is proclaimed. In Dalian, she initially works for the Chinese-Soviet Friendship Society before she moves with her children to Peking. A little later, she gets a job as a photographer for the Soviet news agency Tass and for Xinhua, its Chinese counterpart. Her first reportage trip leads her to the cities of the South: Nanking, Shanghai, Hangzhou, Guangzhou, Changsha and Wuhan. Her husband Emi is a Chinese delegate to the World Peace Council in Prague in 1951, which gives her the chance to meet many important writers, from Pablo Neruda to Ilja Ehrenburg, Guo Moruo, Thomas Mann and Arnold Zweig, once as a photographer, and again as an interpreter at various events in Europe. Eva Siao develops ties with publishing houses in East Germany, which finally publish her picture books on Peking and Tibet.[40] At home again in Peking, she makes portrait photographs of Mei Lanfang and Li Keran, one of the most beloved contemporary Chinese painters. The constant shuttling back-and-forth between East and West is a spiritual struggle for her: "I had to harmonize my love for Emi and for China, as well as my longing for Europe. On the one side, I had to bring China to Europe, on the other side, let my European friends see China through my eyes, and bring China close to them. Only then would my life and my work become meaningful."[41]

Besides her strong-willed character (she does not agree with the campaign against 'rightist deviationists' in 1957, and in many other ways she can never reconcile herself with the communist political campaigns), Eva Siao also reveals her individuality as a photographer. She does not follow the socialist credo, according to which she should show cheerfully smiling, neatly dressed workers, but rather trusts her own subjective understanding in the search for insight and truth. No pedagogical function guides her, but rather the effort to "find" pictures that express what moves her. In her opinion, only a subjectively truthful photograph can make the essence of a person visible. Between 1958 and 1964, she works in China as a film correspondent for East Germany. She is

Figure 4.2
Eva Siao's whole life had been intertwined with China, professionally as well as personally. "I see China with critical eyes, but with loving critical eyes. One must have Oriental patience in China. One cannot run one's head against a wall," she wrote in her memoirs.

repeatedly subjected to the bureaucratic harassment that intensifies as the break of China with the Soviet Union (and thereby also with the GDR) becomes increasingly apparent. Even though Eva Siao exchanges her Soviet passport for a Chinese one in 1964, this does not enable her to get through the turmoil of the Cultural Revolution unscathed: Charged with being a Soviet spy, she spends seven years in solitary confinement. After her rehabilitation, Eva Siao receives a new position with Xinhua. With the start of the policy of opening, she travels back and forth across the world in order to accompany exhibitions of her photographs or to give radio interviews about her rich, but also difficult life.

In the postscript of her autobiography, the independent, sensitive Eva Siao states, "I see China with critical eyes, but with loving critical eyes. One must have Oriental patience in China. One cannot run one's head against a wall."[42] She had to live with this until the end of her life. In China, she states in a personal interview, one always remains a foreigner. "There are a hundred things here that I do not understand."[43] Nevertheless, in her own individual way she tries to increase the Western understanding of the Middle Kingdom and its people. Her own Chinese legacy, the photographic work of three decades, represents a declaration of love for a country that became her new homeland. Her photographic studies do not build on a system, and she does not pose her pictures, but rather only attempts to document the lives of the people and cultural objects that she feels surrounded by and attracted to throughout her life. Similar to her compatriot Hedda Hammer (later Morrison), who lived in Peking before 1946, she focuses her eyes on the street life in the capital, with its markets, street peddlers, and artisans in the parks or on Tiananmen Square.[44] It is astonishing that even after 1949 she prefers to show viewers images of the old China (besides the obligatory pictures of smiling workers zealously studying the works of Mao or the blast furnaces during the Great Leap Forward): Chinese *Lebenswelten* seem for her to possess a timelessness that has not been completely obliterated by the Revolution.

Ruth Weiss

Ruth Weiss is born in Vienna on December 11, 1908, and similar to Eva Siao, develops a great love for the Middle Kingdom. Likewise, she regards the "new China" with a considerably more critical attitude than do her male "Foreign Expert" colleagues. Nevertheless, at the end of her life she was proud to be a Chinese citizen and member of the Political Consultative Conference of the Chinese People.[45] Her father, who has rigidly anti-Soviet attitudes, comes from Galicia, her mother from Upper Franconia in Bavaria. She first becomes aware of her Judaism at school. At the age of ten years, she moves with her mother to her father in Boryslav, in the crude oil producing region assigned to Poland after the First World War. Three years later the family returns to Vienna, now burdened with the stigma of being "Polish Jews." They decide to apply for Czechoslovakian citizenship. Ruth Weiss begins studying German and English in the Danube city and at the same time cultivates many other interests, as she writes in her autobiography, *Am Rande der Geschichte* (On the Edge of History 1999): "Probably it was my Jewish origin that gave me a cosmopolitan viewpoint. For a short time I flirted with emigration to Palestine in order to possibly join a kibbutz with other young people."[46]

Ruth Weiss has her first contact with China when she visits an exhibition of Chinese art works on display in Vienna's Schönbrunn Palace. Furthermore, she attends performances of Puccini's *Madame Butterfly* and Tretyakov's *Brülle, China!* (Roar, China!). Finally, similar to Eva Siao, love for a Chinese man contributes to her interest in the Far East. She earns a doctorate in philosophy in 1932 and has also mastered the fundamentals of the various Chinese schools of thought. As soon as possible, she wants to take a six-month study trip to China, "alone as a freelance journalist." With contributions on China in the Austrian media, she tries to increase her market value as a possible correspondent in the Far East. In a radio report, she deals, for example, with the question of what China can teach us in the twentieth century.

> But what do we know of the people who inhabit that vast country, what does Europe know of the Chinese? In countless films coming from the paper mâché world of the studios, we have encountered them as hypocrites, swindlers and murderers, in short as the embodiment of the cruelly mysterious; products of the lower and even of the higher literature have carried on the tradition of these characterizations, whereby the public is seduced by the fantastic conceptions to a rejecting, contemptuous attitude toward the Chinese people, and even the best educated Europeans often cannot deny their mistrust. This catastrophic error in the judgment of the yellow races stems from the identification of 'foreign' with 'different,' which means not as good as us.[47]

In *Das neue Wiener Tageblatt* (The New Viennese Daily Newspaper) she summarizes an interview with a Chinese pedagogue and writes on classical Chinese theater; in the meantime she treats the history of the Jews in the Far East in the Jewish weekly journal *Die Wahrheit* (The Truth).[48] In September 1933, she boards a ship to sail to Shanghai. Having arrived there, she soon orients herself to the group surrounding Rewy Alley, Hans Shippe, and other progressively oriented foreigners. With Julius Tandler she inspects factories "that represented an inferno of exploitation, deplorable conditions and inhumanity." It is clear to her that she must "place herself on the side of the oppressed." Initially she continues to write articles for *Das neue Wiener Tageblatt,* as well as for the *China Weekly Review*.[49] Later she finds a position as a teacher at a Jewish school. To be sure, it does not please the director that for her Judaism does not mean practicing its religious rites—and so Ruth Weiss has to reorient herself. In those years, she meets Agnes Smedley, the Granichs, Olga Lang, Madame Sun, the gangster boss Du Yuesheng, or Lu Xun, for whom she later creates a memorial with her book *Lu Xun: A Chinese Writer for All Times* (1985). In 1937, she accepts an invitation from the YWCA to come to Sichuan Province to take over the secretariat of the local organization in Chengdu and give German instruction at a missionary school. Subsequently she works as a journalist for the *Chengdu News Bulletin*, teaches English at the medical school, and later she moves to Chongqing.

In 1945, Ruth Weiss returns to Shanghai from the interior of China and a year later relocates to the USA, where she works for a few months as a secretary for the United Nations broadcasting department. Her stay in the West does not last long, because she wants so much to return to China. In 1949, she returns via Hong Kong to her adopted homeland, first to Tianjin, later to Peking whereas her leftist Chinese husband stayed in the US. There she initially works, like Michael Shapiro, as a "polisher" for the magazine *People's China*, before serving as a German expert for *China im Bild* (China in Focus). Occasionally she writes contributions for the *Sächsische Zeitung* (Saxon Newspaper) in Dresden. In contrast to Eva Siao, Ruth Weiss finds the political campaigns "fascinating." "In those years I still believed that the party always told the truth, that thus any complaint was 100% justified! How long one needed to realize that it was not that way at all will become clear later—much, much later."[50] She is one of the few foreigners not harassed during the Cultural Revolution. Only later, when writing her memoirs, does she more clearly grasp how blind she had been. She refers to Mao as a "feudalistic dictator" who tolerated neither opposition nor rational debate on opposing views. Like her compatriot Richard Frey, she reaches the conclusion that after the policy of opening, many of the evils of the old society have reemerged, above all corruption and prostitution. "Nevertheless the situation is not nearly as bad as it was earlier. China is a sovereign country; it makes every effort to eradicate the new plagues. It is to be hoped that the great success will finally be achieved! I probably will not live to see it," she writes in her autobiography.[51] Ruth Weiss spent almost seventy years in China and, "despite all the rigors in the world . . . found a new homeland" there.

Klara Blum

Mein Volk lebt in der ganzen Welt zerstreut
Gehetzt, beschimpft, von Land zu Land vertrieben.
Dein Volk, wenn es sein Reisfeld still betreut,
Es blutet unter räuberischen Hieben.

My people lives scattered over the whole world
Hounded, cursed, driven from country to country.
Your people, even if it calmly cultivates its rice field,
It bleeds under rapacious blows.

In this stanza of "The Shepherd and the Weaver," Klara Blum, born in the Hapsburg city of Czernowitz on November 27, 1904, interprets her love relationship with the theater director and journalist Zhu Xiangcheng as an encounter between two ancient peoples that while different, still have much in common.[52] Ruth Weiss once described the four-years-older Klara Blum as a very sensitive person.[53] Precisely this characteristic predestines her for a complex perception of China. In comparison with Siao and Weiss, her life fate was the hardest and saddest. Her childhood in Galicia is not happy, because her parents often quarrel and she is under pressure from her father. After their divorce, she lives with her mother in Vienna, where the two flee in 1913. Following the First World War, she chooses Romanian citizenship and begins working on a degree in literature and psychology (that she probably never completed). At the same time, she participates intensively in the Zionist movement and—until 1929—often writes articles for Jewish newspapers like the *Ostjüdische Zeitung* (Eastern Jewish Newspaper) in Czernowitz and the *Czernowitzer Allgemeine Zeitung* (Czernowitz General Newspaper). In 1929, she briefly visits Palestine, but cannot decide to remain there permanently. A little later, she joins the Austrian Social Democratic Party but for only three years. From then on, she sympathizes with the communist party, without ever joining it.

In the year when Hitler takes power in Germany, Klara Blum receives a prize for her poem "Ballade vom Gehorsam" (Ballad of Obedience). The prize consists of a two-month study trip to the Soviet Union. This short visit is to stretch into eleven years. In 1935, she obtains Soviet citizenship; three years later, she becomes a member of the Soviet Writers Union. In 1937, there is a—similar to the case of Eva Siao—fateful meeting with a Chinese. For Klara Blum it is with the already mentioned Zhu Xiangcheng, who was born into a wealthy Shanghai family in 1903. The happiness of the lovers from two so different cultural and life worlds is to last only three months: Zhu suddenly disappears in April 1938 without having taken leave of his lover. Klara Blum tries in vain to obtain permission to visit China, because she suspects that the CCP had summoned Zhu home—but in vain. She must wait ten years until in 1947 she finally receives permission to visit China via Shanghai in a roundabout way through Bucharest and Paris and with the support of the Jewish Aid Committee, only to learn there that her lover still cannot be traced. Research and inquiries by Klara Blum and Zhu's friends to official offices meet with the reply that out of consideration for the relationship with the Soviet Union, she should no longer mention the name of the "missing person."[54]

At the start of her "voluntary" Shanghai emigration, Klara Blum lives in the former Hongkou "ghetto" until she finally finds a teaching position at Tongji University (which she must give up after eight months). Her love affair with Zhu Xiangcheng in Moscow inspires her so much that from then on Chinese motifs increasingly assume a central place in her writing. In the year the communists seize power in China, she writes a novel based on her own life story, *Der Hirte and die Weberin* (The Shepherd and the Weaver), which she herself referred to as a monument to her life. After a number of political disagreements, her novel is published in East Germany in 1951.[55] According to the publisher, Karl Dietz, this novel is "written with an infinite love for China," building upon a mythical background of ancient Chinese legends.[56] Lion Feuchtwanger saw in it "the most beautiful descriptions of contemporary China, painted with love and with empathy . . . with their constantly changing natural light they make the huge country exceedingly distinct. I know of no other work that could have given me such a clear picture of the interior landscape of contemporary China."[57] Chinese scenes and themes provide the center of attention; the period of time spans the years between 1929 (in Shanghai) and 1949 (in Peking). Klara Blum thereby documents a period of Chinese contemporary history; many descriptions have a direct historical reference, and she portrays her characters realistically. She is not only enthused about the "new China," but also captivated by the beauty and splendor of its traditions, and sees the political break of 1949 as not a complete break with cultural ties to the past. She retains her positive picture of China over a longer period: in 1939 and as well twenty years later, her writings tell of a "heroic China."[58]

In *The Shepherd and the Weaver,* she rebukes her co-religionists, who as "white" people feel superior to the Chinese. Her lover's homeland represents for her a paradise, a utopian creation of her imagination, as Thomas Lange writes, a "prefiguration of a Jewish-Messianic redemptive expectation."[59] Accordingly, Chinese communism serves so-to-speak as a substitute for a Zionism that has become impossible for Klara Blum. She tries to convey to the reader what is specifically Chinese, for instance the smile of the Chinese that is not always easy for Westerners to interpret, or the strict observance of religious practices that often seem superstitious to the Westerner. The use of traditional Chinese epithets, e.g., "Yuelan" (moon orchid) or "Yueniao" (moon bird), shows that she has become better acquainted with China than many other foreigners. Much the same holds for her use of specifically Chinese expressions and idioms, such as "Nin fei xin le" (they waste their heart) or "Wan fu" (ten thousand times good fortune), which lend the novel an exotic sheen. In the novel *Schicksalsüberwinder* (Overcomers of Fate), which Klara Blum completes in 1962, but that has, however, not been published, she deals with the topic of the "evil foreigner" in China. Some of the former "Foreign Experts" justified their remaining in the PRC after 1949 with their endeavor to undo the harm done by the centuries-long exploitation of China by Western powers. Through her work, she likewise wanted to make amends for the wrongs her colonial predecessors did in the Middle Kingdom.

In 1952, Klara Blum becomes a professor of German language and literature at Fudan University in Shanghai and later also in Nanjing and applies for Chinese citizenship, which she receives two years later. Afterwards, she calls herself Zhu Bailan ("white orchid"). After a dispute with a professor from East Germany, she leaves the former capital city and in 1957 begins teaching at Zhongshan University in Guangzhou (Canton). At the start of the Cultural Revolution, some suspect her of being a spy. She now feels lonely and vulnerable: "Her dreams of having a home and the feeling of belonging to a country and a people were radically destroyed. . . . She no longer knew where she belonged. She was and remained a stranger, an outsider, despite all her efforts. She fell into the deepest sorrow, because she was not adopted and accepted by the Chinese after all, and she could not belong to them," writes the Chinese German scholar Zhidong Yang about her situation then.[60] In May 1971, Klara Blum passes away in Guangzhou without ever having disowned her membership in the Jewish people. Nevertheless, it was the Middle Kingdom where Blum, stemming from a multicultural region of Europe, had the possibility to live as a Jew without playing the role of outsider.

One might, after all, get the impression that most Jews who stayed in China even after the victory of the communists, came to China because of a progressive attitude and not because they were Jews. Perhaps they also thought progressively because they were of Jewish origin.[61]

The experiences of the Jewish wayfarers presented in this book offer contermporary readers differentiated impressions of a country and its people. In their variety their experiences go far beyond the typical images that until the twentieth century shaped over-simplified Western perceptions of the "Chinaman" or the "Yellow Peril."

Groups such as Jewish refugees from Europe or "Spanish doctors" from the Civil War in Franco's Spain were usually almost completely unprepared for their arrival in the Middle Kingdom. Thus they were much less under the influence of anti-Chinese literature than were, for example, the Old China Hands, who were in some cases more familiar since childhood with the commercial fiction of a Sax Rohmer (*The Insidious Dr. Fu-Manchu*) or the pseudo-scientific fact book of a Rodney Gilbert (*What's Wrong with China*).

This lack of mostly negative prejudices permitted some of these visitors to perceive the foreign more objectively. Furthermore, this was additionally facilitated by intensified self-reflection due to their own vulnerability and their insecure position in the Western community of China (as a minority within a minority). Through their "double exile," some developed a particularly strong inclination to reflect on their own attitude toward the "other," be it in newspaper articles or in artistic works.

The engagement and the experiences of "our" protagonists (e.g. revolutionary pilgrims, adventurers, journalists, poets, artists, businessmen, or refugees) have sometimes also contributed to reducing the distance between China and the Occident. Atmospheric descriptions of *Lebenswelten* or chronicles of political and cultural processes and networks can help us to better understand how China has become what it is today. Some of these Jewish wayfarers managed with their descriptions to liberate "the Chinese" from commonplace Western stereotypes, and sometimes even to individualize them. And others (e.g., George Sokolsky, Harold Isaacs) with their detailed knowledge of Chinese characteristics have anticipated theoretical discussions that were carried on by scholars late in the second half of the twentieth century (e.g., Edward Said's "Orientalism" thesis in the field of postcolonial studies or Huntington's "Clash of Civilizations").

In conclusion, we can also maintain that the more these visitors interacted with China, the more positive their overall image of the Middle Kingdom became and the less one-sided their opinions of the country. A fine potpourri of cultural variety instead of a crude phantom image of "China as colossus" is the result of this exchange between West and East, which for some could mean "splendor" and for others "tragedy."

NOTES

1. The (highly political) title "Foreign Friend" was bestowed by the Chinese government starting in the early 1950s on foreigners who volunteered to serve as propagandists, engineers, agronomists, or technicians in the service of the new government. As variants with minor differences in meaning, there are also the titles "Foreign Expert," "International Friend," "Old Friend of the Chinese People," or—as the highest distinction—"Internationalist."

2. See on the institution of the "Foreign Experts," as well as their meaning in the context of Chinese domestic and foreign policy, the various contributions by the New Zealand political scientist Anne-Marie Brady: *Red and Expert* (1996), *Insiders and Outsiders* (2000), *Making the Foreign Serve China* (2002).

3. I personally spoke with Israel Epstein in Beijing (on May 30, as well as on June 2, 2001) and continued regular correspondence with him until his death in 2005.

4. Epstein, *The People's War* (1939). The members of the Left Book Club—besides Gollancz—also included Labour Party MPs, as well as political scientist Harold Laski. Using all possible means, Gollancz tried during the Second World War to enable as many Jews as possible to leave Germany. After the war, Gollancz got into a dispute with George Orwell over his refusal to publish *Animal Farm* and *Nineteen Eighty-Four*. During the "Battle of Britain" a large part of the storage space of Gollancz's publishing house was bombed, and most of the copies of Epstein's book were thereby destroyed.

5. CWR, November 25, 1939, p. 488. The reviewer is John B. Powell, the publisher of this weekly newspaper. Powell does praise Epstein's extensive documentation, but criticizes the author's leftist tone.

6. See, e.g., Johnson, *Peasant Nationalism* (1962).

7. Epstein, *Unfinished Revolution* (1947).

8. *The New York Times*, June 22, 1947, Book review section, p. 29.

9. Various contributions, e.g., in *The New York Times,* mention the "negative" impression made by Epstein's books on influential personalities, such as members of the Institute of Pacific Relations, on whose behalf Epstein likewise collected documentation—e.g., *Notes on Labor Problems in Nationalist China* (1949).

10. Israel Epstein in a conversation with the author in Beijing on May 30, 2001.

11. See, for example, the report by Epstein in: Epstein, *Vignettes* (1979), pp. 277. He summarizes therein his eyewitness reports on trips to Tianjin, Shanghai, Beijing, Guangzhou and Tibet.

12. *China Monthly Review*, January 1952, p. 38.

13. These are—besides Epstein—Eva Siao, Ruth Weiss, Sidney Shapiro, and Richard Frey.

14. *China Reconstructs*, Vol. XXXIV, No. 7, July 1985, p. 35.

15. In summer 2004, an article appears in the daily newspaper *Renmin ribao* (June 23) announcing Epstein's memoirs, which have as their topic his most difficult years in the Middle Kingdom during the Cultural Revolution. The book also appeared in 2005 in English with the title *My China Eye*. There is also a documentary film about Israel Epstein called *Round Eyes in the Middle Kingdom,* directed in 1995 by Ron Levaco.

16. These impressions draw upon the author's visit with Shapiro in Beijing on May 25, 2001.

17. Shapiro's translations from Chinese into English include among others *Outlaws of the Marsh*, a classic from the Yuan Dynasty, or *Family* by Ba Jin. Shapiro once referred to the translation of this book as "my ticket to heaven." The book on the Kaifeng Jews (*Jews in Old China*) appeared in the USA in 1984 (with a later edition in 2000).

18. Shapiro, *I Chose China*: *The Metamorphosis of a Country and a Man* (2000), p. 265. This book is a reworked version of his earlier autobiography, *An American in China* (1979); it later appeared as *My China* (1997).

19. See on this: *China Monthly Review*, August 1951, pp. 68, or November 1951, p. 260.

20. Shapiro, *I Chose China* (2000), p. 159.
21. Shapiro, *Experiment in Sichuan* (1981), for example, p. 6, 31, 46.
22. Shapiro, *I Chose China* (2000), p. 274.
23. Conversation with Sidney Shapiro in Beijing on May 25, 2001.
24. He is labeled a "liar" by Sidney Shapiro, see in: Shapiro, *I Chose China* (2000), p. 298. Other former "Foreign Experts" likewise did not—as I learned in several conversations—give him positive testimonials. Cf. also: Weiss, *Rande* (1999), p. 410. Therein Ruth Weiss writes that in a speech of March 8, 1973, Premier Zhou Enlai referred to Rittenberg as an "evil-doer." The expression "a maverick of remarkable charm" is found in: Milton/Dall, *Wind Will Not Subside* (1976), p. 101. This eyewitness report by the American couple is regarded in the scholarly world as one of the best foreign reports on conditions in China during the Cultural Revolution, at least for the first few years.
25. Milton/Dall, *Wind Will Not Subside* (1976), p. 304. Rittenberg himself understandably denies this rumor. Rittenberg, *The Man Who Stayed Behind* (1993), p. 443. Moreover, he wants to convince the reader that he cried in prison after hearing of the death of Zhou Enlai. However, in his defense, he cannot explain why he—in contrast to the other foreigners imprisoned during the Cultural Revolution—was only released from prison four years later in November 1977.
26. Rittenberg, *The Man Who Stayed Behind* (1993), p. 17.
27. Ibid., p. 74.
28. Ibid., p. 97. Rittenberg aided Anna Louise Strong in Yan'an as an interpreter during her discussions with Mao in 1948. Rittenberg believes that his arrest occurred at the behest of the Soviets, although he himself was never in the USSR.
29. See on this the book by Griffin, *Treatment* (1976). A series of books written by Westerners who had spent time in Red Chinese prisons appeared in the USA from the 1950s until the 1970s, as, e.g., Rickett, *Prisoners* (1957); Rigney, *Red Hell* (1956) or Donovan, *Pagoda* (1967).
30. This official translation assignment involved Volume IV of the *Collected Works of Mao Zedong*, which encompassed the end of the Civil War and the first years of the PRC. On the Western side, the translation team also included Israel Epstein, Frank Coe, Michael Shapiro, as well as Sol Adler.
31. Rittenberg, *The Man Who Stayed Behind* (1993), pp. 276, 371.
32. Ibid., pp. 446, 449.
33. All the information presented here about Sam Ginsbourg is derived from his autobiography, *My First Sixty Years in China* (1982).
34. Ginsbourg, *Sixty Years* (1962), p. 208.
35. Ibid., p. 81.
36. Ibid., p. 209. In another place, he defends, for example, the "Three-Anti Campaign" (1951) and the "Five-Anti Campaign" (1952).
37. Ibid., p. 368.
38. Siao, *China* (1997), p. 568.
39. Individual biographical details stem from an interview that I held with Eva Siao in Beijing on June 2, 2001, a few months before her death. There is also a

documentary film (in German) about Eva Siao by Martina Fluck (from 1992/93) called *Mein Traum, meine Liebe, meine Hoffnung* (My dream, my love, my hope).

40. Siao, *Peking* (1956); Siao/Hauser, *Tibet* (1957).

41. Siao, *China* (1997), p. 266.

42. Ibid., p. 570.

43. Conversation with Eva Siao held on June 2, 2001, in Beijing.

44. See for instance the picture volume by Siao, *Photographien* (Photographs, 1996), and in comparison to this Morrison, *Old Peking* (1999).

45. I visited Ruth Weiss on September 6, 2001, in the Friendship Hotel in Beijing.

46. Weiss, *Rande* (1999), p. 36.

47. Radio speech of January 28, 1933, by Ruth Weiss on the topic: "What does China have to say to the Twentieth Century?" (unpublished manuscript, which was cordially made available to the author by Mr Dierk Detje, Beijing).

48. *Das Neue Wiener Tageblatt*, January 31, 1933 (n. pag.), or of August 21, 1933 (n. pag.); Jewish weekly *Die Wahrheit*, June 30, 1933 (n. pag.), respectively July 14, 1933 (n. pag.).

49. See, e.g., "Der Gefahrenherd im Fernen Osten" (The Source of Danger in the Far East, in: *Das Neue Wiener Tageblatt*, December 7, 1933, n. pag.) or—in the same newspaper—"Europäer in Schanghai" (Europeans in Shanghai, January 20, 1934); China *Weekly Review* of December 23, 1933, p. 152 with the title "Do We Want More Political Troubles?"

50. Weiss, *Rande* (1999), p. 314. Weiss—in contrast to many other "Foreign Experts"—never joined the CCP.

51. Ibid., p. 360. Ruth Weiss died in Beijing in 2006.

52. These verses stem from the poem "Das nationale Lied" (The National Song). It is printed in: Yang, *Klara Blum* (1996), p. 25.

53. Cited from: Yang, *Klara Blum* (1996), p. 6.

54. Only in 1990, twenty years after Klara Blum's death, is convincing evidence found of what many friends had already earlier assumed, namely that Zhu was arrested by officials of the Soviet Interior Ministry shortly before his planned departure for China in 1938 and sentenced to eight years in prison. According to archival information, he died in a Siberian labor camp in 1943. Until the end of her life Klara Blum never gave up hope that she would be reunited with her beloved.

55. Blum, *Hirte* (1951). See on the novel: Yang, *Klara Blum* (1996), pp. 162–192.

56. This legend is mentioned for the first time in the *Shijing,* the classical book of songs.

57. Cited in: Yang, *Klara Blum* (1996), p. 20.

58. See: Lange, *Wahlverwandtschaften* (1995), p. 194.

59. Ibid., p. 194.

60. Yang, *Klara Blum* (1996), p. 6.

61. See on additional "Foreign Experts" of Jewish origin my article "China's Realities" (2008), pp.16–40.

Bibliography

Archives and Papers

American Jewish Archives, Cincinnati, OH
Samuel Sokobin Collection

Center for Jewish History, New York
Leo Baeck Institute: Collections of David Ludwig Bloch, Magdalena Robitscher-Hahn, Willy Tonn
Yivo Institute for Jewish Research: Meir Birman Collection

Columbia University Archives, Oral History Collection, New York
George E. Sokolsky Collection

Harvard University Archives, Cambridge, MA
Theodore H. White Papers

Hoover Institution Archives, Stanford University, Palo Alto, CA
Ben Levaco Collection
Milly Bennett (Mitchell) Collection
George Sokolsky Collection
Georges Spunt Collection

Indiana University, Lilly Library Archives, Bloomington, IN
Emily Hahn Collection

Library of Congress, Manuscript Division, Washington, DC
Paul Federn Papers

Massachusetts Institute of Technology (MIT), Cambridge, MA
Harold Robert Isaacs Papers

National Library of Australia, Canberra, ACT
Papers of Harold Williams

New York University, The Tamiment Library
Grace Maul Granich & Max Granich Papers

University of Washington Archives, Seattle, WA
Erwin Reifler Collection

US National Archives and Records Administration NARA, College Park, MD

Personal Archive of Jacob Avshalomov, Portland, OR

Personal Archive of Carol Goodfriend, New York

Personal Archive of Prof. Tom Grunfeld, New York

Personal Archive of Prof. David Kranzler, New York

Personal Archive of Prof. Peter Rand, Belmont, MA

Personal Archive of Rabbi Marvin Tokayer, Great Neck, NY

Selected Interviews

David Ludwig Bloch, Munich: July 18, 2000

Israel Epstein, Beijing: May 30 and June 2, 2001

Sidney Shapiro, Beijing: May 25, 2001

Eva Siao, Beijing: June 2, 2001

Wang Wu'an, Beijing: September 7, 2001

Books, Articles, and Unpublished Manuscripts

Acton, Sir Harold (1985). *Memoirs* of An Aesthete. A Hamish Hamilton Paperback. 2nd Edition. London.

Ash, Timothy Garton (1999), *History of the Present*: Essays, Sketches, and Dispatches from Europe in the 1990s. Vintage. New York.

Asiaticus (1928). Von *Kanton bis Schanghai* 1926–27. Agis. Vienna, Berlin.

Asiaticus (1938). "Asiaticus" *Criticizes* "Red Star over China" and "Asiaticus" Holds his Ground, in: Pacific Affairs, Vol. XI, No. 2, June, p. 237–244 and p. 248–252.

Avshalomov, Jacob and Aaron (2001). Avshalomov's *Winding Ways*. Composers Out of China. A Chronicle. Xlibris Corporation. Philadelphia.

Balinska, Marta A. (1998). For the *Good* of Humanity. Ludwik Rajchman. Medical Statesman. Central University Press. Budapest.

Ben-Eliezer, Judith (1985). *Shanghai Lost*, Jerusalem Regained. Steimatzky. Jerusalem.

Bennett, Milly (1993). *On Her Own*. Journalistic Adventures from San Francisco to the Chinese Revolution 1917–1927. Edited and Annotated by Tom Grunfeld. M.E. Sharpe. Armonk, London.

Betta, Chiara (1997). Silas Aaron *Hardoon* (1851–1931): Marginality and Adaptation in Shanghai. Ph.D. Thesis. London School of Economics. London.

Betta, Chiara (1999). Silas Aaron *Hardoon* and Cross-Cultural Adaptation in Shanghai, in: Goldstein, Jonathan, Ed., Jews of China, Vol. I. M. E. Sharpe. Armonk, London, p. 216–229.

Betta, Chiara (2000). *Myth and Memory*. Chinese Portrayal of Silas Aaron Hardoon, Luo Jialing and the Aili Garden between 1924 and 1995, in: Malek, Roman, Ed., From Kaifeng . . . to Shanghai. Jews in China. Steyler, Nettetal, p. 375–400.

Blackie, William J. (1972). *The Kadoorie Agricultural Aid Association* 1951-1971. Libra Press. Hong Kong.

Bliss, Charles K. (1965). *Semantography* (Blissymbolics). Self-published. Sydney (1st edition: 1949).

Bliss, Charles K. (1970). The *Invention and Discovery* that will change our Lives. Self-published. Sydney.

Bloch, David Ludwig (1997). *Holzschnitte*. Mukeji. Woodcuts. Shanghai 1940–1949. Edited by Barbara Hoster, Roman Malek and Katharina Wenzel-Teuber. Eine gemeinsame Veröffentlichung des China-Zentrums und des Instituts Monumenta Serica. Steyler. Nettetal.

Blum, Klara (1951). Der *Hirte* und die Weberin. Ein Roman aus dem heutigen China. Greifenverlag. Rudolstadt.

Brady, Anne-Marie (1996). *Red and Expert*: China's "Foreign Friends" in the Great Proletarian Cultural Revolution 1966–1969, in: China Information, Vol. XI, Nos. 2/3 (Autumn/Winter), p. 110–137.

Brady, Anne-Marie (2000). "Treat *Insiders and Outsiders* Differently": The Use and Control of Foreigners in the PRC, in: The China Quarterly, No. 164, December, p. 943–964.

Brady, Anne-Marie (2002). *Making the Foreign Serve China*: Managing Foreigners in the People's Republic. Rowman and Littlefield. Buffalo.

Buck, Pearl (1931). The *Good Earth*. Grosset & Dunlap. New York.

Canham, Erwin D. (1958). *Commitment to Freedom*: The Story of the Christian Science Monitor. Houghton Mifflin Company. Boston.

Chen, Hansheng [Han-seng] (1936). Landlord and Peasant in China. International Publishers. New York.

Cohen, Israel (1925). The *Journal* of a Jewish Traveller. John Lane the Bodley Head Ltd. London.

Cohen, Warren (1978). The *Chinese Connection*. Roger S. Greene, Thomas W. Lamont, George Sokolsky and American-East Asian Relations. Columbia University Press. New York.

Cuthbertson, Ken (1998). *Nobody Said Not to Go*. The Life, Loves and Adventures of Emily Hahn. Faber and Faber. Boston, London.

Davies, John Paton (1972). *Dragon by the Tail*. American, British, Japanese, and Russian Encounters with China and one another. W.W. Norton. New York.

Diner, Dan (1999). Das *Jahrhundert* verstehen. Eine universalhistorische Deutung. Luchterhand. Munich. English: (2008). Cataclysms: A History of the Twentieth Century from Europe's Edge. University of Wisconsin Press. Madison, WI.

Donovan, John F. (1967). The *Pagoda* and the Cross. Scribner's. New York.

Drage, Charles (1954). *Two-Gun Cohen*. Jonathan Cape. London.

Einstein, Lewis (1968). A *Diplomat* Looks Back. Edited by Lawrence E. Gelfand, with a Foreword by George F. Kennan. Yale University Press. New Haven and London.

Encyclopaedia Judaica (1972). Keter Publishing House. Jerusalem.

Epstein, Israel (1939). *The People's War*. Victor Gollancz. London.

Epstein, Israel (1947). The *Unfinished Revolution*. Little Brown and Company. Boston.

Epstein, Israel (1979). *Vignettes* of Past and Present, in: Living in China by Twenty Authors from Abroad. New World Press. Beijing.

Epstein, Israel (2000). On Being a *Jew* in China: A Personal Memoir, in: Goldstein, Jonathan, Ed., Jews of China, Vol. II. M. E. Sharpe. Armonk, London, p. 85–97.

Epstein, Israel (2005). My China Eye. Memoirs of a Jew and a Journalist. Long River Press. San Francisco.

Erling, Johnny, Ed. (1980). *Im Geist Yanans*. Dr. Robitscher-Hahn in Briefen, Gedichten und Selbstzeugnissen. China-Studien- und Verlagsgesellschaft. Frankfurt a.M., Berlin.

Freudmann, Walter (1947). *Tschi-Lai!*—Erhebet Euch! Erlebnisse eines Arztes in China und Burma 1939–45. Neue Zeit. Linz.

Giardinelli, Alisa (2002). *Emigre*. The College as a Place of Refuge. Swarthmore College Bulletin. December, p. 34–40.

Ginsbourg, Sam (1982). My First *Sixty Years* in China. New World Press. Beijing.

Gould, Randall (1945). *China in the Sun*. Doubleday and Company. Garden City, N.Y.

Granich, Max (1938). Days of *Humiliation* are over, in: China Today, May, Vol. 4, No. 8, p. 6.

Griffin, Patricia (1976). The Chinese Communist *Treatment* of Counterrevolutionaries: 1924–1949. Princeton University Press. Princeton, NJ.

Grunfeld, Tom A. (1999). The *Chinese Communist Party* and Revolutionary Internationalism: The Case of Rayna Prohme, 1925–1927. Unpublished manuscript. HSTCC International Conference at Ca'Foscari University, June 30–July 3, 1999. Venice.

Hahn, Emily (1942). *Mr. Pan*. Doubleday, Doran. New York.

Hahn, Emily (1946). *China A to Z*. Franklin Watts. New York.

Hahn, Emily (1955). *Chiang Kai-shek*. An Unauthorized Biography. Doubleday, Doran. New York.

Hahn, Emily (1968). The *Cooking* of China. Time-Life Books. New York.

Hahn, Emily (1988). *China To Me*. Beacon Press (paperback). Boston (first edition: 1944).

Hahn, Emily (2000). *No Hurry to Get Home*. The Memoir of the *New Yorker* Writer Whose Unconventional Life and Adventures Spanned the Twentieth Century. Seal Press. Seattle (original title: "Times and Places," 1970).

Hirson, Baruch (sine anno). From Cape Town to Shanghai. The Life of *Cecil Frank Glass*. In Pursuit of Revolution, 1901–1988. Unpublished manuscript. London.

Holitscher, Arthur (1926). *Das unruhige Asien*. Reise durch Indien—China—Japan. S. Fischer. Berlin.

Hopkirk, Peter (1984). *Foreign Devils* on the Silk Road. The Search for the Lost Cities and Treasures of Chinese Central Asia. Oxford University Press. Oxford.

Isaacs, Harold R. (1958). *Scratches* on Our Minds. American Views of China and India. John Day Company. New York.

Isaacs, Harold R. (1972). *Images* of Asia. American Views of China and India. Harper & Row. New York (originally: Scratches on Our Minds, 1958).

Isaacs, Harold R. (1985). *Re-Encounters* in China. Notes of a Journey in a Time Capsule. Joint Publishing. Hongkong.

Isaacs, Harold R., Ed. (1974). *Straw Sandals*. Chinese Short Stories 1918–1933. MIT Press. Cambridge, MA.

Isaacs, Harold Robert (1968). The *Tragedy* of the Chinese Revolution. 2nd Revised Edition. Atheneum. New York.

Jackson, Stanley (1968). The *Sassoons*. E. P. Dutton. New York.

Jacobs, Dan N. (1981). *Borodin*. Stalin's Man in China. Harvard University Press. Cambridge, MA and London.

Jensen, Fritz (1949). *China siegt*. Stern. Vienna.

Jensen, Fritz (1955). *Opfer und Sieger*. Nachdichtungen, Gedichte und Berichte. Dietz. East Berlin.

Johnson, Chalmers (1962). *Peasant Nationalism* and Communist Power. Stanford University Press. Palo Alto.

Kaminski, Gerd (1983). *China gemalt.* Chinesische Zeitgeschichte in Bildern Friedrich Schiffs. Europa-Verlag. Vienna.

Kaminski, Gerd (1993). *General Luo* genannt Langnase. Das abenteuerliche Leben des Dr. med. Jakob Rosenfeld. Löcker-Verlag. Vienna.

Kaminski, Gerd (1998). Friedrich Schiff: *Künstler* und Chinapionier mit dem Zeichenstift. Zur grossen Schiff-Retrospektive in Shanghai, August 1998, in: China Report, Nr. 129–130, p. 53–64.

Kaminski, Gerd / Unterrieder, Else (1980). *Von Österreichern und Chinesen.* Europa-Verlag. Vienna, Munich, Zürich.

Kaminski, Gerd, Ed. (2003). *Ich kannte sie alle.* Das Tagebuch des chinesischen Generals Jakob Rosenfeld. Aufgefunden und ausgewählt von Ann Margaret Frija-Rosenfeld. Löcker-Verlag. Vienna.

Katz, Richard (1931). *Funkelnder Ferner Osten!* Erlebtes in China—Korea—Japan. Ullstein. Berlin.

King, Frank H.H. (1988a). The *Hongkong Bank* between the Wars and the Bank Interned 1919–1945. Return from Grandeur. Vol. III of The History of the Hongkong and Shanghai Banking Corporation. Cambridge University Press. Cambridge, New York, Melbourne.

King, Frank H.H. (1988b). The *Hongkong Bank* in the Period of Development and Nationalism, 1941–1984. From Regional Bank to Multinational Group. Vol. IV of The History of the Hongkong and Shanghai Banking Corporation. Cambridge University Press. Cambridge, New York, Melbourne.

Klingaman, William K. (1996). Encyclopedia of the *McCarthy Era.* Facts on File. New York.

Kneucker, Alfred (1984). Zuflucht in *Shanghai.* Aus den Erlebnissen eines österreichischen Arztes in der Emigration 1938–1945. Edited by Felix Gamillscheg. Böhlau. Vienna, Cologne, Graz.

Knodel, Arthur J. / Hirson, Baruch, Eds. (2007). *Reporting the Chinese Revolution*: The Letters of Rayna Prohme. Pluto Press. London.

Kranzler, David (1976). *Japanese, Nazis & Jews.* The Jewish Refugee Community of Shanghai, 1938–1945. Yeshiva University Press. New York.

Krasno, Rena (1992). *Strangers* Always. A Jewish Family in Wartime Shanghai. Pacific View Press. Berkeley.

Kuttner, Fritz A. (1990). The *Archaeology* of Music in Ancient China: 2000 Years of Acoustical Experimentation 1400 B.C.–A.D. 750. Paragon House. New York.

Lang, Olga (1946). *Chinese Family* and Society. Yale University Press. New Haven.

Lang, Olga (1967). *Pa Chin* and His Writings. Chinese Youth between the two Revolutions. Harvard University Press. Cambridge, MA.

Lange, Thomas (1995). Exotische *Wahlverwandtschaften*—Dshu Bailans jüdisches China, in: Kubin, Wolfgang, Ed., Mein Bild in deinem Auge. Exotismus und Moderne: Deutschland—China im 20. Jahrhundert Wissenschaftliche Buchgesellschaft. Darmstadt, p. 187–218.

Lattimore, Owen (1935). *Manchuria.* Cradle of Conflict. Macmillan. New York.

Leutner, Mechthild / Titarenko, M.L., Eds. (1996). RKP(B), Komintern und die *national-revolutionäre Bewegung in China*. Dokumente. Band 1: 1920–1925. Russisches Zentrum für die Archivierung und Erforschung von Dokumenten zur neuesten Geschichte. Ostasiatisches Seminar der Freien Universität Berlin. Ferdinand Schöningh. Paderborn, Munich, Vienna, Zürich.

Leutner, Mechthild / Titarenko, M.L., Eds. (1998). RKP(B), Komintern und die *national-revolutionäre Bewegung in China*. Dokumente. Band 2: 1926/27. Russisches Zentrum für die Archivierung und Erforschung von Dokumenten zur neuesten Geschichte. Ostasiatisches Seminar der Freien Universität Berlin. LIT. Münster.

Levy, Daniel S. (1997). *Two-Gun Cohen*. A Biography. St. Martin's Press. New York.

Liberman, Yaacov (1997). *My China*. Jewish Life in the Orient 1900–1950. Gefen Publishing House. Jerusalem, New York.

MacKinnon, Janice R. / MacKinnon, Stephen R. (1988). *Agnes Smedley:* The Life and Times of an American Radical. University of California Press. Berkeley.

Malraux, André (1933). *La condition humaine*. Gallimard. Paris.

McCarthy, Joseph R. (1952). *McCarthyism*: The Fight for America. National Weekly. New York.

Mehnert, Klaus (1964). *Peking und Moskau*. Deutscher Taschenbuch-Verlag. Munich.

Messmer, Matthias (2007). China. Schauplätze west-östlicher Begegnungen. Böhlau. Vienna.

Messmer, Matthias (2008). *China's Realities* from the Viewpoints of 'Foreign Experts,' in: Ehrlich, Mark Avrum, Ed., Jewish-Chinese Nexus. Routledge. London, p. 16–40.

Meyer, Maisie J. (1994). The *Sephardi Jewish Community* of Shanghai, 1845–1939: The Question of Identity. Ph.D. Thesis. London School of Economics. London.

Meyer, Maisie J. (2003). From the Rivers of the Babylon to the Whangpoo: A Century of Sephardi Jewish Life in Shanghai. University Press of America. Lanham, MD.

Milton, David / Dall Milton, Nancy (1976). The *Wind Will Not Subside*. Years in Revolutionary China 1964–1969. Pantheon Books. Random House. New York.

Mirsky, Jeannette (1977). *Sir Aurel Stein*. Archaeological Explorer. The University of Chicago Press. Chicago, London.

Monnet, Jean (1976). *Mémoires*. Fayard. Paris.

Morrison, Hedda (1999). A Photographer in *Old Peking*. Oxford University Press. Oxford, New York, Hong Kong.

Needham, Joseph (1962). *Science and Civilisation* in China. Vol. IV. Physics and Physical Technology, Part I: Physics. Cambridge University Press. Cambridge.

Needham, Joseph (1969). *Within the Four Seas*. The Dialogue of East and West. George Allen & Unwin. London.

Newman, Robert P. (1992). Owen *Lattimore* and the "Loss" of China. University of California Press. Berkeley, Los Angeles, Oxford.

Palmer, James (2011). *The Bloody White Baron*: The Extraordinary Story of the Russian Nobleman Who Became the Last Khan of Mongolia. Basic Books. New York.

Peffer, Nathaniel (1921). *What About China?*, in: The Nation, Vol. 113, No. 2942, p. 591–592.

Peffer, Nathaniel (1927). The *Chinese Philosophy of Life*, in: Current History, Vol. XXVL, No. 3, June, p. 431–433.

Peffer, Nathaniel (1927). The *White Man's Dilemma*. Climax of the Age of Imperialism. The John Day Company. New York.

Peffer, Nathaniel (1930). The *Collapse* of a Civilization. The John Day Company. New York.

Peffer, Nathaniel (1930). The *Death of Chinese Civilization*, in: Harper's Monthly Magazine, Vol. 160, March, p. 499–506.

Rand, Peter (1995). *China Hands*. The Adventures and Ordeals of the American Journalists Who Joined Forces with the Great Chinese Revolution. Simon & Schuster. New York, London, Toronto.

Rickett, Allyn and Adele (1957). *Prisoners* of Liberation: Four Years in a Chinese Communist Prison. Cameron Associates. New York.

Rigney, Harold (1956). Four Years in a *Red Hell*: The Story of Father Rigney. Regnery Press. Chicago.

Ristaino, Marcia Reynders (2001). *Port of Last Resort*. The Diaspora Communities of Shanghai. Stanford University Press. Palo Alto, CA.

Rittenberg, Sidney / Bennett, Amanda (1993). The *Man Who Stayed Behind*. Simon & Schuster. New York, Toronto.

Rudolph, Julius (1940). *Shanghai—City of Refuge*. Jewish Refugees in Shanghai. Edited and revised by Anna Ginsbourg. China Weekly Press. Shanghai.

Schuster, Carl (1935). Some *Peasant Embroideries* from Western China, in: Embroidery, September, p. 87–96.

Schuster, Carl (1937). Peasant *Embroideries* of China, in: Asia, January, p. 26–31.

Schuster, Carl / Carpenter, Edmund, Eds. (1996). *Patterns* That Connect. Social Symbolism in Ancient & Tribal Art. Harry N. Abrams. New York.

Segalen, Victor (1971). *René Leys*. Gallimard. Paris.

Sergeant, Harriet (1990). *Shanghai*. Collision. Point of Cultures 1918/1939. Crown Publishers. New York.

Service, John S. (1981). State Department *Duty in China*, The McCarthy Era, and After, 1933–1977. An Interview Conducted by Rosemary Levenson. With an Introduction by John K. Fairbank. University of California. The Bancroft Library. Berkeley.

Shapiro, Sidney (1979). An American in China. Thirty Years in the People's Republic. New World Press. Beijing.

Shapiro, Sidney (1981). *Experiment in Sichuan*. A Report on Economic Reform. New World Press. Beijing.

Shapiro, Sidney (2000). *I Chose China*. The Metamorphosis of a Country and a Man. Hippocrene Books. New York.

Shapiro, Sidney, Ed. (1984). *Jews in Old China*. Studies by Chinese scholars. Translated, compiled and edited by Sidney Shapiro. Hippocrene Books. New York.

Sheean, Vincent (1937). *Personal History*. Garden City Publishing. New York.

Siao, Eva (1956). *Peking*. Eindrücke und Begegnungen. Introduction by Bodo Uhse. Sachsenverlag. Dresden.

Siao, Eva (1996). China. *Photographien* 1949–1967. Edited by Reinhold Misselbeck. Edition Braus. Museum Ludwig. Cologne.

Siao, Eva (1997). *China*—mein Traum, mein Leben. Econ-Taschenbuch-Verlag. Berlin.

Siao, Eva / Hauser, Harald (1957). *Tibet*. F.A. Brockhaus. Leipzig.

Sokolsky, George E. (1932). The *Tinder Box* of Asia. Doubleday, Doran. New York.

Sokolsky, George E. (1935). *We Jews*. Doubleday, Doran. New York.

Spunt, Georges (1968). *A Place in Time*. G.P. Putnam's Sons. New York.

Spunt, Georges (1980). The Step-by-Step *Chinese Cookbook*. Penguin Books. New York.

Stadler, Friedrich, Ed. (1987). Vertriebene *Vernunft* I: Emigration und Exil österreichischer Wissenschaft 1930–1940. Jugend und Volk. Munich.

Stadler, Friedrich, Ed. (1988). Vertriebene *Vernunft* II: Emigration und Exil österreichischer Wissenschaft 1930–1940. Jugend und Volk. Munich.

Stein, Aurel (1998). On Ancient *Central Asian Tracks*. Book Faith India. Delhi (first print: MacMillan. London, 1933).

Stein, Guenther (1936). *Far East* in Ferment. Methuen. London.

Stein, Gunther (1945). The Challenge of *Red China*. McGraw Hill. New York, London.

Stein, Gunther (1945). The *Other China*, in: Foreign Affairs, October, p. 62–74.

Stein, Gunther (1946). An Interpretation of *China's Conflict*, in: The Yale Review, Vol. 35, June, No. 4, p. 633–648.

Strauss, Herbert A. (et al.), Ed. (1983). *Biographisches Handbuch* der deutschsprachigen Emigration nach 1933. Vol. II. Edited by the Institut für Zeitgeschichte, Munich. K.G. Saur. Munich, New York, London.

Strauss, Herbert A. (et al.), Ed. (1983). *International Biographical Dictionary* of Central European Emigrés 1933–1945. Vol II. K.G. Saur, Munich, New York, London, Paris.

Tandler, Julius (1935). *Volk in China*. Erlebnisse und Erfahrungen. Thalia. Vienna.

Thompson, Edward T., Ed. (1992). *Theodore H. White* at Large. The Best of His Magazine Writing, 1939–1986. Pantheon. New York.

Tonn, Will Y. (1941). *Chinese Chess*, in: The China Digest, September–October, p. 20–23.

Trebitsch-Lincoln, Ignatius Timotheus (1916). *Revelations* of an International Spy. R. M. McBride. New York.

Trebitsch-Lincoln, Ignatius Timotheus (1932). The *Autobiography* of an Adventurer. Henry Holt. New York.

Trebitsch-Lincoln, Ignatius Timotheus [alias Chao Kung] (1932). *Can War Be Abolished?* Kelly & Walsh. Shanghai.

Waley, Arthur (1938). The Analects of Confucius. Allen & Unwin. London.

Wang, Fan-hsi (1980). Chinese Revolutionary *Memoirs* 1919–1949. Translated and with an introduction by Gregor Benton. Oxford University Press. Oxford, New York, Toronto.

Wasserstein, Bernard (1988). The Secret Lives of *Trebitsch Lincoln*. Yale University Press. New Haven, London.

Weiss, Ruth (1999). Am *Rande* der Geschichte. Mein Leben in China. Zeller. Osnabrück.

Werner, Ruth (1977). *Sonjas Rapport*. Verlag Neues Leben. Berlin (Ost).

White, Theodore H. (1979). In *Search of History*. A Personal Adventure. Warner Books. New York.

White, Theodore H. / Jacoby, Annalee, Jacoby (1946). *Thunder* Out of China. William Sloane. New York.

Willoughby, Charles A. (1952). *Shanghai Conspiracy*. The Sorge Spy Ring. Moscow, Shanghai, Tokyo, San Francisco, New York. E.P. Dutton. New York.

Yang, Zhidong (1996). *Klara Blum*—Zhu Bailan (1904–1971). Leben und Werk einer österreichisch-chinesischen Schriftstellerin. Peter Lang. Frankfurt a.M.

Index

About the Author

Matthias Messmer was born 1967 in St. Gallen and received his MA in political science, law, and economics (St. Gallen) and his PhD in social sciences (Konstanz). His research focuses on intercultural subjects and topics related to China and Chinese culture. Furthermore, he is engaged in cultural documentation and criticism in the form of writing and photography. He is the author (in German) of *Soviet and Post-Communist Antisemitism* (1997) and *China—West-Eastern Encounters* (2007) and is currently working on a photo-text book on "China's Vanishing Worlds."

Lightning Source UK Ltd.
Milton Keynes UK
UKOW052249011012

199903UK00002B/1/P

9 780739 169384